Deng Xiaoping

AND THE MAKING OF MODERN CHINA

RICHARD EVANS

Deng Xiaoping

AND THE MAKING OF MODERN CHINA

HAMISH HAMILTON · LONDON

For Grania, Mark and Peter

HAMISH HAMILTON LTD

Published by the Penguin Group

Penguin Books Ltd, 27 Wrights Lane, London w8 5tz, England

Penguin Books USA Inc., 375 Hudson Street, New York, New York 10014, USA

Penguin Books Australia Ltd, Ringwood, Victoria, Australia

Penguin Books Canada Ltd, 10 Alcorn Avenue, Toronto, Ontario, Canada m4v 3b2

Penguin Books (NZ) Ltd, 182–190 Wairau Road, Auckland 10, New Zealand

Penguin Books Ltd, Registered Offices: Harmondsworth, Middlesex, England

First published 1993

1 3 5 7 9 10 8 6 4 2

The author is grateful to the Central Party Literature Publishing
House in Beijing for permission to reproduce thirteen photographs
from their photo-biography of Deng Xiaoping and one from their
biography of Zhou Enlai

Typeset by Datix International Limited, Bungay, Suffolk
Printed in England by Clays Ltd, St Ives plc
Filmset in Monophoto Garamond

A CIP catalogue record for this book is available from the British Library
ISBN 0-241-13031-X

Contents

List of Maps

Acknowledgements

I have accumulated many debts of gratitude during the three and a half years I have spent working on this book.

In China, I am in the debt of Vice-Premier Qian Qichen, Han Xu, President of the Chinese People's Association for Friendship with Foreign Countries, Wu Jianguo, Deputy Director of the Research Department on Party Literature of the Central Committee of the Chinese Communist Party, and several historians of that department, led by Madame Wang Zuoling, head of the Deng Xiaoping Study Group. In September 1991, I wrote to the Vice-Premier to tell him of the project on which I was engaged and to ask for his advice about obtaining interviews in China. His response was to take action which led to my receiving an invitation from the People's Association to visit Peking. I spent ten days there at the end of April 1992, during which time I was entertained to dinner by Han Xu, received by Wu Jianguo and given detailed answers to upwards of forty questions, which I had tendered in advance, about the life and political philosophy of Deng Xiaoping by Madame Wang and her colleagues. Altogether, I spent twelve hours with them. Their answers were very full, and they were ready to answer a large number of supplementary questions. The source notes at the end of the book will I hope make clear how much I owe to them by way of information and guidance over the interpretation of important events.

I am most grateful to Sir Alec Cairncross and the management committee of the Centre for Modern Chinese Studies at Oxford for having agreed that the Centre should pay the cost of my return airfare to China. I am grateful to Ambassador Ma Yuzhen and Wang Yihao, his political counsellor of the time, for having authorized the Consular Department of the Chinese Embassy in London to issue me with a second visa on Easter Sunday when the passport containing the original visa was delayed in the post. Without their help, I would have had to rearrange my visit to China.

In France, I am grateful to Geneviève Barman of the Centre de recherches et de documentation sur la Chine contemporaine for having sent me copies of two important articles about the Chinese worker-students in France and Deng Xiaoping's career there ('La France au miroir chinois' and 'Les années françaises de Deng Xiaoping') by the late Nicole Dulioust and herself. Jean-Philippe Béja of the Centre national de la recherche scientifique presented me with a copy of *Le Tremblement de terre de Pékin*, a very full collection of documents on the democracy movement of 1989 compiled by Michel Bonnin, Alain Peyraube and himself. Without this, I should have found it a great deal more difficult to find my way through the complicated events of the time.

In the United States, Roderick MacFarquhar, Director of the John King Fairbank Center of East Asian Studies at Harvard, kindly sent me the proofs of two chapters in Volume 15 of the Cambridge History of China several months before the volume was published.

Nearer home, I owe a large debt of gratitude to Andrew Nurnberg. It was he who suggested that I should try my hand at writing a biography of Deng Xiaoping and then, after I had agreed, did all those things which only an experienced literary agent can do for a new author. He has given me constant advice and encouragement over a period of almost four years.

At Hamish Hamilton, Andrew Franklin, the publishing director, has given me firm, but always just and shrewd, advice from the moment I sent him first drafts of the earlier chapters. I am greatly in his debt. Also at Hamish Hamilton, Keith Taylor and Charles Drazin have helped me a great deal over preparing my final manuscript for press; Charlie Hartley has given me much helpful advice over the selection and captioning of photographs; and Dinah Benson has turned my sketch-maps into true cartography.

Peter Phillips was a meticulous copy-editor. I am grateful to them all.

Peter Clark and Rodric Wye of the Foreign and Commonwealth Office, both former colleagues in the British Embassy in Peking, made helpful suggestions about books I ought to read. Michael Yahuda of the London School of Economics made and gave me photocopies of several important texts in the collections of the British Library. David Shambaugh of the School of Oriental and African Studies let me read the drafts of several articles which have now appeared in a special issue of the *China Quarterly* ('Deng Xiaoping: an assessment', No. 135, September 1993), of which he is editor. At Oxford, Steve Tsang of St Antony's College lent me several works about Deng Xiaoping by authors in Hong Kong and Japan; Zhang Zhichao, an associate of the Centre for Modern Chinese Studies, helped me translate an article about Deng Xiaoping's activities in Guangxi in 1929 and 1930; and Zhang Yongjin, a former Junior Research Fellow at Wolfson College, acquired for me a copy of Deng Xiaoping's *Selected Works* for the period from 1938 to 1965. I am grateful to them too.

Among friends who read and commented on draft chapters, I am particularly grateful to Bill (Sir Raymond) Hoffenberg, President of Wolfson, and Sir Alan Donald, a friend since the 1950s, when he and I together went through the mill of learning Chinese and shared a house in Peking.

My debt of gratitude to Carole Gough, who typed two drafts of every chapter in the book, and three or four drafts of several chapters, is particularly great. She never overran a target date, even when faced by many pages of reworked manuscript, and was always the soul of patience when I decided to revise a draft which I had told her was in final form.

Still nearer home, I am most grateful to my father-in-law, Brigadier Brian Birkett, for having given me a large-scale map of China. Without it, I should not have been able to make sense of the geography of Deng Xiaoping's military career.

My greatest debt of all is to my wife, Grania, and my sons, Mark and Peter. They have been infinitely tolerant of the quirks and foibles of an author in the house, and full of hope and encouragement when he has found the going hardest.

The book is undoubtedly a good deal fuller and more accurate than it would have been without the help of those I have named. But none of them, nor any of the institutions to which they belong, is in any way responsible for such errors as may remain or for the judgements in the book. Responsibility for these is mine alone.

A Note on the Transcription of Chinese Words and Names

In this book, all Chinese book-titles, phrases and words, and almost all personal and place names, have been transcribed in Pinyin, the official system of romanization of the Chinese People's Republic and the system now used by the United Nations. Among personal names, the only exceptions are Sun Yatsen and Chiang Kaishek, romanizations of these names as pronounced in southern Chinese dialects, and Chiang Chingkuo, a romanization in the Wade–Giles system, which is still in use in Taiwan. Among place names, the exceptions are Peking (for Beijing), Tientsin (for Tianjin), Canton (for Guangzhou), Chungking (for Chongqing), Hankow (for Hankou) and Hongkew and Chapei, two suburbs of Shanghai. All these names have been used by English speakers for a long time, and to continue to use them is comparable to go on using Vienna for Wien or Venice for Venezia.

In Pinyin, 'c' is pronounced like 'ts', 'q' like 'ch' and 'x' like 'sh'. An apostrophe is used to show where the break occurs between syllables when there are two possible choices (for instance, as between Ya'nan and Yan'an, the latter being correct).

CHAPTER I

Farmer's Son, 1904–20

Deng Xixian, who adopted the name Deng Xiaoping as a young revolutionary, was born in the countryside of Sichuan, the largest province of south-western China, on 22 August 1904. In the lunar calendar, the only calendar used at the time in rural China, the date was the twelfth day of the seventh month, and this was the date Deng Xiaoping himself used throughout his youth. The clerks to whom he quoted it as a worker–student in France in the 1920s recorded it as 12 July.

The child's parents were Deng Wenming, a small landowner, and Dan Shideng (meaning wife of Deng from the Dan family), his second wife. They lived in Paifang, a village a few miles from Guang'an, a county town – seat of an imperial magistrate – in the eastern part of the province. In a region of hills and streams, Deng Wenming owned about ten hectares of land, enough to yield ten tons of grain in a good year. Guang'an was a place of some size, with several thousand inhabitants, but it was off the beaten track. The arteries of Sichuan were the Yangtse, which ran through the province from south-west to north-east, and its tributaries. Guang'an stood on a river which flowed into one of these tributaries, the Jialing, but was quite a long way up its valley, with mountains nearby on two sides. The provincial capital, Chengdu, was over two hundred miles away, across several ranges of high hills, and Chungking, the nearest city, about a hundred.

Deng Wenming's forebears had migrated to Sichuan from south China at least two hundred years before Deng Xiaoping's birth. They had originally been Hakkas, members of a Han (ethnic Chinese) group which had lived in north China but had moved to the south, in circumstances which are still mysterious, some centuries before that. The Hakkas spoke a dialect and clung to customs which distinguished them both from other Han Chinese and from the non-Han peoples who were the natives of southern China. The Deng family, however, had shed their Hakka ways, perhaps even before they migrated to Sichuan and certainly by the early eighteenth century, when one of them succeeded in entering the imperial civil service. This man, Deng Shimin, had risen to very high official rank under the Qianlong emperor* before retiring to his native village in 1774. Soon after his death a memorial archway (*paifang*) was built at the entrance to the village, bearing a plaque inscribed in the emperor's own calligraphy, and the village was then called after it. During the Cultural Revolution it was renamed the Anti-Revisionist Production Brigade, to signal the crime for which Deng Xiaoping was then in disgrace, and the archway was destroyed. Though the village has returned to its old name, the archway has not been rebuilt.

Deng Wenming was an energetic, sanguine and gregarious man. In later life, after Deng Xiaoping had left home, he became a person of consequence in Guang'an and its neighbourhood, commanding a militia force of several hundred. Inhabitants of Paifang who remember him have spoken to foreign visitors about his readiness to mix with all members of society and his fairness as an arbitrator in settling local disputes. At home, he was firm but fair, imposing strict discipline on his children, but willing to listen to their stories when their behaviour displeased him. No photographs of him have survived; but he is remembered as a man who had a bald head and a large moustache in middle age. Deng Xiaoping never went bald. In temperament, however, he had traits which it is tempting to see as inherited from his father – confidence, ambition and a liking for decisive action among them.

Deng Xiaoping's mother is a shadowy figure. Deng Wenming had married her when it became clear that his first wife, surnamed Zhang, could not have children. Her family was probably comfort-

---

* Qianlong is a reign name and not the personal name of the emperor. Hence the inversion of name and title.

ably off; her dowry was a mahogany bed, elaborately carved and lacquered in red, a gift which could not have been afforded by poor parents (the bed, in which Deng Xiaoping was born, could still be seen in Deng Wenming's old home in the 1980s). She bore Deng Wenming four children, of whom Deng Xiaoping was the second child and the eldest of three sons. In later life, probably before Deng Xiaoping left home in 1920, she became sickly, and she died, according to one account of tuberculosis, in the late 1920s. No one has written or spoken about her relations with her children, so that it is impossible to judge how she influenced them or how attached they were to her.

Deng Wenming went on to marry twice more. His third wife, surnamed Xiao, bore him another (fourth) son and his fourth wife, Xia Bogen, a ferryman's daughter who was only one year older than Deng Xiaoping, two daughters. Xia had been married before and brought a daughter from this marriage into Deng Wenming's household. Altogether, therefore, Deng Xiaoping had one sister and two brothers, one half-brother and two half-sisters, and one stepsister.[1] Because he left home at the age of sixteen and never returned, he did not meet his half- and stepbrothers and sisters until he was in his forties. It is improbable that he ever met his younger half-sister; she died in 1949, almost certainly before he arrived in Sichuan as the political commissar of the army which conquered Sichuan for the communists.

There is no standard set of given names in China; one or two characters are chosen from the whole vocabulary of the language to indicate the hopes or expectations of parents (often fathers only, at the time Deng Xiaoping was born) for a child or to commemorate some auspicious circumstance of his or her birth. The characters in the name chosen by Deng Wenming for his first-born son, Xixian, mean 'to aspire to' and 'goodness', with an overtone of wisdom. Deng Wenming also gave him a name to indicate his generation. This was Xiansheng. His sister was already called Xianlie, and Deng Wenming went on to give all his other children names which began with the character Xian. The children of Deng Wenming's third and fourth wives used their names in this set all through their lives. Deng Xiaoping and his two full brothers did not.

The house in which Deng Xiaoping was born and brought up was still standing in the 1980s, although altered considerably by local officials, who wanted to turn it into a museum. It was, and is, large but plain. Until one of its two wings, built at right angles to its central section, was pulled down, it had twenty-two rooms, separated by high wooden lintels. Its courtyard was paved, but the roof of the house was thatched during Deng's childhood, and the windows were covered by paper strips on lattice. Some at least of its floor was of hardcore and there was no piped water. It can be taken for granted that Deng ate well and was always warm in bed – in a climate which was raw in winter – but it is unlikely that he lived among many ornaments or pictures or was surrounded by expensive pieces of furniture.

Deng Wenming belonged to the lowest stratum of the scholar-gentry, the ruling class in traditional China. He owed his status neither to birth nor to wealth, but to his education. In the tradition of his ancestor Deng Shimin, he had been educated in the classics of Chinese philosophy and history, written in a language which had long ceased to be spoken. Unlike his ancestor, he had not gone to compete in the examinations which were held at intervals – latterly every four years – to select recruits for the imperial civil service and to award degrees to those who were successful at each of the three levels of competition. He had, however, rounded off his education by spending a year or two at a modern school of law and political science, probably in Chungking. Within his class, his seniors were officials of the civil service and all local degree-holders. His privileges included exemption from liability to corporal punishment and corvée labour.

Deng Wenming was therefore a local notable. He was also a conventional figure. He belonged to a local branch of the Society of Elders and Brothers, one of the oldest secret societies in China and the strongest in Sichuan, in due course becoming its head. He was a devotee of the Faith of the Five Sons, a cult named after the five sons, all scholars or officials, of a philanthropist who had lived centuries before. He worshipped at Buddhist, and perhaps other, shrines all his life, and it was on his way home from a shrine that he was ambushed and killed by bandits or local enemies in 1938. His marriage to Deng Xiaoping's mother while his first wife was still alive, and still living in his household, was very much a conventional act.

In education, however, Deng Wenming was ready to move with the times. Although Deng Xiaoping began his education at 'an old-fashioned private pre-school'[2] – almost certainly a class for boys in a temple or private house, presided over by a degree-holder – he was transferred after two years, at the age of seven, to a modern primary school. After four or five more years, he moved on to a middle school in Guang'an, where he became a weekly boarder. From an early stage, therefore, the child was instructed in 'modern' subjects – mathematics, science and geography – and taught in the vernacular, instead of the classical Chinese which scholars had generally used.

There is nothing in the written record about Deng Xiaoping's school-days and, unlike Mao Zedong and Zhou Enlai, he has never spoken about them to foreigners. There are, however, a few anecdotes. Old men of Paifang, including his maternal uncle Dan Yixing, told foreign visitors in the 1980s that Deng was a lively and intelligent child, fond of playing games with his schoolfellows and very quick to learn. One of them said that he was able to recite a book from memory after reading it three times. (Seventy years later, Wan Li, one of his bridge-partners and closer political associates, told a foreigner[3] that his memory for cards was phenomenally good, and that it was this which gave him the edge over the players who were technically of the same standard.) The old men also said that Deng was a child with ideas of his own, and prepared to act on them even if they were likely to draw punishment for being in violation of conventional morality.

Under the new educational system, Deng would normally have remained at the middle school until he was eighteen or nineteen; then, if he had done well, and if he and his father had so wished,

he would have gone on to one of the institutions of higher
education which by then existed in Chengdu and Chungking. But
at some point in 1918 or early 1919, when he was still only
fourteen, Deng Wenming, on a visit to Chungking, wrote to his
son to say he had seen a newspaper advertisement about the
impending establishment there of a school to prepare young men
(and probably young women too) to take part in a programme of
work and study in France, and to ask him whether he would be
prepared to enter it. Deng Wenming sent a parallel letter to his
brother Deng Shaosheng, who was only three years older than his
son.[4] One or both may have temporized in their replies, but if so
not for long. During the later summer or early autumn of 1919,
they left Paifang to enter the school in Chungking.

On the face of it, Deng Wenming's action is very hard to
explain. Deng Xiaoping was still only a child, quite without
experience of life outside the little world of Guang'an, and his
uncle's experience could not have been much wider. Neither had
been equipped by upbringing or education to cope with the
uncertainties of life in a distant foreign country. Besides, Deng
Wenming must have realized that success in the experiment of
sending his eldest son to France would mean his loss to the family.
If Deng Xiaoping returned to China with industrial qualifications
in his pocket, he would not want to settle down as a farmer, and it
was improbable that he would want to work in Sichuan, where
there was very little industry.

It is conceivable that Deng Wenming was influenced by a
Chinese enthusiast for foreign study or by a foreigner, or that he
had found his son fractious and wanted to send him away. Yet
there is no evidence for any of these possibilities, and the
circumstantial evidence is against them. The founder of the school
in Chungking, Wu Yuzhang, was a teacher in Chengdu, and there
is no reason why Deng Wenming should ever have come across
him. Yang Sen, a native of Guang'an who became known in the
1920s for his ardent advocacy of foreign study, was a contemporary
of Deng Wenming's; but he was not in Guang'an at the time when
Deng Xiaoping was growing up. There was a French Lazarist

mission in Guang'an; but it is as improbable that Deng Wenming, a practising Buddhist, had much to do with it as that the priests who worked in it were enthusiastic about a scheme promoted by revolutionaries, as it was. As to relations between father and son, there is no hint in the stories told by the old men of Paifang that these were other than good. It seems, therefore, that the explanation has to be found, quite simply, in the ambitions of a father and patriot which knowledge of the world had not acted to temper.

There can be little doubt that Deng Wenming took a close interest in national politics. His secret society became involved in a movement to reserve for Sichuan the right to build and operate railways in the province and his action in proposing that his son and brother should go to France is in itself evidence of such an interest. It would not have been difficult for him to learn what was happening elsewhere in Sichuan and in the country as a whole. By the 1900s, there were telegraph offices in most towns of any size, and the circulation of a large number of local newspapers and magazines was a feature of the times. One of the pictures of him which has come down in oral tradition is of his spending a good deal of time in tea-houses, which had always been centres for the exchange of local and national news.

Even if Deng Wenming did not talk much about politics at home, Deng Xiaoping would have been able to follow them for himself from the moment he entered the middle school in Guang'an in 1915 or 1916. It was the custom of middle schools to subscribe to newspapers and it was becoming the habit of their students to take the lead in organizing demonstrations in radical and patriotic causes. According to his official biography, he took part himself in a student boycott of Japanese goods in 1919,[5] when the rights which Germany had enjoyed in the eastern province of Shandong were transferred to Japan by the victorious Western powers at Versailles, even though China had been their ally.

The chief political event of Deng Xiaoping's childhood was the revolution of 1911–12, which swept away the age-old Chinese monarchy and with it the Manchu dynasty which had occupied the throne since 1644. Its roots lay in the protracted failure of the traditional state to give China the strength to resist foreign penetration, military, commercial and cultural. Under successive emperors, three policies had been tried: a closed door; 'self-strengthening', whose essence was the acquisition of foreign technology, military and industrial, but without accepting foreign ideas; and the reform of institutions, from the monarchy downwards. All had failed; and their failure had ultimately brought a revolutionary movement into being.

The leader of this movement was Sun Yatsen. Born in 1865 into a poor peasant family in the southern province of Guangdong, Sun was educated in Hawaii and studied medicine in Hong Kong. In the mid-1880s he became a revolutionary, dedicated to the transformation of the entire political and social order in China, and from 1905 was the acknowledged leader of all those, constitutional republicans, anarchists and Marxists (a very small contingent), who shared this aim and were ready to use force to achieve it. They worked together, though not always harmoniously, in the Revolutionary League, a clandestine organization with its principal base in Japan and more members outside than inside China.

From 1905 to 1911, the league tried to establish bases on the mainland, sometimes in port cities and sometimes in the open countryside, but entirely without success. Its own resources, of men, money and weapons, were slim, its planning was generally poor, and it tended to depend on allies, like secret societies, which were more interested in self-preservation than in fearless action. But it never gave up; and in the autumn of 1911 was making plans to provoke mutinies among the garrison troops of Wuhan, on the middle Yangtse.

It will never be known whether a revolution would have occurred if these plans had matured. As it happened, chance intervened. A group of revolutionaries accidentally set off a large home-made bomb in the Russian-concession area of Hankow, one of the two parts of Wuhan on the northern bank of the Yangtse. The explosion was on such a scale that the police of the Chinese city, who would not normally have entered the concession, went immediately to the scene. There they seized and executed three revolutionaries and found lists of members of the Revolutionary League in army units stationed in the area. In imminent danger of arrest, a group of revolutionary officers hastened to provoke mutinies in several units of the Wuhan garrison and then led these units into battle against those which had remained loyal to the government. The latter were defeated and forced to withdraw. While the government was considering what to do next, mutinies broke out in garrisons in several other parts of China.

Sun Yatsen, who had been in the United States when the first mutinies occurred, now returned home. On 1 January 1912, he was elected the provisional president of a republic in Nanking by delegates from sixteen provincial assemblies. This ought to have led on to his becoming president when the mother of the emperor, a boy of just six, announced her son's abdication five weeks later. But he lacked military support, and a deadlock was created when the empress-dowager in a final edict invited Yuan Shikai, a professional soldier who had trained a modern army for the dynasty and therefore had links with most provincial commanders, to form a republican government. Sun, whose instinct often led him to compromise and who was perhaps genuinely hopeful that Yuan would respect republican and democratic forms, decided to support Yuan and urged a new national council in Nanking to elect him president in his own place, which it duly did. Sun did not become a minister in the government which Yuan then formed, preferring to remain a party leader. In August 1912, he became one of the chiefs of the new Nationalist Party, created through the amalgamation of the Revolutionary League with four smaller republican groups.

The story of the next eight years is one of nationwide political and administrative disintegration. Yuan Shikai quickly made it clear that he was no democrat. When the Nationalist Party emerged as a clear victor in elections to the two houses of a new national assembly, he resisted its efforts to determine the composition of his government and then plotted the murder of Song Jiaoren, the most popular of its younger leaders. He went on to show that he was no republican. He prompted petitions which invited him to restore the monarchy and make himself emperor. His subsequent attempt to act on these was a miserable failure – not least because most surviving monarchists regarded him as having no imperial legitimacy. But the threat and then occurrence of the attempt led to fighting in many provinces, which in turn led to the emergence of that most baneful of China's twentieth-century figures, the local militarist or warlord, and the collapse of effective central government.

The formal name of the movement which Deng Xiaoping joined when he entered the preparatory school in Chungking was the Movement for Diligent Work and Frugal Study. Its progenitor was Li Yuying, a patriot, anarchist and Francophile who had been trying for years to create closer links between China and France and to bring to Chinese workers and students the benefits of education and vocational training in France. A man of means, he had himself been at a French secondary school and had studied at the Pasteur Institute in Paris.

Li's first project dated from 1908, when he had established a bean-curd factory in the outskirts of Paris and set out to instruct its workers, peasants from his native village in China, in written Chinese, French, elementary science and good social behaviour. In the manner of most anarchists, he imposed a strict moral regime; his students were forbidden to drink, smoke or gamble and were required rather than encouraged to study. The experiment did not last for long. The bean-curd factory failed as a commercial undertaking, and Li was obliged to send his guinea-pigs home.

Undeterred, Li went on to devise new and more ambitious schemes. In the immediate pre-war years, he arranged for about 130 Chinese students, of both sexes, to study in secondary schools in Paris and at Montargis and Fontainebleau. During the war, he founded an association to bring basic education, and anarchist values, to the Chinese workers who had been recruited on contract to work in French factories. The association opened a school in Paris, and it seems that at least some contract workers found the time, and had the energy, to attend it.

In 1916, Li – still in France – evolved yet another scheme: to recruit and bring to France a large number of educated young Chinese, this time to work as well as study. His ambitions for them were that they should get over the disdain for manual labour which well-educated Chinese had been taught to feel, bring civility and some education to the 30,000 Chinese workers in French factories, and learn skills useful to China's modernization. He founded a Sino-French Education Association, 'to develop relations between China and France and, especially, with the aid of French scientific and spiritual education, to plan for China's moral, intellectual and economic well-being'.[6] He persuaded friends and well-wishers in China to open branches of the association and to establish schools to prepare recruits for the experience of living and working in France.

Because the political condition of the country was so bad, and also because jobs were hard to come by for the first generation of modern middle-school graduates, a large number of young Chinese were attracted by Li's programme. Between March 1919 and December 1920, almost 1,600 worker-students, about thirty of them women, sailed for France. A few, like Deng Xiaoping, were under twenty, and a few others were in their thirties or even forties, but most were in their early twenties. The largest contingents came from Sichuan and Hunan, Mao Zedong's province. Some were university graduates, but the great majority had not gone beyond a secondary education. They came from the middle of society, the sons and daughters of poorer landowners, merchants or scholars. Most of their families could ill afford the price of a steamship ticket to France, even at the concessionary rate of a hundred silver dollars which was on offer (sometimes chambers of commerce offered to lend, though not give, money for fares, at least allowing families to postpone the day when they would be required to draw on their savings).

Memoirs and other accounts show that most of the worker-students set out optimistically, believing that they would have to work hard but end by acquiring advanced professional and industrial skills. Some also hoped to learn the secrets of France's success in becoming and remaining a democratic republic. In a poem he wrote in June 1920, five months before sailing, Zhou Enlai, with Deng Xiaoping the most famous of the worker-students in later life, spoke of France as the 'birthplace of freedom' and looked forward to the day when the person to whom the poem was addressed – a girl student – would 'unfurl the banner to freedom' in China.[7] On the French side, there were also high hopes. For some time, French politicians and educators had worried about the spread of Anglo-American cultural influence in China, especially through the middle schools and colleges established by Protestant missionaries, and they welcomed the movement as a means of winning admiration for French civilization. Some of them were just as romantic as the young Chinese, claiming that the movement would bring together two civilizations which had much in common. One enthusiast wrote that the Chinese were 'the French of the Far East', because they were philosophers, poets and artists.[8]

The core subjects in the curriculum at the school in Chungking were French, Chinese and basic industrial skills. It is not known how well Deng Xiaoping did in the classroom, though one of his fellow-students wrote over sixty years later that he studied 'very diligently'.[9] Documents in the archives of the French Ministry of Foreign Affairs shed a little more light, showing that he hoped to work in metallurgy when he reached France, that he matriculated from the school successfully and that he passed an examination in the French language conducted by the French consul in Chengdu. After graduation, Deng presumably returned to Guang'an for a short time to pack and otherwise prepare for his sojourn in France and to say goodbye to his family. His leave-taking can only have been painful. It would have been more painful still if he and his parents had known that they were destined never to meet again.

At the beginning of September 1920, Deng set out by steamer from Chungking, with his uncle and nearly a hundred other fellow-students, on the first stage of his journey to France – and to a revolutionary career.

CHAPTER 2

Doctor of Mimeography, 1920–26

Deng Xiaoping, Deng Shaosheng and nearly two hundred other worker-students, about half of them from Sichuan, sailed for France from Shanghai on the Messageries Maritimes liner *André Lebon* on 11 September 1920. They were all fourth-class (steerage) passengers, and as such did not have cabins and could not eat in dining-rooms. They had to spread their bedding on deck or in the hold, where there was very poor ventilation, and to prepare and eat their meals wherever they could. If their voyage resembled the voyages described in the memoirs of worker-students who travelled on other ships, many of them suffered badly from seasickness and quite a few became so homesick that they began to ask about the possibility of returning home long before they reached Marseilles.

Deng and his companions landed at Marseilles on 19 October and immediately travelled on to Paris. There officials of the Sino-French Education Association divided the contingent from the Chungking preparatory school into groups of about twenty and sent each one to a *collège* (non-selective secondary school) in the provinces. Deng and his uncle were members of the group sent to Bayeux, in Normandy.

In a special class, the young Chinese at Bayeux resumed their interrupted study of the French language. If things had gone smoothly, they would have continued as language students until their knowledge of French was good enough to allow them to follow an ordinary programme of secondary education. At this stage, some of them might have transferred to other schools; others would have looked for factory work, with the objects of acquiring basic industrial skills and of earning enough money to finance further spells of education. This latter category would have included all the poorer worker-students – those who had not banked money with the association on their arrival in France or were not receiving remittances from their families.

But this was not to be. In January 1921, the association informed its charges that it had run out of money and that only those students who could pay their own fees would be able to stay at school. The root cause of the crisis was mismanagement. The association had allowed too many worker-students to go to France and had failed to find new sources of income to meet its steadily rising expenditure. The crisis might have been averted if Li Yuying, now back in China, and the movement's other principal backers had been willing to throw themselves into fund-raising. But they were not. All through 1920 they had been losing interest in the movement – partly perhaps because it was so troublesome to administer, but mainly because they had persuaded themselves that a better way to strengthen cultural links between China and France, and to bring useful knowledge to China, was to establish institutions of higher education on the French model in both countries. A particular attraction of the scheme was that it offered the prospect, which the worker-student movement did not, of obtaining funding from the French government, out of money it had received from China under the Boxer Protocol of 1901.*

The worker-students, far from home, had not realized how the wind was blowing. It therefore came as a very great shock when Cai Yuanpei, chancellor of Peking University, announced in Paris that the association, of which he was a co-president, had better things to do than look after them and that they would now have to fend for themselves.

* In this agreement, the Chinese imperial government undertook to pay indemnities to the governments of countries which had suffered damage to life or property during the Boxer rising of 1900. The period of payment was thirty-nine years and the total Chinese liability amounted to about £140 million at 1901 rates of exchange. This imposition was seen to be punitive in China from the start, and by degrees came to be so regarded by most receiving governments.

For Deng, the consequence was the dissolution of his class at Bayeux. He was receiving money from his family at this time and so in theory might have asked the association to find him a place at another school. But he chose, or was persuaded, not to do this, and agreed to enter the Schneider engineering works at Le Creusot, between Paris and Lyons, where several dozen worker-students and about a thousand ordinary Chinese workers were already employed.

Deng's departure from Bayeux ended his only period of modest comfort and security during the whole of his five years in France. For the rest of the time, he lived in factory dormitories or cheap hotels and did work that was often temporary and never skilled. His worst job was the first. According to his official biography, he did 'odd jobs' at the Schneider works.[1] But the company's records show that he was in fact employed in its rolling-mill, where he was one of an army of apprentices and unskilled workers who transferred heavy and still-hot metal plates from a conveyor belt to other parts of the shop. His employment card shows that his daily wage was 6.60 francs, less than the rate earned by apprentices, and that he worked for fifty or more hours a week. In these conditions, and at the age of sixteen, it is not surprising that he decided after only three weeks that he had had enough, and that he would rather risk unemployment in Paris than carry on.

Later, Deng worked in a factory which made rubber tyres and overshoes – his job was to glue together the prefabricated parts of shoes – as a locomotive fireman, as a kitchen help in restaurants, and, right at the end of his time in France, in the Renault automobile works at Billancourt, in the suburbs of Paris. One of his temporary jobs was a week spent making lotus flowers out of pieces of gauze and satin (demurely but dishonestly labelled by his employer as the work of war-widows and orphans). He made little, if any, progress towards acquiring the industrial skills which he had come to France to learn (his official biography says that he was a fitter at Renault but the company's records show that he was an '*ouvrier spécialisé*' – an unskilled worker). Only at one stage, during his time in the rubber-products factory, did he earn enough money to finance a further spell of education. And this was only enough to pay for three months at a secondary school (at Châtillon-sur-Seine, in the winter of 1922–3).

It was against this background of indigence and insecurity that Deng was drawn into politics. His official biography describes the process thus:

In France job-hunting was especially difficult because of the depressed economy. Even those Chinese students who were fortunate enough to find jobs in big factories were paid only half the wages of the ordinary French workers.* Worse still, at this time Deng Xiaoping's family could no longer afford to send him money, so he had to scrape along on his own. His high hopes of studying abroad were crushed by the grim reality.

But new ideas were taking strong hold of the young man. Thanks to the October Revolution in Russia, the workers' movement in France was gaining momentum, and Marxism and other schools of socialist thought were winning more and more adherents. A number of ideologically advanced Chinese students were starting to accept Marxism and take the revolutionary road. Under the influence of his seniors, Zhao Shiyan, Zhou Enlai and others, Deng began to study Marxism and do political propaganda work.[2]

There is a great deal which is vague about this account. In particular, it says nothing about the timing of his conversion to Marxism. The only piece of internal evidence is the reference to Zhao Shiyan and Zhou Enlai. Zhao was working at the Schneider plant when Deng was employed there in April 1921 and overlapped with Deng in Paris from October 1921 to February 1922. Zhou and Deng were both in Paris from May 1921 to February 1922. The only external evidence is that Deng became a member of the Communist Party of Chinese Youth in Europe, an organization which stipulated faith in Marxism as a condition of membership,

* The memoirs of former worker-students make it clear that this was not universally true.

at some stage in 1922. The bracket is therefore fairly wide; it is, however, clear that the decisive period was early on during Deng's time in France.

Vague though it is, the account points clearly to Zhao and Zhou as two of Deng's mentors. This is important. From all accounts, Zhao was a remarkable young man – intelligent, energetic and personally attractive. Zhou was all these things too; moreover, he had already developed an approach to ideology and politics – an inclination to appeal to reason in justifying principles and policies – which distinguished him for the rest of his life. Deng, less cautious and patient by nature, adopted the same general approach; and there is no experience in his revolutionary career other than his association with Zhou which can plausibly explain it. Sixty years later, Deng told the Italian writer Oriana Fallaci that he regarded Zhou as his elder brother.[3] This is a special compliment in Chinese, implying discipleship as well as great affection and respect.

In June 1923, Deng was elected to the executive committee of the European branch of the Chinese Socialist Youth League.* This gave him political work to do; he ceased to be a worker-student who had been converted to Marxism and became a professional revolutionary, doing a job in order to sustain his career as such.

At the very outset of this career, Deng acquired a nickname which appears in many of the memoirs of other worker-students: the Doctor of Mimeography. He was given it – originally by whom is not known – because he was so painstaking in copying the texts of articles for *Red Light*, the league's fortnightly magazine,

---

* Its original title had been the Communist Party of Chinese Youth in Europe. In February 1923, it adopted the extraordinarily cumbersome title of the Chinese Communist Youth League in Europe (European Branch of the Chinese Socialist Youth League). This reflected the simultaneous desire of its members to retain the term 'communist' in its name and the wish of party headquarters in Shanghai to indicate that the league was not a party branch but a branch of its own mass organization for youth.

on to stencils and in rolling off hundreds of copies from the wax. Many of his texts survive, in a calligraphy which is immediately recognizable from the inscriptions he wrote in later life. As with the man, it is consistently sharp and clear.

The office of the youth league was Zhou Enlai's bedroom in a cheap residential hotel at 17 rue Godefroy, near the Place d'Italie in the southern part of Paris. Deng had to work there in a space of only five square metres, much of it taken up by Zhou's bed and other furniture. Only three people at a time could squeeze into the room, even for conversation, so that meetings of the league's executive committee, four or five strong, and larger gatherings, had to be held in local restaurants. In these, Zhou and the rest could normally afford no more than a single vegetable dish and a few bread rolls, and sometimes only rolls and hot water. Deng himself lived at one time in Paris on a diet of milk and croissants – in the process acquiring so much of a taste for the latter that he ordered a whole boxful when his aircraft stopped over in Paris on an official journey in 1974.

Red Light first appeared in February 1924. At some stage, Deng became one of its two editors, and by the end of the year he was writing for it. Three of his articles have survived. All three are attacks on the Chinese Youth Party, a group which was competing vigorously with the league for the allegiance of worker-students and ordinary workers throughout 1924. Clearly influenced by Italian fascism, its line was that China could only be saved by the creation of an authoritarian state. Deng's articles are purely polemical. They heap abuse on the *étatistes*, as the members of the Youth Party were usually known, but attempt no reasoned criticism. The reader will search them in vain for signs that their author would one day be able to argue cogently on matters of theory.

Deng joined the European branch of the Chinese Communist Party in the second half of 1924. This made him a member of the league's parent body, which controlled all its work. Although it had country branches in (at least) France, Germany and Belgium, the European branch was small, with only a few dozen members. It was, however, well-run. It had good security – the French police never discovered any of its secret documents, even after they had set out to find them, as they did in 1925 – reliable if rather slow communications with party headquarters in Shanghai and the headquarters of the Comintern (Third International) in Moscow, and enough of an income to allow it to produce and circulate a good deal of propaganda. Now, in 1993, Deng has been a member of the Chinese party for sixty-nine years, and is almost certainly the longest-serving member of any communist party in the world.

At some point in early 1925, Deng Xiaoping moved from Paris to Lyons, where the party gave him local responsibilities. He was appointed 'special representative to the Lyons area party branch', at which he 'directed the party and league work as well as the Chinese workers' movement'.⁴ At the age of twenty – five years younger than Mao Zedong when he first heard of Marxism – he was given an independent political command. It is quite possible that his work in the labour movement took him back to Le Creusot, where several hundred Chinese were still employed and which was nearer Lyons than Paris. He may also have visited Saint-Chamond, near Saint-Étienne, where there was another large Chinese contingent. He himself worked in a factory somewhere in Lyons.

Deng's stay in Lyons was short. At the end of July, he returned to Paris, registering with the police at Billancourt on the thirtieth of the month. The reason, though not stated explicitly in any French or Chinese document, was undoubtedly the need of the party and the league for his leadership in the capital in the aftermath of the departure of about 150 left-wing militants a few weeks before. About fifty of them had been expelled from France; the others had left of their own volition, but very much under a cloud.

This mass departure was the consequence of the way in which the left-wing worker-students had reacted to the 30 May incident: a confrontation between the police of the International Settlement in Shanghai, under British command, and a large crowd of student and other demonstrators which ended in bloodshed. At least twelve of the demonstrators, who were demanding the release of six students arrested in the settlement for protesting against the action of Japanese guards in firing on strikers at a textile mill, were killed when a British officer ordered his men to open fire on them, at the gates of the police station where the students were being held.

In Paris, the communists and nationalists (now in alliance in China), with the former in the lead, immediately formed an action committee. This body called for a mass demonstration on 14 June which, although held in defiance of a police ban, attracted several thousand participants, French and Chinese. The committee, encouraged by this degree of public support, decided as a next step to mount an attack on the Chinese Legation. This was made on 21 June, a Sunday, and took the police completely by surprise; they arrived on the scene only after a group of young Chinese had broken into the building, found the minister in his apartment and forced him to sign messages of protest about foreign rights and behaviour in China to the French government and his own government. The police cleared the building, but then let the demonstrators disperse freely. This, however, provoked angry comment in some sections of the French press, which spurred the police to strike back; they raided the lodgings of many of the demonstrators – tipped off according to the communists by their political enemies in the Chinese community – arrested nearly sixty of them, detained four of these for trial and secured orders for the immediate deportation of the others. They decided, too, to make it their business to keep a careful eye on the activities of all the militants who remained in France and to penetrate their organizations.

This meant that Deng was under surveillance from the time of his return to Paris. The many police reports of late 1925 which refer to him indicate that he had two main tasks: to rebuild the leadership of the party's general branch, which had been badly disrupted by the summer's exodus, and to make sure that the league continued to function as a going concern. He either chaired or spoke at several meetings in the industrial suburb of Belleville.

He also took work at the Renault plant in Billancourt, seemingly with the double purpose of earning money and keeping in touch with the several hundred Chinese workers, many of them communists or communist sympathizers, who worked at the factory.

Police records also show that Deng and three others, a communist and two social democrats, were suspected of plotting to assassinate the leaders of the Chinese Youth Party. A report said that the four were 'at the head of a movement which aimed at the assassination of Chinese suspected of being in close relations with the French authorities and of being the cause of the expulsions of Chinese communist militants'.[5] Whether the leaders of the anticommunist group in fact helped the police, for instance by providing them with the names and addresses of radicals after the attack on the legation, is uncertain, though certainly plausible. That Deng and his fellows were in fact plotting to assassinate these leaders is extremely doubtful. Political assassination was not a procedure which the party favoured, then or later, and the alleged plotters knew perfectly well that they were under close watch. The charge looks like the invention of men who were keen to deal a final blow to their political enemies.

On 3 January 1926, Deng spoke at a meeting convened by the action committee formed in the summer. He argued in favour of 'fraternization with the government of the Soviet Union'[6] to fight imperialism and encouraged those present to vote for a new ultimatum to the Chinese minister. Having studied reports on the meeting from their informers, the police decided that the time had come to raid three hotels in Billancourt in which Chinese activists were known to live. In the small hours of 8 January, they entered the room which Deng shared with two others, in the hotel of 3 rue Castéja, but found it empty. Nor did they find any illegal or incriminating documents – only some printing equipment, Chinese newspapers and a good deal of propaganda material.

By the time the police entered his room, Deng was in fact on his way to Moscow. He had been planning to leave France for the Soviet Union for some time – he gave notice to his employers at Renault before Christmas, saying that he had decided to return to

China – and it looks as if he escaped arrest because his date of departure had been fixed for the day before the raid. The police, frustrated, could only impound the paraphernalia they found in his room and issue a deportation order, marked 'to be notified',[7] which they had no prospect of being able to serve on him.

Deng Xiaoping arrived in France a patriotic youth, worried about the state of China and anxious to acquire industrial skills, seeing industrialization as the route to the wealth and power which all patriots wanted for their country. But that, according to his official biography, was about all.[8] By the time he left France he had become a Marxist and a professional revolutionary. As a revolutionary, he had built up experience in several kinds of work – starting humbly as an engraver of stencils, he had gone on to be the joint editor of a magazine, a propagandist among Chinese students and workers and the head of a party branch (if a very small one). He had learned, too, what it was like to work under police surveillance and among political enemies. He was not without experience of conspiracy and danger when he was plunged fifteen months later into the cauldron of Chinese revolutionary politics.

How did Deng's years in France affect him otherwise? They certainly inoculated him against the sinocentrism which was so marked a feature in the outlook of Mao Zedong – and of all the other Chinese communist leaders, like Lin Biao, who never lived abroad. Throughout his political career, and especially during his years as China's national leader, he took a great deal of interest in foreigners and in their perceptions of China. He showed, too, grasp of two truths: that China could not ignore the world, if only because the world would not ignore China; and that China could not hope to develop quickly without being willing to learn from the world.

France as such may have influenced him less strongly than the experience of living abroad. By the time he left Paris for Moscow he must have read French without difficulty and spoken French at least passably well. But there is no evidence that he took an interest in French art or literature, or even, as a practical man, in

French engineering and architecture. Nor is there anything in the record – the archives of French government departments, factories and schools, and the memoirs of other worker-students – to indicate that he had French friends. Some worker-students got to know Frenchmen at evening classes run by *L'Humanité*, the communist newspaper, or by taking lodgings in private houses, or by talking about politics to their instructors at school. Not so Deng, it seems.

Deng's character would have developed wherever he had been between the ages of sixteen and twenty-one. But it is hard to believe that he would have become quite so tough or self-reliant, at any rate so young, unless he had gone through the hard school of living by his wits in a world where there was little sympathy, and even less support, for a young Chinese who was down on his luck. Two photographs tell much of the story of how his character did in fact develop. The first, taken of him in a studio with Deng Shaosheng, probably when they were both at Bayeux, shows a boy in rather crumpled Western clothes, awkward in pose and almost expressionless (see plate 1).[9] The second, glued to his employment card at Renault, shows a young man with a firm jaw, a candid gaze and a curl to his lip.[10] He is again dressed in Western clothes, but smartly. He is already recognizable as the Deng Xiaoping of twenty and thirty years later.

CHAPTER 3

Warlords and Bolsheviks, 1926–7

During Deng Xiaoping's five years in France, the state of Chinese politics had changed a great deal. The amount of territory under warlord control had continued to increase, until it extended to the whole country other than the outlying regions of Tibet, Sinkiang and Mongolia (the last of which had broken away, to become a communist republic). The number of warlords, great and small, had swelled until it ran into hundreds. The warlords varied enormously in character and outlook, but had two characteristics in common: they commanded armies loyal wholly or chiefly to themselves and they had territorial bases. The greater warlords managed three alliances or cliques, which intrigued and sometimes fought to acquire more territory or dominate the republican government in Peking. This government eventually controlled no territory of its own. But it had attributes which even the greatest of the warlords did not possess: political legitimacy, under the republic's provisional constitution of 1912; foreign recognition; and, as a function of these two, the power to borrow money, both at home and abroad. For the warlords, therefore, the power to dictate to presidents and prime ministers was a great political prize.

At the same time, a revived revolutionary movement had come into being. One impulse behind it was anger about the failure of the revolution of 1911–12 and shame about its consequences: the imperial government had at least held China together; under Yuan Shikai and the warlords it had fallen apart. Another was anger about the way in which the powers continued to treat China. There had been many humiliations, culminating in the cession to Japan at Versailles of all the rights which Germany had previously enjoyed in the peninsular province of Shandong. A third was the view of a new generation of intellectuals that, in order to modernize and so acquire the power to control its destiny, China would need to undergo a cultural revolution and, in the opinion of more than a few, a social revolution as well. These impulses meant that the ideology and objectives of the revived movement were a great deal more radical than those of the original movement. Its official ideology still consisted of the Three People's Principles, first formulated by Sun Yatsen in 1905 – national sovereignty, popular power and popular welfare – but these were now given more explicitly anti-imperialist and collectivist interpretations. Its agreed objectives were to defeat the warlords, to establish a strong republican government and actively to roll back the host of privileges which foreigners enjoyed on Chinese territory.

The revived movement was also different in composition and organization. The old movement had included a few individuals who called themselves Marxists and some anarchists. The new movement included the Chinese Communist Party, which had been created in 1921 – at a meeting which began on the deserted premises of a girls' school in Shanghai – through the amalgamation of half a dozen local Marxist groups. It was still very small in 1922 and 1923, only a few hundred strong, but it had begun to speak of itself as a 'militant and disciplined party of the proletariat'[1] and to have an orthodox Leninist structure of cells and branches under a permanent headquarters. As important, for itself and for the movement as a whole, it had become a branch of the Comintern in Moscow, thereby undertaking to submit reports to that body and to accept instructions from it. The Nationalist Party, the other – and much larger – organized component of the movement had also leaned towards Moscow, to the point of asking the Soviet Union for political and organizational advice; and in the autumn of 1923, Mikhail Borodin, a Bolshevik with wide foreign experience, arrived in Canton to rewrite its programme and reconstruct it on Leninist lines. From 1924 on, the movement therefore consisted of two Leninist parties, each with a number of subordinate or associated organizations. The parties themselves were linked through a mechanism known as the 'block within': all communists became members of the Nationalist Party, on a personal basis. For the communists, this had both advantages and drawbacks. It allowed them to influence the making and execution of policy in the Nationalist Party, and to proselytize within it; but it also allowed the nationalists to know who the communists were and what they were doing. It came into being because Sun Yatsen refused to agree to a coalition between the two parties and was only accepted by the communists under heavy pressure from their Comintern adviser of the time.

None of this might have produced political change if Sun Yatsen, as much the unchallenged leader of the new movement as of the old, had not become convinced that it must have an army of its own. The old movement had failed because it had depended on fickle military men, and there was in any case no way of defeating the warlords except by deploying military power against them. Encouraged by Borodin, Sun turned to the Soviet Union for help, and in October 1924 General Vasilii Blyukher, who used the pseudonym Galen in China, arrived in Canton to be his military adviser. Dozens of other Soviet officers accompanied or followed him. In the same month, a first consignment of Soviet arms reached Canton on a yacht from the Black Sea port of Odessa.

Five months before Galen's arrival, a military academy had opened at Whampoa, on the Pearl River south of Canton. Fatefully, Sun appointed Chiang Kaishek, a Japanese-trained officer who had supported him staunchly against Yuan Shikai, as its commandant. Strong on military discipline and punctilio, Chiang set to work with great energy and by the end of year had turned out two classes of 500 officers each. At this stage, he appeared to have no particular bias in the politics of a movement which consisted of Marxist revolutionaries, committed to class war against landowners and (ultimately) capitalists, on the left, social reformers, but not revolutionaries, in the centre, and patriots but social conservatives on the right. He worked harmoniously with Galen and in 1925 was prepared to send his son Chiang Chingkuo to Moscow as a student.

The year 1925 was one of gathering storm. In March, Sun Yatsen, who had gone to Peking to take part in a 'national reconstruction conference' called by the warlord who controlled the capital, died there of liver cancer at the age of fifty-nine. From February to May, Chiang Kaishek won a series of victories over warlords with bases near Canton. At the end of this period, the 30 May incident in Shanghai, described in the last chapter, brought great accessions of strength to both the nationalists and the communists; by the end of the year, the Communist Party, which had been barely a thousand strong in 1925, had about 10,000 members and its youth league about 10,000 more. In June, the nationalist leaders established an alternative government in Canton and proclaimed the formation of a National Revolutionary Army. In August, Liao Zhongkai, an ardent advocate of collaboration between the nationalists and both the communists and the Soviet Union, was assassinated in Canton. This caused great tension within the revolutionary movement and, as important for the future, brought Chiang Kaishek into politics through his appointment as one of a committee of three set up to investigate the murder. The committee was unable to pin responsibility for Liao's death on any particular group or individual. But it found that the right wing of the Nationalist Party was conspiring to get rid of, by one means or another, all senior nationalists who favoured reliance on Soviet advice and support and continued alliance with the Chinese communists. This led to a strong tilt to the left in the political balance in Canton. At a Nationalist Party congress in January 1927, left-wing nationalists and communists dominated proceedings and secured control of a new central executive committee (out of all proportion to their numbers in the movement as a whole, the communists secured fourteen out of sixty seats on the committee and three out of nine seats on its standing committee). Known or suspected right-wing conspirators were sent away from Canton, either into warlord territory in the north or – a poetic touch – to Moscow for 'education'. Chiang showed no overt sign of objecting to any of this and worked closely with Borodin, as well as Galen, throughout the winter of 1925–6.

*

Deng Xiaoping spent eleven months in Moscow. To begin with, he was a student at the Communist University for the Toilers of the East, an institution created in 1921 to train Asian workers, from inside and outside the Soviet Union, in revolutionary theory and practice. Dependent on the Soviet government's Commissariat of Nationalities – Stalin's first power-base – it existed for almost twenty years, turning out a steady stream of Uzbeks, Kazakhs, Mongolians and Koreans to run party or government agencies in the Soviet Union and Mongolia and to promote revolution elsewhere. During the 1920s, hundreds of Chinese communists – including two, Liu Shaoqi and Ren Bishi, who were to rise very high in the party – were among its students. Under the perfect control of the Soviet state, and open only to communists, it attracted little international attention and caused no tensions in Soviet politics.

Not so the Sun Yatsen University, to which Deng was transferred after a few weeks. Created by the Soviet party in the autumn of 1925 'in order to train personnel for the [Chinese] revolution',[2] it became an object of controversy in China and both an object and an arena of conflict in the subsequent power struggle between Stalin and Trotsky. After five years, Stalin decided that the university gave more trouble than it was worth and closed it down.

In theory, the university was under the joint control of the central committees of the Chinese Nationalist Party and the Soviet Communist Party, and a well-known nationalist did in fact travel to Moscow to join its board of trustees. How it was financed is still mysterious. One story is that the Soviet party, following the example of the French government in 1920, drew on Boxer indemnity funds; another is that rich nationalist supporters in China were induced to make remittances. Wherever the money came from, the university was lavishly run. All the students were given cash allowances, and they were accommodated, fed and clothed without charge.

The university had a large teaching and administrative staff. Its rector was Karl Radek, a native of Lwów (Lemberg) in Poland who had been an intermediary between Lenin and the German imperial government in 1917. He was a considerable linguist and had the reputation of being a great scholar. An unkempt figure, usually with a pipe in his mouth, he loved to lecture, often for over two hours at a time. Although he had never been near China, his subject was the Chinese revolutionary movement. Many of his listeners must have wondered at his presumption.

Radek, nevertheless, was popular with the students. His deputy, Pavel Mif, an intensely ambitious young man of twenty-five, was not.* A member of the Comintern's Far Eastern secretariat, he believed that the first duty of communist parties outside the Soviet Union was to protect the Soviet state and that it was the principal function of the Comintern to ensure that they did. At the university, his chief object was to find young Chinese who might be open to these views. In his talent-spotting, he looked out for students who were clever and interested in Marxist theory, but who had not had any practical political experience. He had little time for the rest of the students, and they reacted with natural suspicion or dislike. In 1927, after the collapse of the united front in China and the beginning of Stalin's campaign to disgrace Trotsky, he became a remorseless persecutor of the considerable number of communist students who believed that Trotsky's views about Chinese politics had been sounder than Stalin's.

Mif succeeded in making converts of a group which came to be known in China as the Returned Students, the Twenty-Eight Bolsheviks or, even less politely, Stalin's China Section. Its leaders controlled the Chinese Communist Party from 1931 to 1935, implementing a political and military strategy which is now described, and condemned, as the 'third left line'. In 1945, Mao Zedong buried the line in an official resolution on party history which is a masterpiece of mordant criticism, and insisted that its proponents should criticize themselves. The resolution did not say, however, that the line had been made in Moscow or that its

---

* Mif, 'myth' in Russian, was a pseudonym. His real name was Mikhail Aleksandrovich Fortus.

proponents had felt bound to apply it for this reason. The irony is that, although the real villain of the piece was Stalin, Mao was much the most important communist anywhere to come to Stalin's defence when Khrushchev denounced him in 1956. He thereby did more for Stalin's reputation in China than any of Mif's acolytes.

The most important members of the group were Chen Shaoyu (Wang Ming under his revolutionary pseudonym), Qin Bangxian (Bo Gu), Zhang Wentian (Luo Fu) and Wang Jiaxiang. They were all talented in their different ways. Wang Ming wrote and spoke extremely well. Helen Foster Snow, the first wife of Edgar Snow,* has described Bo Gu as he was in 1937: 'He was so typically the Chinese intellectual in appearance as to be a caricature – thin, delicate, overworked, half-sick, and wearing thick-lensed glasses. His thick shock of hair made him seem top-heavy as well as brain-heavy.'³ But he was physically brave (in the early 1930s he risked arrest and execution in Shanghai for longer than almost all the other communist leaders) and he was ready to admit that, as an intellectual, he needed to be taught about how the workers lived and what they wanted. Luo Fu was five or six years older than Wang and Bo and knew rather more about the world. The son of a scholar who had become a successful businessman, he was something of a scholar himself. He had spent two years in California, attending at least some university classes and working on a magazine for the Chinese community in San Francisco, and he spoke good English. Wang Jiaxiang, who did without a pseudonym, was another brave man – he endured a stomach wound with great fortitude before and during the Long March – and he had enough independence of mind to help Deng Xiaoping in 1933, when he was in political disgrace.

* Edgar Snow, an American journalist and writer, visited the communist base area in Shaanxi for four months in the summer of 1936. The book he then wrote, *Red Star over China*, is a classic, both as an adventure story and as a piece of vivid reporting. It gave the world the first account of the Chinese communists which was not a matter of hearsay or nationalist propaganda. Mao Zedong, Zhou Enlai and many others, including Deng Xiaoping, talked to Snow about their early lives.

According to his biographers, Deng did not know the Returned Students in Moscow.[4] This is probably not to be taken too literally: he must have been aware that the vice-rector had collected a group of favourites and at least known them by name and sight. Yet that may have been all. Wang and Bo were in other classes – perhaps because they were Russian speakers – and other sources only mention one classmate who belonged to the group. In any case, with his sturdy patriotism and experience of taking decisions for himself, Deng is unlikely to have had much time for people who were prepared to accept uncritically whatever was said to them by a foreigner who had never worked in the field.

The student body was two or three hundred strong when Deng joined it, and twice as big by the end of 1926. About half of the students were communists, members of the party or the youth league, or both. Of these, only a dozen or so had come from Western Europe; the rest were mostly university graduates and undergraduates from north and east China. The other students were nationalists, quite a few of them the relations of nationalist leaders. Deng had two classmates of this kind: Chiang Kaishek's son Chiang Chingkuo (only seventeen in 1925) and Feng Funeng, a daughter of the warlord Feng Yuxiang. After the collapse of the united front in China in 1927, the composition of the student body altered. The nationalists disappeared. Some asked to return to China; some were compelled to return; and a few were arrested, tried and sentenced to hard labour. Chiang Chingkuo was forced to stay; he was sent to work in a Siberian gold-mine for some time and was held in the Soviet Union until the nationalists and communists formed a new united front in 1937. The nationalists were replaced by communists for whom the party wanted a safe haven. Some of these were older men (Wu Yuzhang, the founder of Deng's preparatory school at Chungking, was one of them); some were party officials; and some factory workers, for whom the university's teaching had to be simplified.

In Deng's time, the academic load was heavy. Seven subjects were taught: foreign languages, history, philosophy, political economy, economic geography, Leninism and military science.

Among foreign languages, Russian was compulsory and English, French and German were optional. History was the history of the 'evolution of social formations' and of revolutions and revolution- ary movements. Philosophy was the dialectical materialism of Marx and Engels and political economy was the political economy of Marx's *Capital*. Leninism consisted of a course based on a series of lectures which Stalin had given at the Sverdlov University in April 1924, shortly after Lenin's death (the lectures were published in book form as *Foundations of Leninism*). Military science included a practical component: training in marksmanship and basic tactics.

Deng's contemporary reaction to this regime is not known. His attitude as an old man to book-learning – and to Marxism– Leninism as a source of wisdom – is quite clear from a speech he made in the spring of 1992:

We should study the essence of Marxism-Leninism, the applicable parts. Long articles are for a small number of experts to study. How should the masses read them? Should they all be required to read thick books? That is formalism. It cannot be done. The first books I read before entering school were the *Manifesto of the Communist Party* and the *ABC of Communism*.* Recently, some foreigners said that Marxism cannot be overthrown. It cannot be overthrown because it contains unbreakable truth, not because there are a lot of thick books on it. Seeking truth from facts is the quintessence of Marxism. This should be advocated, not bookism . . . Practice is the only criterion for judging truth.[5]

While Deng was at his books, the national revolutionary move- ment in China took to the field against the warlords, achieving a string of military successes, but passed politically out of the control of its left wing.

The latter process began in March 1926, when, in a showdown with the army's Soviet military advisers, the left nationalists and

* A primer by Bukharin, one of Lenin's closest associates and Stalin's chief victim when he turned against the Old Bolsheviks who had helped him to defeat Trotsky.

the communists, Chiang Kaishek imposed his will on all three. The crisis began when a gunboat under the command of a communist officer anchored very close to his headquarters at Whampoa, with steam up but without orders he knew about. Suspecting a plot, he declared martial law in Canton, dispatched troops whose loyalty was beyond doubt to disarm the workers' pickets who were guarding many buildings in the city and seized the gunboat. He even detained thirty or so Soviet military men.

Having thus asserted his authority, Chiang went on to insist that three Soviet advisers he particularly disliked should leave Canton, that communist political workers should be withdrawn from the first corps of the army, under his own command, and that measures should be adopted to restrict and make more transparent the activities of communists within the Nationalist Party. Perhaps in order to make it seem that he was even-handed politically, he also demanded that several right-wing nationalist politicians should leave Canton. Galen and Borodin, who had been away in the north at the time of the gunboat incident, could only have resisted at the risk of destroying the united front, and it was dogma in Moscow that this should be preserved.

Chiang also got Galen and Borodin to agree that the army should march north as soon as it was militarily ready. This was another victory. In early 1927, both Stalin and Trotsky wanted the army to stay in the south, because they had concluded that Soviet interests required better relations between the Soviet Union and Japan, and that this in turn required no action by the nationalists which could alarm the Japanese. Leading and rank-and-file communists in Canton undoubtedly wanted early military action. But the central executive committee in Shanghai had echoed the overt Soviet line that such action might be premature. By no means for the last time, it made itself vulnerable to internal criticism by doing as Moscow wished.

The northern expedition began in late June 1926. There was heavy fighting in Hubei, where Wuchang was only taken after a siege of forty days, and in Jiangxi, where Nanchang, the provincial capital, was only captured at the third attempt. Some units, including several of the best, suffered heavy casualties. As the army advanced, a mass movement developed behind it. Its chief targets were unpopular landlords – 'local tyrants and evil gentry' in Mao Zedong's phrase[6] – and foreigners. In January 1927, the British concessions in the Yangtse cities of Hankow and Jiujiang were overrun and occupied. In Hunan, there was much explicitly anti-Christian agitation, leading to the evacuation of some mission stations and the closure of most mission schools.

By the end of 1926, the army had wrested from warlord control most of the territory south of the Yangtse. Its degree of success had surprised the world and entirely altered the balance of power in China; it had begun to look as if, with its second wind, Sun Yatsen's revolutionary movement would succeed after all. Chiang himself, now commander-in-chief and an international as well as a national figure, was in an even stronger political position than he had been before leaving Canton, and in this had begun to make clear that he was opposed to a social revolution in either the cities or the countryside and that he wanted only limited action against foreigners and foreign interests. The communists perceived the trend clearly and with great alarm. A central committee report of January 1927 contained this analysis:

The right wing of the Kuomintang [Nationalist Party] is daily becoming more powerful ... There is currently an extremely strong tendency within the Kuomintang to oppose Soviet Russia, the communist party, and the labour and peasant movements.

The tendency towards the right is due first to the belief of Chiang Kaishek [and others] ... that only one party should exist in the country, that all classes should cooperate, that class struggle should be prohibited, and that there is no need of a communist party ...

The second reason is their idea that the national revolution will soon succeed, that there will soon be a movement for class revolution, and that the greatest enemy at present is not imperialism or militarism but the communist party ... For these reasons a great anti-communist tide has developed within the Kuomintang ...[7]

*

It was the activities of Feng Yuxiang, a warlord, which were responsible for Deng Xiaoping's return to China.

A more appealing figure than most of the other warlords, Feng has gone down in history as the Christian general. As well as being a Christian, he was a high-minded Chinese traditionalist, believing that it was the duty of a leader to exemplify virtue and to care about the welfare of the common people. As a soldier, he dressed simply, eschewing the elaborate uniforms favoured by most warlords, mixed with his men and relied as much on example and exhortation as on abuse and punishment in his man-management. He encouraged his troops to sing on the march and taught them Christian hymns as marching songs. Partly because of his eccentricity, but mainly because he was regarded as an honest man, keen to do good for his country, he became a popular figure well outside the ranks of his army.

In 1924, Feng, whose base was in north-west China, sought Soviet aid, to bolster his position against Wu Peifu and Zhang Zuolin, the other principal northern warlords, after he had occupied Peking while they were fighting one another. On the recommendation of Borodin, who had travelled from Canton to take his measure as a potential ally, both for the Soviet Union and for the nationalists in the south, the Russians decided to provide him with arms, money and military instructors. They also sent him political advisers – whom he was less willing to accept – and offered places for his officers in Soviet military academies. In parallel, the Chinese communists decided to send young men from Shanghai and Peking, including some who had been given military training in the Soviet Union, to work in the ranks of his army.

In spite of this aid, Feng's army suffered a series of defeats at the hands of Zhang Zuolin, the master of Manchuria, in early 1926. Feng resigned his command – a common move for a defeated Chinese general – and made plans to visit Moscow. The Russians may not have wanted him. But he was determined to go, no doubt calculating that it would be impossible for them to refuse to receive a man who had accepted their aid and who would count for a good deal, politically as well as militarily, now that the northern expedition was about to begin. He made his way by easy stages to Ulan Bator, the capital of Outer Mongolia (the Mongolian People's Republic) and there had a series of meetings with Borodin, whose standing in Moscow could have suffered if he had not been able to intercept, question and brief Feng before he arrived. After a month-long stopover, Feng travelled on to Moscow at the beginning of May.

Feng stayed in Moscow for fully three months. He met most of the Soviet leaders of the day (though not Stalin), and visited Sun Yatsen University, making a speech to the students – Deng Xiaoping presumably included – which was full of revolutionary rhetoric and was enthusiastically received. He played his cards adroitly. Knowing that the Russians urgently wanted him back in China, he was able to exploit their anxiety to exact extremely good terms. There are several versions of these, but they all speak of large financial grants, considerable quantities of military equipment and a generous programme of training for Feng's officers. When he was satisfied, Feng undertook to make an open and formal declaration of support for the nationalist cause. He was quick to honour his word. On 17 September, having recrossed Mongolia, found his army and formally resumed its command, he led his officers in making a 'mass pledge' of support for the nationalist revolution in the desert town of Wuyuan, on the great northern bend of the Yellow River.

On his return journey, Feng was accompanied by a new contingent of Soviet military advisers and by several Chinese communists. According to Deng Xiaoping's official biography, he had invited the Comintern to 'send a number of its Chinese comrades to work in his army'.[8] It is rather more likely that the Comintern persuaded him to accept them, arguing that he ought to have communists in his army to symbolize his acceptance of the revolutionary united front. Whatever the precise give and take, he allowed the Comintern to send a new wave of communist activists into his army.

The leader of the Chinese group was Liu Bojian, a former secretary of the youth league in France who had undergone

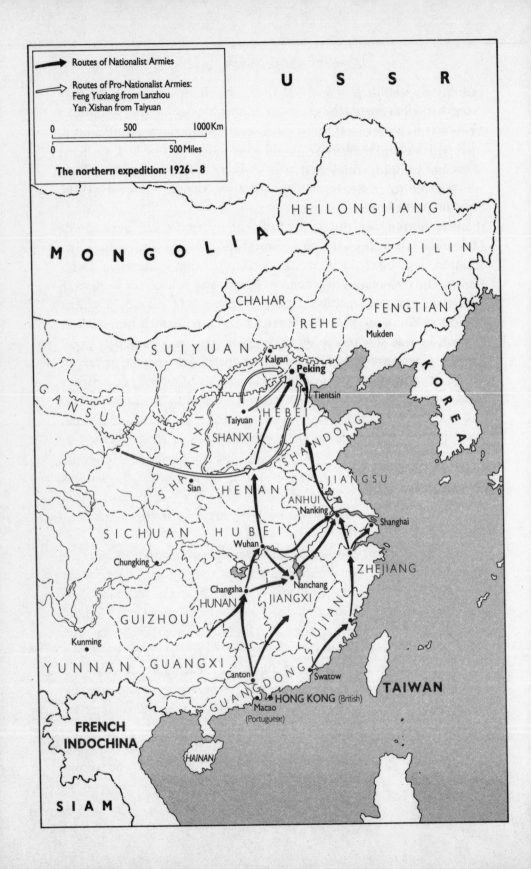

The northern expedition: 1926 – 8

Routes of Nationalist Armies

Routes of Pro-Nationalist Armies:
Feng Yuxiang from Lanzhou
Yan Xishan from Taiyuan

0   500   1000 Km
0   500 Miles

USSR

MONGOLIA

HEILONGJIANG

JILIN

CHAHAR

REHE

FENGTIAN

Mukden

SUIYUAN

Kalgan

Peking

Tientsin

GANSU

SHANXI

Taiyuan

HEBEI

SHANDONG

KOREA

Sian

HENAN

JIANGSU

SICHUAN

HUBEI

ANHUI

Nanking

Shanghai

Chungking

Wuhan

Changsha

Nanchang

ZHEJIANG

HUNAN

JIANGXI

FUJIAN

GUIZHOU

Kunming

YUNNAN

GUANGXI

Canton

GUANGDONG

Swatow

TAIWAN

HONG KONG (British)

Macao
(Portuguese)

FRENCH
INDOCHINA

HAINAN

SIAM

military as well as political training in Moscow. By the spring of 1927, he had become deputy director of the political department of Feng's army at Xian, the site of its new headquarters, and had set up a political and military academy in the city.

Deng Xiaoping followed. Perhaps, as his biography says,[9] he was selected to go by the Comintern; perhaps Liu Bojian asked for him; or perhaps he volunteered (though his biographers say that there is nothing in the record to indicate that he met Feng in Moscow). His journey began at the end of 1926 and took him to Xian by way of Ulan Ude on the trans-Siberian railway, Ulan Bator, and Yinchuan and Lanzhou on the Yellow River. He started by train, went on by truck and then rode on camel and horseback for long distances.[10] The least comfortable stage must have been the one in the Gobi Desert, which he crossed in an ammunition lorry. The January temperature in the desert can fall to −30°C and there are five hundred empty miles between Ulan Bator and the Yellow River. He reached Xian in February 1927.

CHAPTER 4

In Peril, 1927–31

Deng Xiaoping returned to a country in the throes of civil war and for much of the time during the next four years was in danger of his life. His only spell of comparative safety was the four months he spent at Xian immediately after his return, when he worked as a political soldier in Feng Yuxiang's National People's Army.

At Xian, Deng had three posts, two open and one secret. He was head of the political section in the Sun Yatsen Military and Political Academy, the training school established by Liu Bojian (who became his chief), a political instructor there and secretary of the communist party's underground organization inside it. In his open jobs, he had two functions: to indoctrinate officers in Sun Yatsen's Three People's Principles, in the process no doubt giving a great deal of emphasis to Sun's policies of alliance with the Soviet Union, cooperation with the Chinese Communist Party and support for workers and peasants, and to spot and befriend potential recruits to communism. In his secret job, he dealt with the day-to-day work of an organization which was expanding all the time. At least several dozen students at the academy became communists, and one of Deng's tasks must have been to distribute them among the widely scattered units of Feng's army. The officers who passed through his hands included some who led insurrections in the countryside near Xian in 1928 and others who became leaders of the small Red Army whose base became the refuge of the main Red armies at the end of the Long March in 1935 and 1936.

While Deng was at Xian, the national revolutionary movement, under increasing internal strain ever since the death of Sun Yatsen, split in two. The most important reason was that most officers in the army came from landowning families and were therefore unalterably opposed to social revolution in the countryside. A second reason was that Chiang Kaishek and a sizeable group of nationalist politicians became hostile to action against foreign interests which could prejudice the early recognition of a nationalist government. If for different reasons, they became as keen to avoid giving offence to the powers, above all Japan, as Stalin and Trotsky had been in early 1926.

The split was provoked by Chiang's deliberate policy, put into effect in March 1927 and pursued relentlessly right through the spring and summer, of purging all organizations, official and unofficial, of communists and left nationalists in the provinces under his control (all those which the army had occupied south of the Yangtse except for Hubei, Hunan and a part of Jiangxi). The introduction of the policy was signalled when a military commander arrested and executed the communist leader of the labour union in Ganzhou, the largest town in southern Jiangxi, in March. It was made open and systematic in Shanghai in April, when nationalist troops and local gangsters, some of them disguised as workers, moved to break the authority of the city's general labour union over its port and industrial workers. Hundreds were killed in street fighting and searches of buildings. A story which has passed into legend is that railwaymen were pushed into the lighted furnaces of locomotives at the railway depot. This does not seem to have been true. But there can be no doubt that many union organizers and ordinary workers were executed after arrest, often in public, or that troops fired into unarmed crowds whenever these gathered to demonstrate or protest. Many communists perished, including Wang Shouhua, the head of the labour union (who was seized as he was leaving the house of a leader of the Green Gang, Shanghai's most powerful underworld organization, after dining with him) and Zhao Shiyan, Deng Xiaoping's mentor in Marxism. Zhou Enlai, the senior communist in the city, escaped by the skin of his teeth. He was arrested, but had the good fortune to be taken to the headquarters of an officer who was willing to let him go.

The massacre was followed by others in Nanking, Canton and the smaller industrial towns of the Yangtse delta. These were followed in turn by counter-terror in cities controlled by the left nationalists or by armed workers and peasants; in Wuhan, a score of anti-communist labour leaders were executed in public and many businessmen with foreign connections were killed in Changsha. Politically, the left nationalists reacted by expelling Chiang from the party. He responded by setting up an alternative government in Nanking. By the end of April, the break between left and right was complete and seemed irretrievable.

The split confronted the communists with a choice – between going their own way and continuing to collaborate with the left nationalists, in the hope of bridling and controlling them. Some of their leaders, including Mao Zedong, who was convinced that millions of peasants in Hunan – his native province – were ready to rise in revolution, favoured the bolder course. But others, including Chen Duxiu, the general secretary, were inclined to temporize, even if they took a gloomy view of how the nationalists were likely to behave towards the communists in the long run. And Stalin, now with a point to make against Trotsky, whose line was little different from Mao's, was demanding that what was left of the united front should remain in place. At a meeting of the Comintern's executive committee in late May, he quoted Borodin's judgement that the nationalists would resist social revolution in the countryside even at the price of a break with the Comintern, but argued – successfully – that the communists should 'manoeuvre' rather than break with them. The committee's final resolution required the communists to continue to operate 'directly in alliance with the left Kuomintang'[1] and instructions were then issued to Borodin and Chen accordingly.

From then on, things went from bad to worse for the communists. In June, a newly arrived Comintern delegate (M. N. Roy, who became a fascist in his native India during the Second World War) showed Wang Jingwei, the most influential of the left nationalist leaders, a telegram from Stalin himself which instructed Chen and his colleagues to encourage militant peasants to seize land and to curb by means not explained, the 'excesses' of counter-revolutionary generals. This alienated a key potential protector. In the same month, Feng Yuxiang, who had spoken fair words to Wang Jingwei at a meeting in the north, announced that he intended to collaborate with Chiang Kaishek and told a group of journalists that it was his desire to 'extirpate' communism as well as militarism. Several powerful generals who were still loyal to the left nationalists began to demand openly that the party should be purged of communists.

In July, the Comintern instructed the communists to withdraw from the Wuhan government, in which they held several important posts, but to stay on as members of the Nationalist Party, seeking to change its leadership and policies 'from below'. It was too late. The nationalist central executive committee had already begun to consider putting a formal end to the united front and the political council now ordered all individuals who were members of both parties to resign from one or the other. Within a few days, martial law was imposed in Wuhan, and nationalist troops began to hunt for known or suspected communists.

Chen Duxiu, trapped all through the summer between the sheer unreality of the Comintern's instructions and reluctance to call for social revolution himself (Mao later said because he feared it), now resigned as general secretary, although he stayed on for a while in Wuhan. Many other senior communists made their way to Jiangxi, where the most powerful military leader was thought to be sympathetic, or sought refuge in Hankow's foreign concessions.

To escape a purge of communists which Feng Yuxiang was widely known to be planning, Deng Xiaoping left Xian in June and made his way to Wuhan. He reported for duty to the party's military commission, run by Zhou Enlai, in Wuchang, on the southern bank of the Yangtse, but was soon ordered to join Chen Duxiu at party headquarters in Hankow, on the northern bank. Here he became a secretary of the central committee, for the first time working within the apparatus he was one day to control.

From this point of vantage, Deng was able to watch the last

rites of collaboration between the Chinese nationalists and the Soviet Union. Borodin, deeply depressed about the failure of his mission, left Hankow on 27 July, on a train loaded with baggage and the trucks and heavy-duty touring cars he and his fellow Russians would need to cross the Gobi Desert. It would have been in Stalin's nature to blame and punish him for the failure of his own China policy. Yet he was not disgraced at the time. He survived the 1930s in second-rank posts, and it was ultimately anti-semitism and not China which destroyed him. Together with many other Jewish party members, he was arrested in 1949. He died in a prison camp in 1951 in his late sixties.

It was at about this time that Deng changed his name to Deng Xiaoping. This must have been because he wanted the slightly greater degree of safety from arrest, and from interrogation if once arrested, that he would enjoy under an assumed name, even with the same surname. Many other prominent communists used assumed names at one time or another. Some, like Wang Ming and Bo Gu among the Returned Students, did so because it was a Bolshevik habit to adopt *noms de guerre*, and many others, like Zhou Enlai, for the sake of security when working underground. Deng was unique among them in choosing a name which was an incomplete disguise, but which he stuck to when disguise was no longer needed. 'Xiao' means small and 'ping' peaceful, even or balanced.

On 7 August, an emergency meeting of all available members of the central committee was held in Hankow. The meeting elected a new provisional politburo, though not a new general secretary, and adopted four documents. One of them, in one account dictated by Besso Lominadze, a new Comintern delegate, accredited to the communists alone, condemned the former party leadership for 'opportunism'; the other three called on the party to seek to overthrow the nationalist governments in both Nanking and Wuhan and to organize armed uprisings* with the object of

---

* The Chinese word of which 'uprising' is the conventional translation means a rebellion or insurrection in a righteous cause.

setting up local or provincial soviet governments. For tactical reasons, however, the rebellions were to be staged under the flag of the 'revolutionary left Kuomintang'. Deng Xiaoping attended the meeting as an official of the committee, and was therefore present when the Communist Party, in the bitterness of defeat, turned to an altogether new strategy.

The communists embarked on this strategy in thoroughly unpromising circumstances. In Moscow, Stalin and the Comintern, having forced the communists to remain in alliance with the left nationalists all through the summer, now wanted quick insur-rectionary victories – just what they were ill-placed to achieve. In the cities, their union organizers had been killed or driven underground. In the countryside, peasant militancy was on the wane, after the killing of many rural activists. In the army, party members and communist sympathizers commanded several armies or regiments, and were strong in the political departments of other forces, but held their commissions as nationalist officers. Besides, the disgrace of Chen Duxiu had left leadership in the hands of a group of men who were without military experience. The acting head of the new politburo was Qu Qiubai, a writer, and there was not a single military man among its ten other members (Mao Zedong, an alternate, had worn uniform as an ordinary soldier in the army of a Hunanse militarist in 1912, but never as an officer).

By the time of the emergency meeting, a first uprising had already taken place, in the form of mutinies provoked from above, in two corps of the army stationed in and near Nanchang, the capital of Jiangxi. These led to the seizure of the city and the creation of the first military force, about 15,000 strong at the outset, under direct communist control. But it was a triumph whose glow faded fast. After a long march from Nanchang to the coast east of Canton, the new army, its ranks greatly thinned on the way by desertion and the defection of a divisional commander with all his men, was defeated piecemeal by nationalist troops and was unable to reunite. Most of its leaders then made their way to Hong Kong or Shanghai. Zhou Enlai, who had coordinated the original mutinies, arrived in Hong Kong a very sick man, and had

to spend some time in hospital in Kowloon. Zhu De, the future commander-in-chief of the Red Army, stayed on with his men and in
the end managed to lead about 600 poorly armed survivors to join
Mao Zedong in his mountain base of Jinggangshan in April 1928.

The autumn harvest revolts which followed in August also
failed. In Hubei, a ragbag peasant force was quickly disarmed by a
militia unit which its leaders had expected to be an ally. In Hunan,
Mao Zedong was in charge. Under orders to capture Changsha, he
soon decided that his motley army, consisting of four 'regiments'
of mutinous soldiers, miners, peasants and former bandits, could
not hope to do this. He assembled the troops which remained to
him after a series of disastrous battles, including one in which two
of his regiments fought one another, in a town far from Changsha
and managed to persuade most of them to follow him to
Jinggangshan, the highest and remotest part of the mountain
range which divides Hunan from Jiangxi. After a march of several
weeks, he reached his objective with a few hundred men. A haunt
of bandits from time immemorial, Jinggangshan had become the
base of two bands of outlaws. Mao persuaded their leaders to
become his allies, and then settled down to a winter of great
hardship, but some military security, in the crags and pine forests
of a region as inaccessible as any in the south of China.

The third and last uprising of the year, in Canton in December,
was the greatest failure of all. The plan was to use local units
under communist command and armed workers to seize the city,
establish a municipal soviet government (a commune) and create
an island of Red territory which would last. The outcome, after
several days of desperate fighting, was the complete destruction of
all the party's local organizations, the death of several of its
national leaders and the slaughter of several thousand workers,
including many who had not taken up arms. From Stalin's point
of view, there was an additional setback: nationalist troops killed
several Russians in the streets and raided the Soviet consulate.
Stalin had tried hard to keep the activities of the remaining
Comintern advisers in China separate from those of his diplomats
there, but the disaster in Canton showed that nationalist command-

ers saw no distinction between them. Thus was alliance between the Soviet Union and the Chinese nationalists brought to a bloody end, and in the city where Sun Yatsen and Borodin had sealed it.

In the autumn, Qu Qiubai decided to move party headquarters from Wuhan back to Shanghai, where it had been until the spring. Deng Xiaoping, still a secretary of the central committee, made his way there in late September or early October, travelling with Li Weihan, whom he had known in France and who had now been promoted to the politburo. He thereby closed a cycle of travel on which he had set out almost exactly seven years before.

Quite soon after his arrival in Shanghai, Deng was appointed chief secretary of the central committee, and as such became responsible for looking after the documents kept at headquarters and for its 'confidential work',[2] communications and financial affairs. Onerous responsibilities at the best of times, they were doubly so in the conditions in which he now had to work. The party was a proscribed organization and its members in the cities were in daily danger of arrest. Nationalist troops and police had no scruple about using torture to extract information from suspects, so that there was the constant danger of one arrest leading to others. In the industrial world, where the communists were keenest to re-establish their influence, many labour organizers belonged to the Green Gang or other anti-communist underworld societies. Paid informers abounded; and the police of the International Settlement and the French Concession were as hostile to communism and communists as the police of the Chinese city. They searched for communists on their own account and quite often turned over suspects to the city police.

The offices of the party and its subsidiary bodies were spread over a large area. Most of the central committee's departments were in central Shanghai; those of the Jiangsu provincial committee were in the industrial suburbs of Chapei and Hongkew; and some of the youth league's bureaux were in the French Concession. Zhou Enlai was in charge of security at party headquarters and in due course laid down the rule that one or two members of the politburo and its standing committees should always be absent from meetings of those bodies, to avoid arrest in the worst case of a police raid. Ad hoc meetings of politburo members and officials were often held in safe rooms inside public buildings, including hospitals, and it is recorded in Zhou's biography that Deng often went to meetings in a hospital in Weihaiwei Road, in the heart of the city. Two members of the politburo were given away, arrested and executed in August 1929, at about the time Deng left Shanghai for the south-west, but security was on the whole effective during the two years he lived underground there.

At some point in 1928 or early 1929, Deng got married. His wife Zhang Qianyuan, was a party member and had held a party post of some sort in a small base area which had been created by local communists in the mountains between Jiangxi and Fujian. It is not known when or how Deng met her, though the likeliest case is that he came across her when she was sent to Shanghai as a courier.

Whatever the circumstances in which Deng and Zhang met and married, their marriage ended tragically after only a short time. Zhang had a miscarriage and died soon afterwards. Different sources give different dates for her death, but they agree that it occurred at a time when Deng was not in Shanghai. The record about his activities in 1928 and 1929 is thin, but it is improbable that he left Shanghai often, if at all, during the time when he was the principal official at party headquarters. The assumption must be that Deng became a widower after he had left the city and this function. The blow must have left its mark on him. But, always a private man about his private life, he has not allowed any word about his feelings to go beyond people who could keep secrets, and his official biography does not mention even the fact of the marriage.

For the communists, the chief political event of 1928 was the sixth party congress. Because there was nowhere in China where several dozen delegates could meet safely for any period of time, it was held outside Moscow, in what had been a large country house.

The contingent from China included most members of the politburo, though not Li Weihan, who stayed in Shanghai. Deng Xiaoping remained behind with him. At the congress, Bukharin, who had sided with Stalin against Trotsky over China but who was soon to come under attack for his 'rightist tendency' and 'rich-peasant line' in the Soviet Union, was much to the fore as chairman of the Comintern's executive committee. An eccentric figure, who sometimes appeared on the platform in shooting clothes or with a falcon on his wrist, he steered the congress towards the adoption of decisions consistent with those in a resolution his committee had adopted in February.

At the end of debates which lasted for most of June, the congress defined the current stage in the Chinese Revolution as 'bourgeois-democratic' (and not socialist) and the prevailing situation as an interval between two 'revolutionary high tides'. It condemned 'opportunism' (as allegedly practised by Chen Duxiu, who had refused to attend), but also 'putschism' (desperate military undertakings of the kind ordered by Qu Qiubai). It adopted a ten-point programme, in which three objectives were to overthrow the 'Kuomintang warlord government', to confiscate the land of all landlords and to 'unite with the world proletariat and unite with the Soviet Union'. Sixteen years later, Mao Zedong, who had by then worked out a complete theory of his own about the nature of the Chinese Revolution, said that the programme was correct, but ought to have been set in a context which stressed the protracted nature of the revolution and the 'very great importance of rural base areas'.

In the middle of 1929, Deng Xiaoping's career took an entirely new turn. The politburo replaced him as chief secretary of the central committee and sent him off to Guangxi, in the far south-west, on a special mission with three tasks: to make contact with the province's governor and pacification commissioner, who, though both were appointed by Chiang Kaishek, were planning a military move against him and had expressed interest in collaborating with the communists; to take charge of all provincial party work; and to prepare an armed uprising. It was a difficult and dangerous mandate. Although the pacification commissioner was a secret party member and the governor had communist sympathies, their local authority was weak. And, if they once moved against Chiang, it was far more likely than not that they would be defeated. Guangxi had good communications only with French Indo-China and Canton, now firmly in anti-communist hands, and was hundreds of miles from any part of the country where communist troops were active. It is no wonder that the Far Eastern office of the Comintern, operating secretly in Shanghai, firmly advised against responding to the overtures of the two conspirators.

Deng reached Nanning, the provincial capital, in early September, having made his way there by sea to Haiphong in Indo-China and then overland across the province. He was followed by several other party members, including Zhang Yunyi, who had received military training in the Soviet Union. Having met the governor, Deng achieved an immediate sucess by persuading him to appoint Zhang the commander of one of the two regiments of the provincial garrison and the commandant of a training unit for junior officers. Deng and Zhang then waited for the governor to set out on his expedition against Chiang Kaishek, which he soon did, taking the pacification commissioner with him. As soon as they had gone, the two communists ordered one battalion of the Nanning garrison to march north-west into the hills and another to establish itself in a blocking position on the highway from Nanning to Hanoi. They also sent reliable men to take over the provincial arsenal, which contained 5,000 rifles, some mountain guns, mortars and machine-guns, a few radio sets and a great deal of ammunition – a haul beyond the dreams of Mao Zedong, now at large in southern Jiangxi with two or three thousand men.

The adventure of the governor and the commissioner soon came to an end. Their army was defeated on the border between Guangxi and Guangdong and they both became fugitives. The moment Deng and Zhang heard this news, they transferred the entire contents of the arsenal on to steamers they had assembled in the port of Nanning and began to pull their troops out of the city. One contingent, led by Deng, travelled on the steamers up the Yong River and then the northern of its two main tributaries. At Pingma (now Tiandong), it waited for the second contingent, led by Zhang, which marched all the way. The combined force then moved on to Bose, a market town and county seat in the remote western corner of the province, where Deng and Zhang began to plan the uprising which was to signal the extension of the soviet movement to a new part of China.

On 11 December, a date chosen because it marked the second anniversary of the insurrection in Canton, the hammer and sickle was hoisted in the centre of Bose in the name of the seventh army of the Chinese Red Army of Workers and Peasants. Downstream in Pingma, an assembly of representatives of workers, peasants and soldiers elected a soviet government of workers and peasants. There was no armed resistance in either town. Now the political commissar of the new army and secretary of its front committee, the instrument used by the party at this time to control its military units, Deng made his way almost at once to the area to which he had sent a battalion of the Nanning garrison in the autumn, and there organized a second uprising. At the beginning of February 1930, the creation of a another soviet government and of another Red Army, the eighth, was proclaimed at Longzhou, a town very close to the Indo-Chinese border.

At this juncture, mysteriously, Deng returned to Shanghai. According to his official biography, his purpose was to report to party headquarters. It is possible that he received a summons from Shanghai, which was linked with Longzhou by radio (through a relay station in Hong Kong), but it seems more likely that he decided to go of his own volition. Party headquarters would have had little reason to call him back at a time when both new bases needed consolidation. He, on the other hand, faced at least one difficult political problem: how to handle Li Mingrui, the former pacification commissioner, who had made his way to Longzhou after his defeat in eastern Guangxi and had then helped Deng to organize the uprising there. Li was bound to want a place in the new military scheme of things, and Deng may have wanted to talk to party headquarters about what this should be. More humanly, he could also have been worried about his wife.

Deng was away from Guangxi for about two months, until late April. In Shanghai, party headquarters decided to appoint Li Mingrui commander-in-chief of the two new armies and Deng their political commissar. This settled the question of what to do with Li and showed that party headquarters, now dominated not by Xiang Zhongfa, the general secretary, but Li Lisan, the head of the organization department, was satisfied with what Deng had achieved so far.

Deng returned to a situation which had deteriorated badly in his absence. Li Zongren and Bai Chongxi, two of the three warlords who had controlled Guangxi before 1926, when they joined the northern expedition, had returned to Nanning and then moved quickly to attack the eighth Red Army. A small force – perhaps less than 2,000 strong – it was defeated in battle and driven from its base. The seventh Red Army tried to relieve pressure on it by advancing on Nanning, but was defeated in its turn, forced to retreat, and driven into the mountains beyond Bose.

Apparently taking a large risk with his own security, Deng spent the spring and summer working on a 'project of agrarian reform' in an area where there were few, if any, Red troops. Collaborating with Wei Baqun, a local communist who had led a peasant band in the hills for several years, and Li Mingrui, he 'mobilized the masses to expropriate local tyrants, distribute land [and] carry out agrarian revolution'.[3] It seems that this was a full-blooded undertaking, in the spirit of the party's official policy, which was to confiscate the land of all landowners. If so, it was a stronger policy than the one practised for most of the time by Mao Zedong in Jiangxi, and the one Deng himself came to favour later on. Perhaps he had yet to learn that thoroughgoing agrarian revolution usually led to lower farm output and so to more difficult conditions for the peasants on whom the Red armies had to rely for political and physical support.

In June 1930, the seventh Red Army left the mountains and re-established itself around Bose. Deng now rejoined it and became active in its training. He also turned his hand to politics and administration, helping to create several soviet governments at county level. By the end of the summer, the base area had been reconstituted to cover about twenty counties, with a total population of over a million.

It is just possible that the base could have survived, if with shifting frontiers, if Deng, Li Mingrui and Zhang Yunyi had been left to their own devices by party headquarters. But they, like all other communist leaders in the field, became victims of what came to be called the Li Lisan line – a grandiose strategy for the seizure of power by the communists 'in one or more provinces'.

The *locus classicus* for the line is a politburo resolution of 11 June 1930, stating that China was the 'weakest link in the chain of world imperialism', that China was ripe for revolution and that world revolution might immediately follow revolution in China. It was the case in China that Chiang Kaishek was deeply engaged in civil war with Feng Yuxiang and Yan Xishan, another northern warlord, and that the communists now had more than 50,000 men under arms, in three larger and quite a few smaller base areas. It was also the case that the capitalist world was sinking into slump. All the same, it passes belief that Li could have brought himself to believe that the communists were powerful enough to seize and hold Wuhan, Canton and many other large cities, which was his chief military assumption.

In Li's grand design, the tasks set for the seventh army were to capture Liuzhou and Guilin, large towns in north-eastern Guangxi, then to establish a base area in Guangdong (to prevent hostile forces in that province from moving against communist armies further north) and finally to occupy Canton. In August, an emissary from party headquarters, Deng Gang, arrived in Guangxi with Li's orders. His official biography says that Deng Xiaoping 'doubted the possibility of taking these cities and expressed his disagreement'. But, it adds, 'most of his comrades maintained that they should obey the representative's instructions and Deng was

The march of the seventh Red Army: 1930 – 1

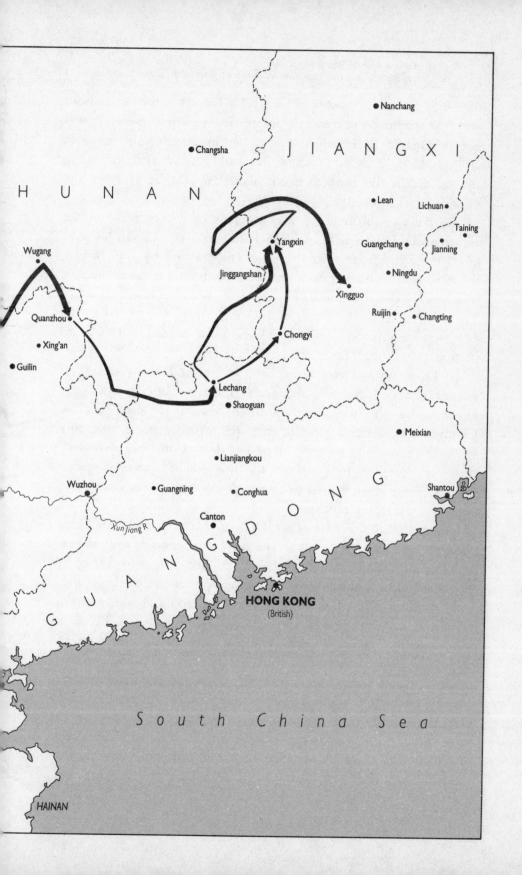

therefore obliged to act accordingly'.[4] This is a moment about which it would be particularly interesting to know more. It was not in Deng's later nature to act on instructions he thought wrongheaded, and in Guangxi he had greater authority than anyone except the emissary from Shanghai. Yet he accepted the view of the majority.

The army, reinforced by a contingent of survivors from the eighth army, left its base in late September 1930. It soon lost one of its three divisions, when the one commanded by Wei Baqun, the local man, turned back to the west (with fatal consequences: it was quickly destroyed and Wei was later betrayed and executed). The other two, led by Deng and Zhang Yunyi, continued to the east, setting out on a march which, as it turned out, was to prefigure the Long March of five years later.

To begin with, Deng and Zhang did their best to act on Li Lisan's orders. They led the army towards Liuzhou and only abandoned a plan to assault the town when they heard that Bai Chongxi was marching on it with reinforcements. It was only when the army had suffered 'repeated defeats and heavy losses'[5] that they decided to give up all thought of attacking urban centres. This, it seems, led to a showdown with Deng Gang, Li's emissary, who then left them.

It is not clear precisely when Deng and Zhang concluded that the only sensible course was to aim for Mao Zedong's central base area in Jiangxi. An account of the army's movements by one of its veterans makes it clear that it zigzagged for several weeks, apparently without any fixed objective, in the mountains of western Hunan in the late autumn.[6] In the end, however, the conclusion was reached. The army, now less than 4,000 strong (out of an original 10,000), was reorganized and the line of march became straight. Conditions were miserable. Most of the troops were wearing cotton clothes and straw sandals, and so suffered severely from the cold. Food was short too. In February 1931, the two or three thousand survivors came under attack while in the process of crossing the Lechang, a wide and rapidly flowing river in the mountains of northern Guangdong. One part of the army was driven away from the boats in which the other, larger part had already reached the opposite bank. Thus split, it was unable to reunite for months. Deng was with the forward contingent, which he and Li Mingrui then led into Jiangxi, at a point not far from Mao Zedong's original base on Jinggangshan.

Deng now left his troops. His official biography states that he was sent to report to the central committee in Shanghai.[7] During the Cultural Revolution, however, a Red Guard flysheet accused him of having abandoned his men. Its story was that, having heard the sound of firing from their lines when he was returning from a reconnaissance, he decided on the spot to make off for 'the beautiful world of Hong Kong'.[8] It may have been the case that he turned back when he realized that his choices lay between so doing and risking death or capture by walking into a battle. But that does not mean that he behaved discreditably. He was not the field commander, and he had in any case been authorized by the army's front committee to make his way to Shanghai. There is a story, too, that the incident was investigated by a committee of inquiry after he had reached Jiangxi later in 1931 and that he was acquitted of all blame.

A remnant of Deng's little army survived. After several months of fighting near Jinggangshan, it was incorporated into the army of the central soviet area in July 1931.

CHAPTER 5

Long Marcher, 1931–5

When Deng Xiaoping visited Shanghai in the spring of 1930, Li Lisan had been in effective – even imperious – charge of party headquarters. Now, a year later, he was gone, summoned to Moscow to answer for the failure of his line. Examined by the Comintern's far eastern department and then by its executive committee, he was forced to make two humiliating confessions of error, though not before he had infuriated several of his inquisitors by asserting that the Comintern, in faraway Moscow, did not understand the Chinese Revolution and was therefore not qualified to lead the Chinese Communist Party (some of them also objected strongly to his having said in China the summer before that loyalty to the Comintern was one thing and loyalty to the Chinese Party quite another). He was punished by being kept in the Soviet Union, doing nothing of any consequence, for nearly fifteen years.

While Li was on trial, Pavel Mif, now very high in Stalin's favour, was in or on his way to Shanghai. His purposes were to get the Chinese party to condemn the Li Lisan line and to compel it to reconstitute its leadership, and he succeeded in both. In early January 1931, he presided over a one-day meeting of the central committee which condemned the line root and branch and then altered both its own composition and the composition of the politburo. It heard confessions of weakness and error from Xiang Zhongfa, the general secretary, Zhou Enlai and Qu Qiubai. At least three of the young men who had belonged to Mif's circle at the Sun Yatsen University, including Wang Ming, became members of a new politburo of sixteen full and alternate members. Qu Qiubai was dropped.

These proceedings led to a schism between the new leadership and a group of veteran labour leaders who had opposed Li Lisan and his line, but who had also objected to the reconstruction of the party leadership by the leadership itself (they wanted an emergency conference with a wider participation) and to Mif's list of candidates for promotion. The veterans were arrested by the police of the International Settlement in mid-January, turned over to the nationalists and shot by them in early February. There was strong suspicion in the party that the place and time of the meeting at which they were arrested had been given away by someone in the new leadership.

Another disaster followed. In April, Gu Shunzhang, under Zhou Enlai in day-to-day charge of intelligence and counter-intelligence at party headquarters, was arrested by the nationalists in Wuhan. He apparently made no attempt to keep from his captors the great deal he knew about the whereabouts of senior party members. If the party had not had an agent in a counter-intelligence office in Nanking, who warned headquarters about the amount Gu had disclosed, it is probable that most of the party's top echelon in Shanghai, including Deng, would have been rounded up. As it was, Xiang Zhongfa, the general secretary, was arrested in May and executed in June. Gu's collaboration did not save him; the nationalists executed him once he had revealed all they thought he knew. In revenge, quite a few members of Gu's family were shot by the communists – on the orders of Zhou Enlai, according to a story which has never been officially denied.

Xiang Zhongfa was not replaced as general secretary. Instead, first Wang Ming and then Bo Gu became the de facto leader of the party, described as 'the comrade exercising overall responsibility'.

In the late summer of 1931, Deng made his way from Shanghai to what had become known, because of its size and situation, as the central base area. The statement in his official biography that he went there 'with the approval of the central committee'[1] implies that he asked to go, which would not have been surprising in his and the party's circumstances.

Deng's journey took him to the port of Shantou (Swatow), on

the coast of Guangdong to the east of Hong Kong and from there by steamer or launch up the Han river into western Fujian.[2] In his memoirs, Nie Rongzhen, a future marshal of the People's Liberation Army who used the route at the end of 1931, says that it had been open since 1928, that it was used by 'many leading comrades of the central committee' and that all medical supplies and radio equipment bought in Hong Kong and Shanghai were sent to the base area along it.[3] The members of Nie's party wore the long gowns of scholars and were told to speak as little as possible to people they met on the way, lest the fact that they could not speak the local dialects should arouse suspicion. The journey from the coast to the border of Fujian took them about five days.

By the middle of 1931, the base area was well established. Its core consisted of about 10,000 square miles of hilly and mountainous country on each side of the boundary between Jiangxi and Fujian. Within it, the Red Army* was in unchallenged military control and local government, in the form of regional and county soviets, was in communist hands. It was more than self-sufficient in food, but had almost no industry, so that industrial goods, including cotton cloth and modern drugs and medicines, had to be obtained by trade. So did salt. Its climate was hot and dry during the summer, but very wet during the winter and spring. During these seasons there was frequent mist and fog, which often helped the Red Army in its campaigning.

Around the core was a zone in which there was much marching and counter-marching by the Red Army, but which was not under settled communist control. The communists were generally stronger in the countryside, with party branches in many villages, and the nationalists in the towns. When it came to fighting, the

---

* From 1927, all communist troops belonged in name to a national Red Army of Workers and Peasants. In November 1931, when the communists proclaimed the establishment of a national soviet state, a revolutionary military commission was created as one of its principal bodies. Zhu De became both its chairman and the Red Army's commander-in-chief. He held both posts until the soviet state was abolished and the Red Army turned into armies of Chiang Kaishek's National Revolutionary Army in August 1937.

Red Army could always defeat the militia of local landowners and by 1931 was more than a match for isolated brigades, and even divisions, of provincial armies. But it was too lightly equipped to take well-defended walled towns. A few months after Deng's arrival in the base, it failed to capture Ganzhou, the hub of southern Jiangxi, even though it used well over 10,000 troops in a series of attacks and the garrison was only a few thousand strong. Its lack of artillery and other heavy equipment was a handicap which it never overcame in Jiangxi and which was to have serious consequences when Chiang Kaishek's Central Army adopted a strategy of fortifying all newly occupied positions during its advance into the base area in 1934.

Though things were to change by degrees, Mao Zedong was the dominant political and military figure in the base in 1931. In the army, he was political commissar of the first front army, a formation about 30,000 strong, created through a complicated series of amalgamations to carry out Li Lisan's military strategy, and secretary of its front committee. In the party, he was an alternate member of the politburo and a member of the central bureau for the soviet areas, a body set up by party headquarters in January 1931 to control front committees and party branches in all soviet areas (Zhou Enlai, at this time still in Shanghai, was the bureau's secretary). But he owed his dominance chiefly to what he had achieved. Every peasant in southern Jiangxi and western Fujian knew that he had arrived in their region in the spring of 1929 with only 2,000 ill-clad and poorly equipped troops, forced out of their base on Jinggangshan, but in the space of two and a half years had turned this force into an army over twenty times the size and had created a little state in which the writ of nationalist magistrates and the local landowners no longer ran. He had brought the peasants into local government and given land to many labourers and tenants. For many, he had become a folk-hero, in the tradition of scores of peasant leaders who had challenged provincial governors, and occasionally the emperor himself, all through Chinese history.

*

On his arrival in the base area, Deng became secretary of the party committee of Ruijin county, a post of upper middle rank. As a former chief secretary of the central committee, he could perhaps have looked forward to something more senior. On the other hand, he may have been given the post to deal with a crisis; many officials in the county had been arrested and there was widespread popular discontent.

The crisis had grown out of a confrontation, which led to fighting, between Mao Zedong, ultimately supported by Zhu De, the commander-in-chief of the Red Army, and a group of military and civilian leaders in south-western Jiangxi in the winter of 1930–31. This came to be known as the Futian incident, after a town in the centre of the province from which some of these leaders had fled after being rescued from gaol by a local Red Army unit. In due course, the leaders were expelled from the party (by the central bureau for the soviet areas) and then captured or recaptured. There followed a purge of their supporters during which hundreds may have perished. The leaders were attacked for being members of the Anti-Bolshevik League, a clandestine nationalist organization. In fact, however, they seem to have been latter-day supporters of Li Lisan (Mao described them as such to Edgar Snow),[4] against whom Mao began to move as soon as he knew that Li had fallen from grace.

His official biography says that Deng at once acted 'to rehabilitate the cadres and ordinary people who had previously been wronged'.[5] But it does not say why those he rehabilitated had been in trouble in the first place. If they had been accused of being members of the Anti-Bolshevik League, it would be surprising to find people facing this charge in Ruijin, a hundred miles from Futian, nine months or so after the beginning of the purge. It would be even more surprising to find Deng, a comparatively junior member of the party (he was still outside the central committee) and a newcomer to the base area, acting to rehabilitate the victims of a campaign which Mao himself had launched and was known to have launched. And yet there are no records of any other political campaign at the time. Perhaps the most plausible explanation is that those he helped were indeed alleged members of the Anti-Bolshevik League, and that he intervened on their behalf because he had been asked to do so at party headquarters before he left Shanghai. This fits all the known facts in Jiangxi; and contemporary documents show that there was disquiet in Shanghai about the severity of the purge which had followed the original incident.

After a few months at Ruijin, Deng was made secretary of the party committee of Huichang, a county further south, and then became responsible for 'directing the work' in a zone of three counties. Sometime later in 1932, he became director of propaganda of the party's Jiangxi provincial committee. These were steps upward.

During the summer of 1932, Deng married for the second time. Like his first wife, his new wife, Jin Weiying, was a party member. Known to her friends as A Jin, she seems to have been a young woman of spirit. But she was inconstant too. When Deng found himself in political trouble a year later, she left him to marry Li Weihan, one of those who had attacked him most strongly. She was one of the thirty or so women who made the Long March, though only at the cost of serious damage to her health. She died in Moscow, where the party had sent her for medical treatment, a year or two later.

In January 1933, Bo Gu (who had replaced Wang Ming as de facto party leader when the latter returned to Moscow in the autumn of 1931) and Luo Fu (now a member of the politburo) moved from Shanghai to the central base area. They lost no time in moving to discredit and punish all local leaders who had criticized a set of policy prescriptions which they had put to the politburo and was known collectively as the 'forward and offensive line'.

The positions of Bo's and Luo's opponents are described thus in Deng's official biography:

They opposed the theory of 'making the cities the centre of the Chinese revolution' and advocated building strength in the vast rural areas, where the enemy's forces were relatively weak. They rejected military adventurism in favour of luring the enemy in deep. They were against expanding the Red Army's main forces at the expense of local armed forces and urged that both should be expanded simultaneously. They opposed the 'left' land distribution policy which would have left former middle and rich peasants destitute.[6]

These were all positions which Mao Zedong had adopted and which have been deemed to be correct ever since he became the party's unchallenged leader. But because of his local prestige, and perhaps also because the Comintern had been urging Bo and Luo to avoid open conflict with him, they did not attack him by name. And he, for his part, was careful to keep his powder dry. He made no attempt to protect those who were attacked by name, even though one of them was his own brother, and he gave public support to at least some of Bo's and Luo's policies. In July 1933, he wrote a newspaper article in which he attributed victory over Chiang Kaishek in the latter's fourth campaign to destroy the base area, achieved in the spring, to a forward military strategy and declared that all communists must set themselves 'against any underestimation of the new revolutionary situation [and] against those opportunists who would retreat and escape in panic before the [next] . . . campaign of the enemy'.[7]

Deng was an early target of the Returned Students' campaign. On 15 April, Luo Fu attacked him by name in a newspaper article and on 6 May Li Weihan, who had worked so closely with Deng in Shanghai, demanded 'brutal struggle' against him in another article. Li alleged that he had opposed the party's 'forward and offensive line', stood out against its policies of attacking large cities and expanding the Red Army to a strength of one million, and shown lack of confidence in the party's new leadership and distrust of the Comintern. This last charge is particularly interesting. It shows that, whatever Deng may have thought of the Li Lisan line, he was on Li's side as a patriot. What does not emerge from Li Weihan's article is when and how Deng had expressed his views. What is clear is that, even at this stage in his political career, he disdained to conceal his views on larger issues of policy.

Deng may have been imprisoned. He was certainly forced to write statements of self-criticism, deprived of the right to bear arms and sacked as director of the propaganda department of the provincial party committee. His sentence was to be given 'the most serious warning'. He was then sent to a county on the northern fringe of the base area, to work there as 'an ordinary inspector'.[8] It was presumably when he was in detention or exile that his wife abandoned him to marry Li Weihan.

According to one Chinese historian, the party's leaders may have feared that Deng would defect to the nationalists from his outpost.[9] Whether or not this was so, he was transferred after only a few weeks to the general political department of the Red Army, to become its secretary-general. This was full, or more than full, rehabilitation. He owed it to Wang Jiaxiang, one of the Returned Students, and Luo Ronghuan, a professional soldier. As director of the department, Wang was an influential figure; but he was junior to Bo Gu and Luo Fu in the party, and his action showed moral courage.

Sometime in the summer of 1933, Deng was moved to the propaganda division of the general political department, where he became editor-in-chief of *Red Star*, its new weekly newspaper. In this job, his life ran smoothly for a year. He was a long way from the front (though this grew steadily closer from the spring of 1934); and he was outside the circle which had to decide policy as it became clear that Chiang Kaishek's fifth campaign against the base area, launched in October 1933, threatened its survival.

For his fifth campaign, Chiang Kaishek had mobilized nearly a million men, of which at least half belonged to the Central Army under the direct control of the Ministry of War in Nanking. Chiang had prepared for it by giving special training, including political indoctrination, to more than 7,000 officers and working out both a general strategy and detailed operational plans. The general strategy was to advance into the base area from the north and to block any escape from it on the other three sides. A central feature of the operational plans was to fortify, as they were occupied, all points which commanded ground. Between October 1933 and October 1934, over 14,000 blockhouses, some of them large enough to accommodate several hundred men, were built around and inside the base.

The Red Army had no answer to these methods. Mao Zedong later claimed that it would have been able to save the base if its commanders had continued to apply the strategic principles which he had worked out between 1927 and 1932, especially those of luring the enemy in deep and of concentrating superior force to wipe out enemy formations one by one. But Chiang had developed his operational plans precisely in order to prevent the communists from being able to use their mobility; and his commanders in the field were careful both to avoid being lured into rash advance and to support one another as they moved methodically forward. It is most improbable that Mao would have been any more successful than those who were in fact in charge of military operations – Zhou Enlai (as political commissar of the first front army),* Bo Gu (as party leader) and Otto Braun, a military adviser from the Comintern who had arrived in October 1933 – in stopping Chiang. Politically, however, the fact that these three had failed gave him the platform from which he was ultimately able to strike out for party leadership.

Zhou, Bo and Braun decided during the summer that the base could not be held and that the army must leave it if it was to survive. Its escape was well planned. With a large supply train, it had been on the move for about two weeks before the nationalists realized that it had gone, and it had marched for 500 miles before they were first able to bring it to battle. But the three planners had not decided where it should go. They had simply set an interim objective: to reach the open country of southern Hunan, from where several options, including a march north to reach a small base area in the north-west of the province and a march west into

* A post in which he had replaced Mao Zedong in October 1932.

territory still under warlord control, would be open. None of them, certainly, supposed that the operation they had planned and ordered, which they described as a strategic 'shift', would turn into the Long March – a journey lasting a full year and covering nearly 6,000 miles.

Deng Xiaoping was still the editor of *Red Star* at the beginning of the Long March. The army set out on the march with huge quantities of equipment, almost certainly including the press used to produce the newspaper, but most of this was lost when it was attacked from three sides while crossing the Xiang river, in north-eastern Guangxi, in late November. Nevertheless, an edition of sorts was produced six weeks later, at Zunyi in Guizhou, when the army paused for its first rest. Deng could have had a hand in putting it together. On the other hand, he had recently become chief secretary of the central committee – replacing Deng Yingchao, Zhou Enlai's wife, who was ill – for the second time in his career and would have had plenty to do in that capacity.

The pause at Zunyi is famous for an enlarged meeting of the politburo which was held there from 15 January to 17 January. In the official Maoist account, the meeting 'put an end to the domination of the "left" line in the central leading body' and 'inaugurated a new central leadership, headed by comrade Mao Zedong'.[10] In reality, the outcome was rather less clear-cut. What is shown by contemporary documents is that Mao succeeded in getting a majority of the six full members of the politburo on the march to agree to a meeting to discuss the defeat in Jiangxi; that he seized the occasion to attack the military strategy of Zhou Enlai, Bo Gu and Otto Braun in a long set-piece speech; and that most of the others present then supported him. At or immediately after the meeting, he became a member of the politburo standing committee (or secretariat),[11] the inner circle, and became Zhou's military assistant within the party. But it was not until three weeks later that he was able to press his victory home. Then, at a further enlarged meeting of the politburo, held a long way from Zunyi, long and short resolutions setting out the main points in his Zunyi speech were adopted and more changes were made at the top of the party. Luo Fu, who had supported Mao at Zunyi, replaced Bo Gu as 'the comrade exercising overall responsibility'. Wang Jiaxiang, who had come to Deng's rescue in 1933 and who had likewise supported Mao, became a full member of the politburo. In the army, Mao became political commissar of a new front command headquarters in March and then, with Zhou Enlai and Wang Jiaxiang, a member of a new military troika. Zhu De, commander-in-chief all the way through, accepted these changes as placidly as he had earlier accepted the dominion of two civilians and a foreigner. Otto Braun, discredited and unpopular, had already been sent off to watch the exercise of field command at a subordinate headquarters.

Deng was present at the Zunyi meeting and, as chief secretary of the central committee, would have had a lot to do in preparing and issuing its resolutions. Thereafter, he was probably idler than he liked to be until another enlarged meeting of the politburo was held at Huili, in his native Sichuan, in the middle of May. At this, there was a backlash against Mao. Although the army had succeeded in crossing the Yangtse at the beginning of the month, it had only managed to do this after making an enormous sweep through Guizhou and the far south-western province of Yunnan, losing many men from exhaustion in the process. Some senior commanders complained that the army had been ill-led, and they were supported by Luo Fu. But Mao beat them off, showing that he was as formidable in defending himself as he had shown at Zunyi that he was formidable in attack.

Most of the following summer was taken up by negotiations between Mao, more or less steadily supported by the other political leaders from Jiangxi, and Zhang Guotao, the political commissar of the fourth front army, a part of the Red Army which had been operating in Sichuan since 1932. It was five or six times larger than the first army, whose size had been reduced from about 70,000 to not much more than 10,000 during eight months of marching and fighting. For this reason, and because Zhang had long been a full member of the politburo, Mao was up against someone he could not treat lightly.

Several important issues, political and military, were at stake, above all the issue of where the amalgamated army of more than 70,000 men ought to go. Should it go north, to put itself close to Soviet territory? Or should it stay in Sichuan, which was physically a long way from Nanking and politically beyond its control? In the end, after four conferences, an operational plan, a new command structure and a distribution of forces between two 'routes' were agreed. Mao, who wanted the army to go north, got his way over strategy; but Zhang became political commissar of the amalgamated army, displacing Zhou Enlai, and managed to subordinate the whole of the first army to his own headquarters or to a detached headquarters in which both the commander and the political commissar were men from the fourth army.

These arrangements, finally settled in late August, held for barely two weeks. In early September, Zhang decided that the whole army should turn back to the south and issued orders accordingly. The left route obeyed him, and so did his own men with the right route. But Mao and the other party leaders, accompanying the right route, did not. Invoking party authority, they ordered Zhang to start moving north again ('no objections: no delay: no disobedience')[12] and then started to move north themselves, taking with them about 5,000 men.

At some stage during the summer, Deng Xiaoping left party headquarters and joined the political department of the first army group, commanded all through the march by Lin Biao. His job was to explain to Lin's two or three thousand men, the survivors of an original 18,000 what Mao's little army was trying to achieve and why. It would therefore have fallen to him to convey and explain the decisions of a politburo meeting on 12 September which marked the final break between Mao and Zhang. These were that Mao's force should continue to move north (Mao had suggested that the aim should be to 'open a base area on the border near the Soviet Union, and then to develop towards the east'),[13] that it should be reorganized, with Peng Dehuai as its commander and Mao as its political commissar (Zhu De was at

The Long March of the first front army: 1934 – 5

general headquarters with Zhang), and that it should be called the Shaanxi–Gansu Branch Brigade of the Chinese Anti-Japanese Army.

For Mao's army, the Long March ended at Wuqizhen, a small town near the Great Wall, on 18 October, almost exactly a year after it had begun. There it could at last rest, having entered the base area of a small Red Army which had been active in the north-west since 1931.

There is nothing in the (now abundant) published material about the Long March to suggest that Deng was ever in physical danger. He was a political worker throughout and so did not take part in any of the set-piece battles or actions by small groups of volunteers which were the military highlights of the march (three of these actions were to secure landing-places on the far side of rivers: the most famous of them was an action in western Sichuan, when twenty-two men, of whom eighteen survived, crawled under fire across the chains of a suspension bridge from which most of the carriageway of planking had been removed).

Otherwise, however, the Long March must have been as much of an ordeal for Deng as his march with the seventh Red Army from Guangxi to Jiangxi four years before. There was the same need for constant physical exertion, the same vulnerability to wind and weather, the same anxiety about where food for the troops was to be found and the same uncertainty about the dispositions of the enemy. During the second half of the march, the army twice travelled through regions where conditions were particularly harsh. One was a high mountain range, treeless and snow-covered, in western Sichuan, and the other a huge tract of marshland on the plateau between the basins of the Yangtse and the Yellow River. Many soldiers died of exposure in each.

The region in which Mao's and Peng's little army finally found sanctuary was poor, remote and sparsely populated. Its remoteness was an asset. Nationalist generals were always disinclined to send their troops into parts of the country which were far from good lines of communication and large towns. But its poverty was not. Nor was the sparseness of its population. There were few able-bodied men for the army to recruit or to mobilize to do work in its support.

The region belongs to the loess country of north and north-west China – an area as large as France and Germany put together – where the soil consists only of wind-blown silt, fertile but easily eroded. In a treeless landscape, the climate is harsh. It seldom rains; but when it does the loess becomes mud and there is sudden flooding. In the spring, there are blinding and freezing sandstorms, whipped up by strong winds straight from the Gobi Desert.

To begin with, the communists established their headquarters in Baoan (now called Zhidan, after a local leader who was killed in battle in 1936), a small town of brown huts. In 1936, they moved to Yan'an, a walled town with a population of perhaps 20,000. Today the walls have gone. But a clifftop pagoda of nine storeys survives. So do the cave-dwellings, tunnelled out of the loess, in which Mao Zedong and his closest associates lived for the next eleven years. Both have become important in the symbolism of Chinese communism – the pagoda as a symbol of pride and defiance during a time of adversity and the caves as sites to show that Mao, Zhou Enlai and the rest lived lives of exemplary revolutionary virtue, practising what they preached about the importance of industry, simplicity and thrift, during their Yan'an days.

CHAPTER 6

Soldier in the Hills, 1935–45

On 1 August 1935, when Mao Zedong and Zhang Guotao were arguing in a remote corner of Sichuan about where their combined armies should aim to create a new base, Wang Ming issued a manifesto in Moscow which called in the name of the Chinese Communist Party for the establishment in China of an anti-Japanese united front. Out of radio contact with Moscow since the middle of 1934, when the party's relay station in Shanghai had been found by the nationalist police, neither Mao nor Zhang knew anything about this development at the time. It was not until late November, six weeks or so after he had reached Shaanxi, that Mao heard about it from Lin Yuying, an uncle of Lin Biao's who had been sent from Moscow to find the party's leaders in the field and brief them about developments there – and it was probably a matter of luck that Lin, who had travelled through the Mongolian desert, found Mao and his colleagues even as soon as this. Zhang heard about it later still, when Mao chose to tell him about it on the radio link he maintained with party headquarters in Baoan.

Wang's manifesto stemmed from a new Soviet policy towards Japan. Worried about the ambitions of the generals and admirals who had the largest say in making Japanese external policy, Stalin had decided that the Soviet Union's chief object in the Far East should be to deter Chiang Kaishek's China from making common cause with Japan in an anti-Soviet and anti-communist alliance. This required that political relations between the Soviet Union and China (diplomatic relations had existed since 1932) should become closer, which in turn required that the civil war in China should cease. To help make this possible, Stalin and the Comintern wanted the Chinese communists to abandon their claim to have established a separate state, greatly modify all their social policies and give up the vituperative attacks on the Nationalist Party and Chiang Kaishek personally which had been their stock-in-trade since 1927.

Mao Zedong was even keener than Stalin that China should stand up to Japan and believed that defiance, and if necessary armed resistance, could best be organized within the framework of a national united front. But he detested Chiang Kaishek, as a man as well as for his politics, and so wanted to find a way of creating a united front which did not assume that Chiang was its only possible leader. His preferred strategy was to build a front from below, developing the line of the national soviet government (of which he was chairman) in January 1933, when it had offered to conclude an agreement for joint resistance to Japan with 'any armed force' which was willing to stop attacking Chinese soviet territory, grant 'democratic rights' and arm the masses.

Mao moved quickly. At the end of December 1935, the politburo met at Wayaobao, a poverty-stricken village in the depths of northern Shaanxi, and adopted a political resolution in which the key passage read:

Our task is to unite all possible anti-Japanese forces … to make all Chinese people who have strength deliver their strength; all those who have guns deliver their guns; all those who have knowledge deliver their knowledge – not to miss one single patriotic Chinese … This is the party's general line: a line of the most broad national united front.[1]

A few days later, in a speech to a meeting of party activists, Mao said that the 'Japanese invasion' had altered class relations in China and that it was now possible 'not only for the petty bourgeoisie but even for the national bourgeoisie to join the anti-Japanese struggle'. But he still spoke of Chiang Kaishek as an enemy, linking his policy of 'betraying China' with the Japanese policy of 'subjugating China'.

This remained the party's platform, made known by every possible means, throughout 1936. Meanwhile, Mao and his colleagues worked hard to rebuild the strength of the party and the army, both enormously reduced by the Long March. This entailed three operational objectives: to consolidate the north Shaanxi base area; to achieve non-aggression agreements with the commanders of the regional armies Chiang Kaishek had ordered to invade it; and to persuade the fourth front army, now reinforced by a smaller force, the second front army, to march north to join the first army. They achieved all three, but the third of them only at a very heavy cost.

This cost was the loss of about two-thirds of the fourth army in an expedition towards Sinkiang. Zhang Guotao, who had begun to lead the second and fourth armies towards the north in July 1936 but who was reluctant to reamalgamate his forces with Mao's, was chiefly responsible. But Mao, as chairman of a reshuffled revolutionary military commission, must take some of the blame; at the least he acquiesced in a 'combat project' under which the expedition was planned. The military effect was to reduce the once-proud fourth army to a rump; the political effect was to destroy both the reputation and the power base of Zhang Guotao, leaving him open to attack for his whole record as a leader when he finally reached Yan'an.

It did not take the communists long to conclude non-aggression agreements with the commanders of the regional armies which surrounded them. They were greatly helped by the background and experience of these men. One of them, Yang Hucheng, had been an ally of Feng Yuxiang's at the time when communist workers had been active in Feng's army in 1927; and the other, Zhang Xueliang, was the son of Zhang Zuolin, the Manchurian warlord, whom the Japanese had murdered in 1928. He and most of his men were far more eager to fight against the Japanese than against the communists. After negotiations in Yan'an and Xian, pacts which provided for 'non-encroachment', trade and the maintenance of radio links were concluded in the spring of 1936.

Chiang Kaishek became tougher in his attitude to Japan during 1936. But it was still his first priority to destroy the communists and he was therefore infuriated by Yang's and Zhang's behaviour. In the early autumn, he sent elements of his own Central Army to the north-west, and in December he flew to Xian, to present Zhang and Yang with the choice between attacking the communists and receiving orders to move their armies to central China, far from their bases.

Chiang installed himself at Lintong, a little spa with hot springs in the hills east of Xian. On 9 December, a large procession from Xian, led by students, marched there, to demand an end to civil war and the proclamation of national resistance to Japan. Zhang Xueliang told the demonstrators that he sympathized with them and apparently promised them 'a definite reply in action within one week'.[2] Three days later, troops acting on Zhang's orders seized Chiang – according to one account, in a small hilltop pavilion to which he had fled in his nightshirt when he heard soldiers outside his bedroom door – and then brought him as a prisoner to Xian.

The communists have never claimed that they were in any way responsible for this coup or even that they knew about it in advance. That they were as much taken by surprise as the rest of the world is in any case suggested by their reactions. To begin with, they organized a mass meeting in Baoan to celebrate the capture of their chief enemy and there was talk there among Mao and the other leaders of killing Chiang. A few days later, however, it became clear that they were ready to contemplate his release in return for undertakings both to call off hostilities against themselves and to negotiate about cooperative resistance to Japan. This shift had something to do with pressure from Moscow (now linked by radio with Baoan) but sprang too from the realization of cooler heads that Zhang's action had given the communists an opening which they could not have created for themselves.

On 16 December, Zhou Enlai flew to Xian, in a private aircraft provided by Zhang. On Christmas Day, Chiang was released, having put nothing on paper, but having given Zhou enough by way of oral promises to get the latter to press Zhang (and a rather more reluctant Yang, who feared revenge) to let Chiang go. Zhang agreed to accompany Chiang to Nanking – a quixotic decision for which he paid a very heavy price. Arrested almost immediately, he was tried and sentenced to ten years' detention. Yang, too, was punished; Chiang transferred and then dissolved his army in early 1937 and he was never again given a national command.

The communists acted quickly to follow up Zhou Enlai's diplomacy. In February 1937, Mao and his colleagues sent a telegram in the name of the central committee to the Nationalist Party's central executive committee, offering to abandon armed struggle and to integrate the soviet areas and the Red Army into the nationalist state and army in return for an end to armed attacks, the release of all political prisoners and the initiation of active preparations for war against Japan. These proposals were not accepted, but had the effect of setting an agenda for serious bargaining. During the next four months, Zhou Enlai met Chiang Kaishek five times, and a good deal of progress was made. This led on to the conclusion of a set of formal agreements soon after the outbreak of war with Japan in July 1937. In these, the communists undertook to put an end to armed struggle and the expropriation of landlords; to dismantle their soviet state; to rename the Red Army and to put it under the command of the central government; and to work for the implementation of Sun Yatsen's Three Principles. In return, the nationalists allowed the Communist Party to open liaison offices in several cities, to circulate a national newspaper and to nominate representatives to the Nationalist Party's advisory bodies. They also agreed to pay the communists sizeable subsidies. Flesh was put on these bones when the northern Shaanxi base area became the Shaanxi–Gansu–Ningxia Border Region of the Chinese Republic, with its own regional government, and the Red Army turned into the eighth route and new fourth armies of the National Revolutionary Army.*

Deng Xiaoping fell seriously ill towards the end of the Long

---

* The new fourth army was formed from the survivors of troops left behind in Jiangxi at the beginning of the Long March.

March. He caught typhoid and, according to one account, was too ill either to ride or to walk by the time he reached Shaanxi. Once he had recovered, he became deputy director of the political department of the first army group (the designation in 1936 of the troops who had entered Shaanxi with Mao Zedong and Peng Dehuai). This was promotion. It was also a move which fixed him in the career he was to follow for the next sixteen years – the years in middle life when he made his name throughout the party and army and showed that he was qualified to become a national leader.

In this career, Deng was both a political soldier and a military politician. As a soldier, it was his job to ensure that the army was responsive to political training and instructions; as a politician, it was to ensure that the party understood military realities and did not ask either too much or too little of the army. Later, the job became one for specialists – regular officers who had received special training. In the 1930s and 1940s, however, it was usually taken on by civilians with high party rank; at one time or another, Mao Zedong, Zhou Enlai and Liu Shaoqi were all the chief political officers of whole armies. Like Mao (especially), Deng found the dual role of the job entirely congenial. His experience had made him a skilful politician; his temperament fitted him for military life.

In the Red Army and the eighth route army the politico-military hierarchy consisted of political commissars and political departments at every level from front army to division. At each level, the political commissar was normally senior to the military commander in party rank. He also had greater authority. The commissar could issue orders and instructions in his own name; but, except in moments of crisis on the battlefield, the orders of the commander were only valid if countersigned by the commissar.

As a political soldier, the commissar had very wide responsibilities, extending from the 'political consciousness' and political reliability of the party members in his formation or unit to the morale and welfare of all troops. It was as much his job to organize an athletics meeting as to brief party members about the significance of party resolutions or instructions. He was also responsible for arranging basic instruction in literacy for the large number of 'fighters' who were 'word blind'. Outside the army, he was responsible for winning the trust and support of the civilian population. Until 1937, landlords were treated as class enemies and it was normal practice to appropriate their money and property, including their houses, even if small plots of land were sometimes returned to them to cultivate themselves. Even then, however, the army could not live off such exactions alone and needed to work with farmers who were willing to sell a fair proportion of their stocks or new output of food and to provide recruits. Civil work was particularly important in areas where the hold of the Red Army was not secure and where cooperation with the communists could expose local people to retaliation from returning landlords or nationalist troops and administrators.

The war between China and Japan lasted for just over eight years, from July 1937 to August 1945. At the beginning of that time, the communists possessed just one base area: a desolate loess plateau in the distant north-west. By the end of it, they occupied nineteen areas, covering twelve times as much ground as the original base (known as Shaan–Gan–Ning, from the abbreviated names of the three provinces it covered), and inhabited by nearly 100 million people. As in Jiangxi, these areas had inner and outer zones; each area had at least one core under settled communist control. A dozen areas formed a block in northern China, stretching from Shaan–Gan–Ning in the west to the tip of the Shandong peninsula in the east. Only two areas were entirely isolated: one in the mountains of Hainan island, in the far south, and the other the area through which the Pearl River ran, between Hong Kong and Canton.

The army and the party grew at rates to match this territorial expansion. In late 1937, the combined strength of the eighth route army and the new fourth army was about 50,000. By the spring of 1945, it had become nearly 900,000. The party had a strength of about 40,000, concentrated in Shaan–Gan–Ning, in 1937. By the spring of 1945, it had become 1.2 million, with a wide geographical spread.

All the new base areas lay behind Japanese forward positions, wholly or in part. This was in consequence of a strategy the communists had adopted at the very outset of the war. In 1937, several political and military leaders argued that the eighth route army should engage in mobile warfare against the Japanese, operating with complete divisions or brigades, and collaborating as closely as possible with nationalist commanders. Mao Zedong, now the secretary of a revived party military commission, strongly opposed them. At a politburo conference in August 1937, he insisted that the Japanese Army was altogether more formidable than the nationalist armies which the Red Army had fought for ten years and that to engage in mobile – let alone positional – warfare against it would expose the small eighth route army to early destruction. In deference to the advocates of mobile warfare – some of whom feared that a strategy of guerrilla warfare alone would expose the communists to the charge that, for all their brave words about the need to fight the Japanese, they were concerned only with building up their own military and political strength – he agreed to the adoption of a concept which allowed for the conduct of mobile warfare 'when conditions were favourable'. But it was settled that the army should 'basically' confine itself to guerrilla operations.

The process of building base areas, at first only in mountainous regions but later in many parts of the north China plain, was arduous and suffered many setbacks. Everywhere – in the mountains and on the plain – the condition for the creation of a base was the establishment of settled military control. Only when this was firm could the party move in to turn an occupied area into a base. When it did, its first move was usually to create a new local-government structure, consisting of consultative and executive committees at the level of the village and upwards, elected on the basis of wide or universal suffrage. It preserved its own power by putting up party members for election and making sure that the majority of the members of executive committees took their instructions from party branches. Its next normal step was to act to improve the lot of the poorer members of local society and – as important – to diminish the wealth and authority of traditional power-holders. It used three principal instruments: rent reduction, the reduction of interest rates and the reallocation of tax burdens. The guideline for rent reduction was 25 per cent, a proportion which had once been pledged by Sun Yatsen. Interest rates were not always cut very deeply, lest the provision of credit, on which many poorer peasants depended for survival during the lean spring season, when food stocks were nearing exhaustion, should dry up. But scales of taxation were sometimes made steeply progressive.

The communists never neglected social and patriotic propaganda in the base areas. But the key to their success in mobilizing popular support, for the existence of which there is much Japanese and nationalist testimony, lay in their ability to provide order and security in regions where these had been destroyed, directly or indirectly, by the Japanese invasion and to do this in a form which was more congenial to most of those concerned than the form which had existed before the invasion.

In four parts of northern China, one or more base areas became border regions. These regions, which covered parts of two, three or four provinces, had their own governments, with elected administrative councils. Party members were usually, but not invariably, in a majority on these councils, which had nominal authority over a layer of executive offices and departments. Besides Shaan–Gan–Ning, only one border region was ever recognized by Chiang Kaishek as having legitimate existence.

Deng Xiaoping was not present at the conference which settled strategy for the war, but was appointed deputy director of the political department of the eighth route army on the day it ended. As such, he spent the autumn of 1937 in the Wutai mountains, a group of peaks covered with Buddhist and Lamaist temples and monasteries in north-eastern Shanxi. He was there when the 115th division, commanded by Lin Biao, ambushed and destroyed the supply train of a Japanese division in a narrow ravine nearby. This, the first Chinese victory of the war, yielded no prisoners and little equipment, but did a great deal for the national prestige of the communists.

In January 1938, Deng was appointed political commissar of the 129th division, to succeed a man who had died. This move brought him into the formation in which he was to spend the whole of the rest of the war. The division was about 13,000 strong[3] and consisted chiefly of survivors of Zhang Guotao's fourth front army, so that its morale may have been lower than that of the eighth route army's other two divisions.

The division's commander was Liu Bocheng, a Sichuanese like Deng, who had been a professional soldier for the whole of his grown-up life. Born in 1892 and so twelve years older than Deng, he had been an officer in the armies of several Sichuanese militarists before becoming a communist in the early 1920s. After taking part in the Nanchang rising of August 1927, he had been sent by the party to the Soviet Union, where he spent about three years at a Red Army academy. Chief of staff of the first front army during the Long March, he had kept out of the disputes about strategy into which other commanders, especially Lin Biao and Peng Dehuai, had been drawn. Blind in one eye, he always wore spectacles. Very much a soldier's soldier, popular with his troops, he seems to have made it his rule to leave politics to others. He and Deng got on extremely well; in his official biography, Deng is quoted as having said years later that people were right to describe Liu and him as inseparable: 'We did feel inseparable in our hearts.'[4]

By the time Deng joined the division, it had established itself in the Taihang mountains of south-eastern Shanxi, a 'high and perilous' region, 'easy to defend but difficult to attack'.[5] The Japanese in fact made no attempt to attack it; having captured Taiyuan, the capital of the province in November 1937, they concentrated on setting up fortified posts on the railway lines which ran into Taiyuan from the north, the south and the east. In their mountain fastness, Liu and Deng began to build a base, and to consider how to deal with the impact of the Japanese invasion on the province as a whole. The governor had fled, local government had collapsed and its unoccupied areas were full of deserters from retreating nationalist armies.

During the next two years, 1938 and 1939, Liu and Deng concentrated on base-building and army-building, avoiding contact with the Japanese. They consolidated the base in the Taihang mountains, created another in the mountainous centre of Shanxi and then founded two more bases in the north China plain, east of the railway, much used by the Japanese, between Peiping and Wuhan. In each base, they recruited and trained two kinds of auxiliary troops: local forces, which had full-time military responsibilities, but which remained in the areas in which they had been raised; and militia groups, which were part-time, but which could be given duties to free regular and local forces for military operations. The auxiliaries also provided a pool of recruits for the division itself.

In 1940, Liu and Deng went over to the offensive, first against the nationalists and then the Japanese. In March, they attacked a nationalist army which had advanced into the Taihang base as part of a drive by Chiang Kaishek to re-establish the authority of the nationalists in the many areas outside Shaan–Gan–Ning where the communists had replaced it. They defeated it and then went on to defeat the troops of Yan Xishan, the provincial governor, which had joined in. These victories gave them a much freer hand politically, in the base areas and outside.

Liu's and Deng's victories also created conditions in which all the communist commanders in Shanxi could contemplate aggressive action against the Japanese. With or without authority from Mao's military commission in Yan'an, they made plans to attack Japanese posts on the railways of north China and to block or cut the lines themselves. The sabotage operations began in late August and led to fighting which lasted for over three months. To begin with, the communists committed a force of twenty-two regiments – about 40,000 men. Later, as the scope of the campaign was extended to include attacks on other Japanese garrisons, and as the Japanese began to mount counter-attacks, up to five times as many units and troops were thrown in.

The Hundred Regiment Campaign, as it came to be known, had mixed results. It led to the interruption for a few weeks of Japanese lines of communication in Shanxi and Hebei and the capture of quite a few towns. It also heartened the whole country at a time when there was much more bad news than good (since the autumn of 1938, when the Japanese had taken Hankow and Canton, the nationalist armies in the centre and south had stood entirely on the defensive). But it revealed to the Japanese the fighting capacity of the eighth route army, making retaliation inevitable, and to the nationalists how successful the communists had been in their base- and army-building. In Yan'an, Mao Zedong reacted badly to publicity for the campaign in the nationalist press and there are stories that he was displeased about the conduct of the campaign. Peng Dehuai, the field commander of the eighth route army at the time, has written that he 'triggered' the campaign ten days before it had been due to start and before formal approval to launch it had been received from Yan'an. This would have been quite enough to annoy Mao, who was now as jealous of his own authority as he had once been ready to flout the authority of others. In any case, it is likely that Mao thought it rash for Peng and the others concerned, including Deng, to extend the scope of the campaign after the success of its first phase, to the point where up to 200,000 men were committed and exposed to counter-attack. Peng has also written that Mao sent him a telegram of congratulation 'when news of our victory reached Yan'an'. But this could have been early on in the campaign; and it did not save Peng from being attacked for his handling of it at a conference in Yan'an in the summer of 1945, five years later. Today, the verdict on the campaign itself is favourable. The two sentences about it in Deng's official biography read: 'Beginning in August 1940, Liu and Deng, with 38 regiments under their command (not including local forces), participated in the Hundred Regiment Campaign. Fighting 529 operations, big and small, they dealt heavy blows to the Japanese and puppet troops and greatly strengthened the whole nation's confidence in victory.'

Nevertheless, there is implied criticism in the first sentence of the next paragraph: 'In 1941 the war of resistance behind enemy lines in north China entered the most difficult stage, when the Japanese troops concentrated their attacks on the rear.'[6] This change is not attributed to the campaign; but it is not explained in terms of anything else.

The two years which followed were indeed years of great difficulty in all the northern base areas. The Japanese, who did not thin out their armies in China after the beginning of the Pacific War in December 1941, set out to destroy all communist-controlled forces in the bases and to sweep them clean of communist influence. Under the watchword 'kill all, burn all, loot all', their troops now stayed in target areas for weeks or months at a time, making little attempt to distinguish between communists and the rest of the rural population. There were many atrocities and it became common for growing crops to be burned and stocks of food to be destroyed or carried away. By the end of 1942, the bases in the plains, including the two created by the 129th division, had been turned into areas where there were no forces of any size under communist control. In the mountains, the communists lost many of the towns they had captured during the Hundred Regiment Campaign.

It is from this time, when he was living rough in the bare hills of eastern Shanxi, that it is first possible to form a clear picture of Deng Xiaoping as a mature man. As for no earlier period, some of his speeches and writings are in the published record, and for the first time since his days in France there is a store of anecdotes about him.

Deng was a very small man. He had stopped growing, at a height of barely five feet, at about the time he went to France. He is alleged to have attributed this to the poverty of his diet there, but it is more likely that his short height was inherited: his father was a small man, and none of his own children is tall. He was also stocky, even in early middle age, with a short neck and broad shoulders. He had a large, rather square, face, with a strong chin and deeper-set eyes than most Chinese.

Like many small men, Deng was quick in his movements and outstandingly energetic. He was physically tough too; except when he had typhoid at the end of the Long March, he was never seriously ill during his youth and middle age, even though he lived for much of the time in areas like Guangxi and Shanxi, where many kinds of serious disease were endemic. At some stage, he had become a heavy smoker – like Mao Zedong, but unlike Zhou Enlai – but there is no hint in the tales of his associates that he ever suffered from serious side-effects.

Deng was choleric in temperament. Although he had learned early on to keep his temper under control, it never faded, and there were times when he chose to let it show. Later, when he was China's national leader, his temper was feared by his colleagues and subordinates, and so became important politically. With his temper went a natural impatience, though it was one of his characteristics in maturity to insist that rapid action should always be preceded by careful thought. His open impatience was reserved for procrastination or muddle once a decision had been taken.

Deng had a fine natural intelligence, though there is more than a hint of regret in his many later speeches about education that his own education had effectively been cut short at the age of sixteen. He was a good political and military analyst and very clear in presenting a case, both orally and on paper. His speeches and essays of the early 1940s, of which nine appear in the first volume of his *Selected Works*, are cogent, even if rather too heavily tabulated to make exciting reading. They show that the cast of his mind was concrete, but also that he had good grasp of theory and that there was nothing hidebound about his approach to problem-solving. He relished facts and figures, and made himself something of an expert on subjects, like trade and taxation, which he had never dealt with before, but which mattered greatly for the survival of the bases of the 129th division and popular support for the border-region government which Liu and he superimposed on them in 1941. The principle he adduced for all economic work was 'to restrict to a certain degree the savage exploitation of the past ... [but] to stimulate capitalistic production, which is at present beneficial to the development of the national economy'.[7] It was characteristic both that he used no euphemism for 'capitalistic production' and that he used the words 'at present' before 'beneficial', making it clear that it was not in the communists' scheme to tolerate capitalism for ever.

At the beginning of 1943, Japanese pressure on the base areas began to slacken. The communists reacted by pushing out their frontiers, to cover new as well as old ground, especially in Shandong. Deng was largely responsible for directing this process. During the second half of 1943, Peng Dehuai, Liu Bocheng and Nie Rongzhen, the three senior commanders in the northern base areas, were all recalled to Yan'an. Deng replaced Peng as the acting secretary of the party's northern bureau and also took charge of day-to-day work at the headquarters of the eighth route army, assuming control of about 300,000 regular troops and as many in local forces.

In the spring of 1944, the Japanese launched their largest offensive in China since the first year of the war. Code-named Ichigo, it had two purposes: to establish control over the railways of the centre and south, in order to lessen Japanese dependence on seaborne transport, which had become increasingly vulnerable to American attack, and to occupy the airfields in the south-west from which American aircraft had been operating in growing numbers. The offensive began in April in Henan and continued during the summer and autumn in Hunan and Guangxi. There was strong Chinese resistance, supported by the aircraft of General Claire Chennault's fourteenth air force, at some points in Hunan, but not a great deal elsewhere. By November, the railways had been cleared of Chinese troops and the airfields occupied. The losses of Chiang Kaishek's army were enormous and hundreds of thousands of civilians were killed. The offensive revealed to the world the extent to which the efficiency of nationalist troops had declined since the early days of the war and how corrupt, faction-ridden and inefficient the central government had become. It did enormous damage to the prestige of Chiang Kaishek himself,

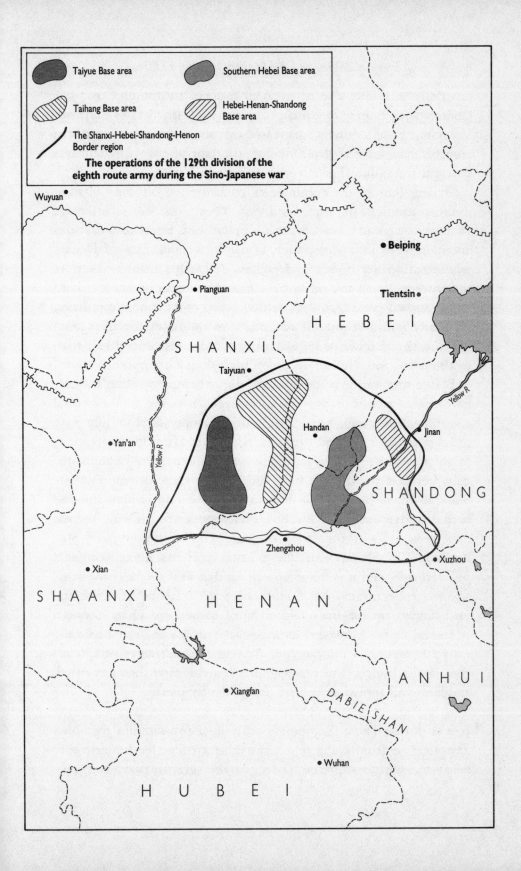

The operations of the 129th division of the eighth route army during the Sino-Japanese war

Wuyuan

Beiping

Pianguan

Tientsin

HEBEI

SHANXI

Taiyuan

Handan

Yellow R

Jinan

Yan'an

Yellow R

SHANDONG

Xian

Zhengzhou

Xuzhou

SHAANXI

HENAN

ANHUI

Xiangfan

DABIE SHAN

Wuhan

HUBEI

especially at home, and to national morale. By the end of 1944, China was a country in which, to quote Professor Lloyd Eastman, 'economic production had decreased sharply . . . inflation was out of control, the army was hapless before the Japanese, government was corrupt, and political disaffection suffused all levels of society'.[8]

During Ichigo, the communists concentrated on consolidating their positions in the north and east. They launched no offensive to relieve pressure on Chiang's armies, but were also cautious about moving into areas, such as the whole province of Henan, where nationalist power had collapsed. Deng's main tasks were therefore to beat back subsidiary Japanese attacks on the northern bases, and to persevere with settled social and economic policies, especially rent and interest reduction, in the bases. By the spring of 1945, the number of regular troops under his control had risen to about 500,000. He had become a big fish in a big pond.

Before the summer of 1945, Deng returned to Yan'an only twice: in September 1938 for an enlarged meeting of the central committee (of which he was still not a member) and in July 1939 to take part in a politburo conference. Soon after this conference, he married for the third time. His new wife was Pu Zhuolin, the daughter of a prosperous ham and sausage merchant in Yunnan. She had made her way to Yan'an from Beiping, where she had been a student, in 1937. Twelve years younger than Deng, she has now been his wife for fifty-four years. Unlike the wives of Mao Zedong, Liu Shaoqi and Zhou Enlai, she has never sought a political role, and it is not even certain that she is a party member. She has concentrated on looking after her husband at home and on bringing up the five children born to her and Deng between 1940 and 1952. Slim and almond-faced in youth, she became a matronly figure in middle age. Among the marriages of China's communist leaders, this marriage has lasted longer than any other, and has to all appearances been one of the happiest.

It was during Deng Xiaoping's years in the mountains that Mao Zedong rose from being one member of a collective leadership to being the party's supreme leader. At the seventh party congress, held in Yan'an from April to June 1945, he was elected chairman of the central committee, a new post, and, in virtue of this, chairman of the politburo and of the secretariat, the small inner committee which made all the most important decisions, and his 'thought' was enshrined in the party's new constitution as the guide to all its work. He acquired both a formal position and an ideological status beyond any to which Stalin ever aspired.

Mao's formal rise followed rather than led his accumulation of authority and reputation. As early as 1936, when he was junior in the secretariat to Luo Fu, Bo Gu and Zhou Enlai, his authority was greater than that of any of his colleagues and he was presenting himself to Edgar Snow as the party's effective leader. But, in the conditions of the day, when the Chinese party was a branch of the Comintern, he could not have gone further without the sanction of that body. It was therefore a key moment when Wang Jiaxiang, who had been the first to speak in Mao's support at Zunyi and who had subsequently gone to Moscow for medical treatment, returned to Yan'an in July 1937 with a directive by Dimitrov, the chairman of the Comintern's executive committee, which described Mao as 'the leader of the Chinese people'.[9]

In spite of Dimitrov's accolade, Mao had a very difficult year between November 1937, when three members of the politburo who had been in Moscow – Wang Ming himself, Kang Sheng and Chen Yun – returned to China, and November 1938, when the central committee, meeting for the first time in Yan'an, adopted documents which largely reflected his views on political and military strategy. All through this year, Mao found himself at odds with Wang on the crucial issue of whether the communists should adopt an arm's-length attitude towards the nationalists in the new united front or agree, or even seek, to operate within the institutions of the nationalist state, including the army. Wang's slogan was 'everything through the united front'.

Wang was an articulate and (to begin with) confident adversary. In 1931, when in Shanghai, he had written and circulated a pamphlet, *The Two Lines or The Struggle for the Further Bolshevization of the Communist Party of China*, which set out the complete political programme of the Returned Students and was the guidebook of Bo Gu and Luo Fu when they controlled party headquarters. Back in Moscow as the Chinese party's senior delegate to the Comintern, he became a member of that body's executive committee and considered himself entirely within his rights to issue the manifesto of 1 August 1935, calling for the creation of a new united front, in the name of his party.

According to one source, Mao was 'in a minority and sometimes completely isolated for about half a year'[10] after Wang's return. Then the tide turned, largely because of Wang's political naïvety. Instead of staying in Yan'an, where he could have influenced other leaders and kept in touch with Moscow, he chose to spend the summer of 1938 in Wuhan, engaged in (ultimately fruitless) discussions with nationalist commanders and politicians about the possibility of organizing a popular defence of the city on the model of the defence of Madrid by the republicans in Spain. When he returned to Yan'an, he found that the balance of opinion in the politburo had shifted against him. The politburo did invite him to give the keynote report at the then imminent central committee meeting, but then rejected his draft and asked Mao to give the report instead.

Thereafter, Wang's star waned steadily. After the central committee meeting – which 'corrected in the main the right capitulationist errors made by Wang Ming in the early days of the anti-Japanese war'[11] – he continued for a while to be head of the party's united-front work department and to write a good deal in the party press. But he was in due course replaced as head of the department by Zhou Enlai and then became inactive as a writer. He was re-elected to the central committee at the party congresses of 1945 and 1956, but in very low positions. In the 1960s, he came under public attack during the Cultural Revolution; presumably with help from the Russians, he escaped to the Soviet Union and died there, an embittered exile, in the 1970s.

His legitimacy and political authority both now secure, Mao went on to reinforce his position by tackling matters of theory. In this realm, his influence on the party, enormous at the time, is still strong: and it has left its mark indelibly on Deng Xiaoping.

In the light of what came later, Mao's most important pieces of analysis were about the stages of the revolutionary process in China and relations between the communist party and society. Mao divided the pre-socialist stage of revolution in China into two phases: a phase, which had lasted at least until about 1918, during which it 'came within the old category of the bourgeois-democratic revolution'; and a phase during which, while remaining bourgeois-democratic in its social character, it became part of the 'proletarian socialist world revolution' and required the establishment of a state system 'under the joint dictatorship of several revolutionary classes', including the proletariat and the peasantry. He called the second phase the phase of New Democracy and went on to define the political, economic and cultural programmes which were appropriate to it. It was within this framework that he later put forward policy proposals, especially for a national coalition government in 1945 and a communist-led united-front government in 1949.

In writing about the party and society, Mao tackled head-on, and in a way which went beyond Leninist orthodoxy, the problem of reconciling the requirement for dictatorship (which he never doubted) with the claim that the party stood for and practised democracy. The key element in his scheme was the 'mass line', on which he wrote:

In all the practical work of our party, all correct leadership is necessarily 'from the masses, to the masses'. This means: take the ideas of the masses (scattered and unsystematic ideas) and concentrate them (through study turn them into concentrated and systematic ideas), then go to the masses and propagate and explain these ideas until the masses embrace them as their own, hold fast to them and translate them into action, and test the correctness of these ideas in such action.[12]

This mass line has twin roots: in the Chinese millenarian tradition, and in the non-Chinese tradition of Rousseau and the Jacobins of the French Revolution. Mao emphasized the role of the party in synthesizing the ideas which reached it from below. But he was firm in regarding the ideas of the masses as the raw material for policy-making in the party's practical work, and thereby introduced an abiding element of populism into China's modern political culture.

In order to purge the party of Wang Ming's ideas and to substitute his own, Mao launched a 'rectification movement', which began in Yan'an in February 1942 and spread outwards from there to all the base areas during the two following years. He selected three particular modes of thought and behaviour for attack: 'subjectivism', 'sectarianism' and stereotyped party writing. In his scheme, the first two were double-sided; each had an aspect which was too harsh and another which was too lax (in subjectivism, the harsh aspect was 'dogmatism' and the soft aspect 'empiricism'). During the movement, it was the aspects which were too harsh – too 'left' – which were chiefly condemned. No names were named until the movement was officially over. Then, in 1945, Wang Ming and Bo Gu – though not Luo Fu and Wang Jiaxiang, to whom Mao had debts – were identified and pilloried as dogmatists in a central committee resolution.*

The rectification movement was conducted under the slogans 'cure the disease to save the patient' and (from the summer of 1943) 'arrest few and kill none', to distinguish it from the purges which the Returned Students had carried out in all the base areas of the early 1930s. But its long sessions often became extremely tense and unpleasant, and could be followed by 'struggle meetings'. Several freer spirits among the writers who had flocked to Yan'an from Shanghai and other cities since 1937 had to face relentless attack. Almost all of them made confessions of error in the end. But an author who had written satirical essays about the hypocrisy of many of Yan'an's loudest moralists refused to give in. He was imprisoned, and then executed in secret a few years later. The person responsible for his death was Kang Sheng, who had been

* The resolution also criticized unnamed 'empiricists' who had supported Wang and Bo during their years of political ascendancy. The only leaders of the Jiangxi period who plausibly answer to this description are Zhou Enlai and Zhu De.

trained in police methods in the Soviet Union and had known Jiang Qing, Mao's third wife, whom he married in 1939, for many years. During the rectification movement, Mao curbed Kang when the latter tried to reintroduce harsh treatment for party members with blemishes on their records. Twenty-five years later, during the Cultural Revolution, he gave Kang his head.

Deng Xiaoping returned to Yan'an for the first time since 1939 in June 1945, to attend a meeting of the central committee which had been elected at the seventh congress. He was now for the first time a member of that body, ranking twenty-eight among its forty-four full and thirty-three alternate members. Perhaps because he had not been present at the congress, and so had been unable to make any direct impression at it, this position did not quite do justice either to the responsibilities he had carried since 1943 or, as his next appointments were to show, to the view of his abilities taken by Mao and his associates.

CHAPTER 7

Soldier on the Plain, 1945–52

The surrender of Japan on 14 August 1945 made inevitable a renewed contest between the nationalists and the communists for national political power, and now on terms a great deal more even than before the war. Was it inevitable, however, that this contest should take the form of civil war?

On the one hand, the statements and actions of the two sides during the period which followed the Japanese surrender show that each side was prepared to give a fair amount of ground for the sake of creating, or seeming to create, a framework within which the contest could be conducted by political means. The pressures on them to do this were strong. After eight years of war against Japan, during which many millions had died, and nearly thirty years of internal military conflict, all classes in the nation were profoundly war-weary. The Americans, whose political, military and economic support was as badly needed by the nationalists as it had been during the war, very much wanted peace and were prepared to use pressure as well as their good offices to obtain it. The Russians, whose troops had occupied Manchuria during August 1945, wanted peace too, to spare themselves the need to make embarrassing political choices and to make more likely a rapid American military withdrawal. Moreover, each side had positive reasons for wanting to avoid civil war. The communists could by no means be certain of survival in such a war, let alone of victory. The nationalists, for their part, faced enormous political and economic tasks, not least those of re-establishing their authority in Japanese-occupied areas and of restoring a shattered national economy.

On the other hand, each side lacked trust in the other. More profoundly, neither side had a place for the other in its ideal scheme of things, so that any political settlement, or less comprehensive form of agreement, would have been likely to break down as soon as there was a significant shift in the balance of power. Once this had happened, there would have been nothing to prevent fighting so long as the communists retained armed forces under their control, as they were determined to do. It is hard to escape the conclusion that civil war was bound to break out sooner or later, although not necessarily as soon as it did.

As things turned out, there were two phases of serious negotiation before full-scale fighting began. The first phase was from August to October 1945, when Chiang Kaishek and Mao Zedong, the latter supported by Zhou Enlai, and both under pressure from the Americans, negotiated in Chungking for six weeks about all the matters, political and military, at issue between them. In the background was a race between nationalist and communist forces to occupy territory in Manchuria, in which the Russians on the whole did more to help the former. Each side made concessions. On their side, the communists gave up their demand that Chiang should form a coalition government to include themselves and agreed to withdraw altogether from nine of their nineteen base areas. But one issue remained intractable: the form of the future administration in the other ten communist bases. Mao flatly rejected Chiang's demand that the communists should allow these bases, all in the north or north-west, to be integrated into the nationalist state. This issue had to be left unresolved when Mao returned to Yan'an in October and was never settled.

In the second phase, from December 1945 to June 1946, General George Marshall, sent to China as President Truman's special envoy, worked hard to stop fighting and to promote political and military accords. To begin with, he achieved a good deal: a cease-fire agreement in January 1946, under which tripartite truce supervisory teams were set up, and a set of political and military agreements during the following month. Under one of the military agreements, a committee of three worked out a plan for the balanced reduction of the armed forces of the two sides. But effective action did not follow. One reason was that there was no paramount authority to insist on implementation. A second was that the issue of who was to administer the communists' northern base areas remained unresolved. A third was that serious fighting broke out in Manchuria in March, when the communists hastened to occupy cities evacuated during that month by Soviet troops and the nationalists reacted by sending troops to evict them. From then on, violations of the cease-fire became steadily more frequent. Marshall managed to arrange a two-week truce for Manchuria in early June, but the negotiations on issues of substance which took place while it was in effect did not lead to agreement. In early July, Chiang Kaishek, who had for months been preparing a full-scale offensive against the communists, ordered it to be launched.

Liu Bocheng and Deng Xiaoping remained in partnership after the end of the Pacific War, and became embroiled in fighting even before Mao had left Chungking. In the autumn of 1946, they fought campaigns against nationalist armies in both the west and centre of their border region (or liberated area, as was becoming its more usual name).

The first campaign was against Yan Xishan, their adversary of 1940, who decided in September 1945 to re-establish his authority as the governor of Shanxi and to begin by recovering Taihang and Taiyue, the communist bases in the east and centre of the province. But Liu and Deng were ready for him and having lured his army deep into the mountains, attacked and defeated its scattered divisions one by one, on classic Maoist lines. Over 20,000 prisoners, including many senior officers, fell into communist hands. The campaign showed that elements of the eighth route army could take on and defeat larger nationalist formations. Its lesson for Chiang Kaishek was that he would have to wage all-out war to take from the communists any territory which they were not prepared to give up at the negotiating table.

The second campaign followed almost immediately, fought by Liu and Deng offensively against a nationalist force of 40,000 which was advancing north along the Beiping–Hankow railway through the heart of their liberated area. In the first battle, at Handan, a large town on the railway, about a third of the nationalist troops defected to the communists under their commander, foreshadowing many later defections. The rest retreated, but were soon surrounded and forced to surrender. This campaign carried the message for Chiang that the communists were not prepared to let nationalist armies make strategic movements across areas under their control. In a statement issued shortly after the end of the campaign, Mao Zedong made no attempt to prevaricate about this:

The Kuomintang authorities are mustering large forces and are trying to swamp all the liberated areas as in a great flood. Following the failure of several attacks in September and October, they are preparing new attacks on an even larger scale. And one way to obstruct these attacks and effectively check the civil war is not to let them transport their troops by rail.

During the next nine months, the communists stepped up the prosecution of class war in the areas they controlled. From 1937 to 1945, they had exercised steady political pressure on landlords and moneylenders – often also landlords – to reduce rents and lower interest rates. Usually, however, local party branches had not mobilized tenants and borrowers to harass the rich. Now, however, Mao called for popular action; in a directive of November 1945, he wrote that rent-reduction must be 'the result of mass struggle, not a favour bestowed by the government' and, quoting a report he had written in 1927 on the peasant movement in Hunan, that 'excesses can hardly be avoided'.[1] The landords became 'struggle objects'. On the purpose of struggle, a party directive of May 1946 stated that the time had come to move on from rent-reduction to the confiscation of the property of landlords, including their houses. It spoke of several methods, ranging from the sale of land under gentle persuasion to forcible expropriation. In the atmosphere of the times, with civil war imminent, most local party leaders chose to use methods at the stronger end of the range. In many places, landlords were haled before mass meetings, denounced for harsh or insensitive behaviour towards their tenants and sentenced to punishments which, at the minimum, entailed the loss of most of their property. Besides being intended to show that the communists had not forgotten their old social agenda, the purposes of the drive were to destroy the power and prestige of the ruling class in the countryside and to swing the poorer members of rural society firmly behind the party and the army. The second purpose was not achieved everywhere; many peasants were frightened of retribution at the hands of the nationalists in altered military circumstances and others were unwilling to leave newly acquired plots of land to face the rigours and dangers of military service, the form of support the party and army most wanted from them.

Deng was the son and the brother of landlords (his second brother, Deng Shuping, had taken over the management of Deng Wenming's land in Guang'an after the latter's death) and he had opposed the expropriation of landlords and rich peasants in Jiangxi in 1933. But there is no evidence that he had qualms about the new policy. Rather the reverse. As a political commissar, he must have wanted recruits; and documents show that the party in his liberated area believed that land reform was effective in producing them. In any case, he had never doubted that land reform ought to be at the heart of the party's programme for the new democratic phase of the revolution.

In the first year of the civil war, from July 1946 to June 1947, the People's Liberation Army, as the eighth route army and the new fourth army had been renamed on the eve of its outbreak, was on the defensive in all parts of the country except Manchuria. In that theatre, the field army commanded by Lin Biao, one of the four armies into which the whole army was now divided, advanced several times from its base in the forests and mountains near the Soviet border and gradually gained the strategic initiative.

Liu Bocheng and Deng Xiaoping led the field army which held the vital central sector on the southern front. If it had broken or been destroyed, the nationalists would have been able to surround another field army to its east and open secure lines of communication with Beiping and Manchuria. For a whole year, it fought against larger nationalist forces in western Shandong, on either side of the railway which runs from east to west south of the Yellow River. It inflicted heavy casualties, at moderate cost to itself, but was forced to give a lot of ground. By January 1947, the nationalists had taken twenty-four of thirty-five county seats in one of its old base areas on the north China plain, and by the summer it had been forced to retreat across the Yellow River. Elsewhere, the communists were also in difficulties. In the east, the nationalists had made a lot of headway; and in the north-west, Yan'an had been lost and Mao and his colleagues at party headquarters forced to take refuge in the bare loess hills of northern Shaanxi.

After a year, therefore, the map suggested that the situation of the communists was serious, even grave. But the map did not tell the whole story. It did not reveal the casualty ratio during the first year, which was about three to ten in favour of the communists, or the low state of discipline and morale in many nationalist formations. Nor did it show that many nationalist divisions and brigades in the war zones were acting as garrison troops and were therefore not available for offensive use. Yet, for many in nationalist China, it seemed to compensate for a darkening political picture. Behind the lines, on what Mao called the 'second front', inflation was accelerating, corruption and carpet-bagging among nationalist politicians and administrators were rampant, and a peace movement which blamed the nationalists more than the communists for the fact of civil war was developing.

In this situation, Mao made the key decision that the communists should go over to the strategic offensive. Justifying this in a directive of September 1947, he wrote:

Our army will of course meet many difficulties in carrying out the policy of fighting on exterior lines and bringing the war into the Kuomintang areas ... But they can and must be overcome. For the enemy will be forced to spread out even more, and vast territories will be available to our army as battlefields for mobile operations, so that we will be able to wage mobile warfare; the broad masses in those territories hate the Kuomintang and support us; and though a part of the enemy forces still has a comparatively high combat-effectiveness, on the whole the enemy's morale and combat-effectiveness are much lower than a year ago.[2]

This reads convincingly. But the risks were in fact very great. In spite of their difficulties, military and political, the nationalists had by no means lost the will to fight and were at the time pressing their offensives in the east and north-west. Besides, the policy of 'fighting on exterior lines' carried the very real danger that one or more communist armies would be blocked, surrounded and destroyed.

It fell to Liu and Deng to make the first move. At the end of June 1947 (after Mao had made his decision, but more than two months before he issued his directive), a part of their field army, led by them, recrossed the Yellow River and attacked the nationalists in south-western Shandong. In a month of fighting, it inflicted over 50,000 casualties and captured the headquarters of four nationalist divisions. Then, in a second surprise move, it began a forced march to the south, striking out for the Dabie mountains, a range between Nanking and Wuhan, deep inside nationalist territory. During an advance of 300 miles in twenty days, it was in trouble several times, particularly when it threaded its way through a treacherous belt of marshland on the diverted wartime course of the Yellow River* and when it had to cross a wide river under fire from behind. By the end of August, however, it had reached the mountains, perhaps 50,000 strong.

The next few, very difficult, months are described in one of the few passages in Deng's official biography where feeling creeps into the narrative:

The troops under Liu and Deng were exhausted from continuous marching and fighting and were unfamiliar with the terrain.

---

* The nationalists had destroyed the dikes on the lower river in 1938. This had switched the river's course from a channel north of the mountains of Shandong to one south of them.

Furthermore, since they had only just arrived in the new area, they had no time to set up local governments and to mobilize the people, so they were short of food, clothing and ammunition. [After Liu had led a part of the troops away to the west], Deng Xiaoping and Li Xiannian were left to command a crack force whose task was to continue stubborn resistance in the mountains. Calling on the soldiers to be selfless, Deng said that there were two loads to be carried, and one was heavier than the other. If they in the Dabie mountains carried the heavier load, other armies in other regions would be able to destroy large numbers of enemy troops and carry out intensive work among the masses, which would be greatly to the general advantage. They should therefore hold on firmly, no matter how weak they became and what hardships they had to endure. Sharing the hardest conditions with their men, Deng and Li manoeuvred in the mountain gullies day and night, often on empty stomachs.[3]

Clearly based on the recollections of survivors, it is tempting to think that Deng himself had a hand in composing this passage. It in any case makes clear that there were times when his troops were in danger of defeat and that the boldest throw of Mao's military career could have ended in disaster. The most difficult period was from November 1947 to January 1948, when Bai Chongxi, who had once hunted Deng's seventh Red Army in Guangxi and who was now Chiang Kaishek's deputy chief of staff, sent a force of 200,000, chiefly collected from the war zones in the east and north-west, into the mountains. At one time, Deng was reduced to leading a hunted contingent of only 500 men.[4]

Relief came in the spring of 1948, when other communist troops began to fill the gap between the Yellow River and the mountains. Deng himself was able to leave the mountains and to make his way to northern Henan. There, in May, he became secretary of the party's central plains bureau and political commissar of the central plains military command, still in association with Liu Bocheng.

Deng was appointed to these posts during a general lull in the war. The nationalists and communists both wanted to rest and take stock. On the communist side, Mao was uncertain about how the communists should follow up their victories of the spring. In his memoirs, Nie Rongzhen describes conversations Mao had with himself and others at this time about strategic plans, including one in which Mao was dissuaded from ordering the field army in the east to cross the Yangtse straight away.

Also at this time Mao, who was unwell after spending a winter in conditions of extreme discomfort in Shaanxi, received an invitation from Stalin to go to Moscow for medical treatment. He declined it – for reasons which are not hard to fathom. Acceptance would have led to his leaving China for a minimum of several weeks at a time when the civil war was moving towards a climax and when it had become possible for the communists to think for the first time in terms of the 'fundamental overthrow' of the nationalist state. In any case, he must have suspected an ulterior motive. From 1927 onwards, Stalin had consistently tended to lean towards the nationalists rather than the communists in decisions about China which meant favouring one side or the other. This had been so over the creation of a second united front in 1937, over the supply of military aid during the war against Japan and over help for the armies of the two sides in Manchuria in 1945 and 1946. The obvious conclusion for Mao was that Stalin wanted to cross-question him about his fundamental military and political objectives and, having heard them, to set out how their achievement would impinge on the Soviet Union's geopolitical interests.

Whatever his suspicions, Mao soon learned at only one remove about Stalin's views. In the summer of 1948, Anastas Mikoyan, a senior member of the Soviet politburo, paid a secret visit to the party headquarters, now re-established in the mountains of Hebei. The very fact of the visit was unknown to any but a few in China and the Soviet Union until the early 1970s, when the text of a talk by Mao in which he had spoken about it began to circulate abroad. References to it have since appeared in several open sources, including the memoirs of Nie Rongzhen. Nie says that Stalin sent Mikoyan to China (via Dalian in Manchuria, where there was a Soviet air-force base) to 'talk with comrade Mao Zedong to find out how strong the Chinese revolution was and how many men we had to fight battles'. He comments that 'the Soviet comrades had the impression that the revolutionary army led by the Chinese Communist Party had been greatly diminished over years of war and only dwindling numbers of troops were left. This showed how they always underestimated the strength of the Chinese revolution.'[5] In fact, Mikoyan had been told to remonstrate as well as inquire. His line was that it would be wrong for the Chinese communists to go for complete victory in the civil war, because this could lead to American intervention on the nationalist side, with incalculable consequences for the world balance of power, as well as the communists themselves. The right course for the communists, therefore, was to abstain from sending their armies south of the Yangtse and to content themselves with political control of the northern half of the country. Mao rejected both the analysis and the proposal – scornfully in his own account of this remarkable episode.[6]

The outcome of the war was decided by three campaigns fought between September 1948 and January 1949. Each of the three was initiated by the communists and each resulted in an overwhelming communist victory. Together, they resulted in the complete destruction of the nationalist armies in Manchuria and in north and central China. Nearly one and a half million nationalist troops were killed or captured.

Deng Xiaoping's military career reached its apogee in one of these campaigns: the Huai-Hai campaign,* fought in central China, between the Yellow River and the Yangtse, from early November to mid-January. In it, the communists deployed two field armies, including Liu Bocheng's and some local forces, all under the command of a general front-line committee, a party body, of which Deng was secretary and therefore the executive chief. In the field, about 300,000 troops were supported by an army of civilian

* Huai is the name of a large river; *hai* means sea or ocean in Chinese.

labourers – as many as 5.4 million according to Deng's official biography – who carried stores and ammunition and dug trenches and ditches (the ditches in order to block and trap the many thousands of vehicles, including tanks, which the nationalists wanted to use). On the nationalist side, eight armies of about 100,000 troops each became drawn in.

There were four main battles, fought to the east, south-west and west of the railway junction town of Xuzhou, in Jiangsu, where Liu Zhi and Du Yuming, two of the principal nationalist commanders, had their headquarters. In each of the first three, a nationalist army of about 100,000 men was destroyed; in the fourth, two armies suffered the same fate. In all four, the battlefield strategy of the communists was to encircle a nationalist force whenever it was incautious enough to move into open country from its base. Some nationalist troops fought on until their supplies of food or ammunition were exhausted, but others surrendered as soon as serious fighting began. The nationalists had complete command of the air, but proved incapable of using their air arm either to cause the communists serious casualties or to supply enough food and ammunition to surrounded forces of their own. They also failed to make effective use of their armour, even though the campaign was fought on an open plain and the winter ground was hard.

Chiang Kaishek himself intervened frequently in the direction of operations. This, however, only confused his field commanders, who were already badly handicapped by poor logistics, inadequate intelligence and faulty communications. Again and again, they were taken by surprise and forced to fight at times and places of their enemy's choosing. They paid heavily for their failings; Du Yuming and an army commander were captured and two other army commanders were killed. Altogether, about 550,000 nationalist troops were put out of action.

This enormous nationalist defeat meant that the road to the south was open to the communists and that they were in a position to dictate terms for peace. Mao set these out in a statement issued on 14 January 1949, four days after the surrender of the last nationalist troops on the Huai-Hai battlefield. Amounting to a demand for complete surrender, they included the abolition of the nationalist state, the punishment of 'war criminals' (including Chiang Kaishek), the integration of all remaining nationalist forces into the People's Liberation Army and the formation of a 'democratic coalition government' to replace the 'reactionary Nanking Kuomintang government'. Chiang rejected the terms, but then immediately resigned as president of the republic. A former vice-president, Li Zongren – a survivor of the northern expedition and one of the few nationalist generals who had won a battle against the Japanese – then became acting president and opened negotiations with the communists in Beiping, which had now fallen to them. But the latter were in no mood to compromise and in April Li's negotiators had to carry back to Nanking a draft agreement on internal peace which embodied all the original terms. Li rejected the draft on 20 April; on the following day, the communists answered by crossing the Yangtse on a front of several hundred miles.

Except in Hunan, where Bai Chongxi held Lin Biao's field army, moved to the south from Manchuria, for three months, there was little organized nationalist resistance from this time on. Li Zongren, based in Canton, worked hard to rally it; but he found his efforts undermined by Chiang Kaishek, who had decided that the only possible way of preserving the nationalist state and party was to transfer them to the island province of Taiwan. Although formally in retirement, he set up a headquarters there and, using all his old links with nationalist politicians and commanders, organized the removal to it of about half a million troops, much of the navy and the air force and the whole of China's gold and foreign-exchange reserves. His hope was that the United States, where anti-communist sentiment was becoming steadily stronger as the Cold War took hold in Europe, would never allow Taiwan to be invaded. For the longer term, it was that a third world war would allow him to return to the mainland with the support of American arms.

Liu's and Deng's field army fought two campaigns during the war's final phase. In the first, it captured Nanking and occupied most of the lower Yangtse valley. This ought to have brought the war to an end for Deng. It was the party's plan to put him in political charge of eastern China, the former nationalist heartland, and it had already appointed him secretary of the party's east China bureau.

But this plan was changed in July, when the party decided that the danger of 'capitalist encirclement' (American military intervention) had receded, and that it could press on with the conquest of what remained of nationalist China. A consequential decision was that Deng should stay with Liu's field army.[7] In early October, he and Liu left Peking, where they had been to hear the proclamation of the establishment of the Chinese People's Republic on the first of that month, for Hunan, to which their army had meanwhile been moved. They travelled by train, an unaccustomed luxury, and caught up with their troops near the stretch of the Xiang river where the first front army had so nearly been trapped in November 1934.

In this second campaign the army's mission was to conquer the whole of south-western China. It was quickly accomplished. Although the nationalists made Chungking and then Chengdu the last stops for their government on the mainland, there was little fighting in Sichuan or anywhere else. Several nationalist commanders came over to the communists – with all their troops – and so did two provincial governors. Unfortunately, it is not known with what emotions Deng, in December, entered Chungking, the city he had left for France as a callow youth twenty-nine years before and never revisited. But he would have noticed how much it had grown during the intervening years and how much damage it had suffered from Japanese bombing during the war. Perhaps such observations had something to do with his early appointment as its mayor, responsible for its rehabilitation, a job he might have been too senior to get without asking for it.

Under the Common Programme, the blueprint for New Democracy adopted in September 1949 by a conference of nearly 700 delegates from the Communist Party and eight small groups from the political centre, China was divided into six regions, in four of which a military and administrative commission became the governing body. In the south-west, Deng Xiaoping became a vice-chairman of the regional commission, under the chairmanship of Liu Bocheng. He also became political commissar of the military command and first secretary of the regional party bureau. This last post was the most important. It gave him seniority over Liu, and everyone else, in the controlling institution of the new regional order and made him responsible to the party secretariat in Peking for every aspect of regional affairs.

The region consisted of the four provinces of Sichuan, Guizhou, Yunnan and Xikang, which varied greatly in character. Sichuan was large, populous and generally fertile; but it had suffered from over twenty years of warlord rule and then from being used during the war against Japan as the chief tax base and source of recruits for the nationalist government and army. Guizhou was poor and mountainous. So was Yunnan, which bordered on Burma (where many defeated nationalist troops had taken refuge) and Indo-China. Ethnically and physically, Xikang was a part of Tibet.* In all four provinces, but especially Yunnan and Xikang, large areas were occupied by non-Han peoples, who had traditionally regarded the Han Chinese as enemies. The total population of the region was probably in the neighbourhood of 150 million; its area was about 500,000 square miles.

Deng, Liu and their colleagues set themselves three principal tasks: to establish law and order, to promote economic recovery and to carry out land reform. Because of the legacy of warlordism

---

* Tibet within the borders drawn for it by the nationalists was outside the south-west military and administrative region and remained so until the region was abolished in 1954. The Qing emperors had regarded Tibet as a part of their realm, and both the nationalists and the communists considered it to be under Chinese sovereignty. In 1951, the central government and a Tibetan delegation signed an agreement under which Tibet became an autonomous region of the People's Republic. Deng Xiaoping was active in organizing the military pressure which persuaded the Tibetans that they had no option but to negotiate and it was troops from his command which ultimately entered Lhasa.

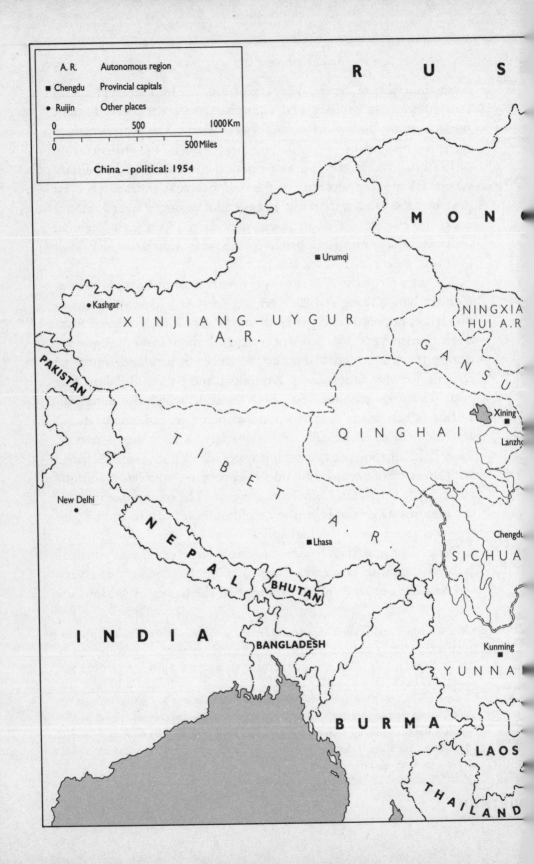

China – political: 1954

A. R.　　Autonomous region
■ Chengdu　Provincial capitals
● Ruijin　Other places

0　　　　500　　　　1000 Km
0　　　　　　　500 Miles

and the physical and ethnic character of the region, all three were difficult. The mountains were full of armed bands, including many made up of former nationalist troops. A great deal of land was used to grow opium poppies, especially in Guizhou and Yunnan, and whole districts lived off their cultivation. Except in central Sichuan, communications were poor; everywhere, the level of literacy was low and life expectancy short. Within two years, however, the party and the army cleared the region of armed vagrants and set up a new pattern of local government, modelled on the one developed in the base areas of the north. Because the party had never had more than temporary bases in the region, and there were few officers with experience of civil administration in the army, many officials who had worked for the nationalists were kept on, and new administrators were recruited from the recent graduates of local schools and universities.

Except in wholesale commerce, industrial and commercial recovery was left to follow the establishment of law and order and – a very high priority – the conquest of inflation. As in all other parts of China, inflation was tackled both by restraining demand and by stimulating supply. On the demand side, savings were vigorously encouraged through the sale of bonds and the indexation of deposits to the value of a bundle of commodities. The ability of private banks to lend was restricted by making it compulsory for all enterprises and official and military bodies to deposit their cash with branches of the newly established People's Bank of China, and official bodies were compelled to balance their budgets. On the supply side, communications were restored and state-owned companies were established to handle the wholesale trade in food and agricultural raw materials. These measures, adopted in a new climate of political certainty, produced very rapid results. The regional rate of inflation fell with the national rate, which declined from one in the hundreds of thousands to 20 per cent in 1951 and to well below 10 per cent in 1952.

In Sichuan, the railway protection movement of Deng's childhood had contributed to the overthrow of the dynasty, but not to the construction of any railways; in 1949, there was still not a kilometre of standard-gauge track in the whole of the province. There is nothing in the published record to show that Deng and Liu, both Sichuanese, considered this to be a reproach to their native province. This, however, is the natural explanation for their decision, taken early on, that scarce resources should be allocated to building a 300-mile line from Chungking to Chengdu. It was opened to traffic in July 1952, just before Deng left the region. The inclusion in his official biography of three photographs taken on the day of the opening ceremony suggests that he is still proud of his part in planning the project.

Among the three tasks, it was land reform which gave the programme of Deng and the others its revolutionary character. The first paragraph of the agrarian reform law of June 1950 sets out the purposes of reform very clearly: 'The land ownership system of feudal exploitation by the landlord class shall be abolished and the system of peasant land ownership shall be introduced, in order to set free the rural productive forces, develop agricultural production, and thus pave the way for New China's industrialization.'[8]

This abolition of 'feudal exploitation' amounted at one and the same time to a social, political and economic revolution. For millennia, the landowning class had controlled the social life of the Chinese countryside, including its market towns, and, because the empire and the republic had not provided government below the level of the county, its political life as well. In the myriad villages of China, the administration of justice, the maintenance of law and order, the upkeep of roads, canals and systems of irrigation, and the handling of representations to the county magistrate and his staff had all been in its hands. Acting with local self-help organizations, it had also had a lot to do with the maintenance of temples, the management of trade and the provision of relief in times of disaster. Now, in the space of two years, from the middle of 1950 to the middle of 1952, it was eliminated; its members, perhaps fifteen million people (including dependants), were deprived of most of their property and reduced to living off small plots of land and any income they might have from activity in industry or commerce. Tens of thousands, and probably hundreds of thousands, of them were killed. This, the greatest social revolution in Chinese history, was also the greatest social revolution in the whole history of the world.

Land reform brought the party into every village in China. During the campaign itself, party work teams mobilized the land-less and other poorer peasants to draw up charge sheets against the landlords and then to challenge and denounce them, so that old habits of subservience were broken and responsibility for revolutionary action could never be disowned. But the party did not then withdraw. It set up branches in the villages, recruiting into them many peasants who had come forward as leaders during the campaign; and these branches became the nerve-endings in a system of political control which penetrated rural society far more deeply than any which had been dreamed of before.

Economically, land reform created quite new patterns of owner-ship. Poor peasants – owners of no land or amounts inadequate for subsistence – gained most and former landlords lost most. The size of holdings and the size of farms both became much more uniform. Whereas the former had varied on average between 0.4 hectares for poor peasants and 8 hectares for landlords, it now varied on average between 0.8 hectares for former landlords and 1.5 hectares for rich peasants; and whereas the latter had varied between zero for landlords, who lived off rent, and 3 hectares for rich peasants, it now varied between 0.8 hectares for former landlords and 1.5 hectares for rich peasants.* Moreover, as these figures show, the size of holdings and the size of farms came to correspond. Nationally, over 300 million peasants gained from the process of confiscation and redistribution, and about eighteen million landlords and rich peasants lost from it.

Deng Xiaoping promoted land reform just as vigorously as any

* These holdings are very small by comparison with the holdings of family farmers in Western Europe and, even more, North America. There was, however, hardly any dairy farming or ranching in Han China.

other communist leader, even though it meant the dispossession of his own relations – Deng Shuping, his second brother, certainly, and perhaps others as well. But, in a move for which he was violently attacked during the Cultural Revolution, he arranged for Deng Shuping, his stepmother Xia Bogen, her daughter Deng Xianfu and his sister Deng Xianlie to be brought to Chungking and accommodated in the compound in which he himself lived and worked. As Deng Wenming had been popular in Guang'an, and as Deng Shuping and the others were known by the local communists to be his relations, they might have been spared violence during the process of reform. But Deng's action guaranteed their safety – and saved him from the uncomfortable choices he would have had to face if they had been threatened and then sought his help or if local party leaders had asked him for guidance about how they should be treated.

In July 1952, with or without warning, Deng Xiaoping was transferred to Peking. He had spent only two and a half years in the south-west, but had had time to add to his already very wide range of experience. This, and his performance over the years, must have counted for a great deal in the decision of Mao and his colleagues to bring him to the capital. Indeed, they were probably decisive. As he had spent almost the whole of the previous fifteen years in the field, it would be wrong to suppose that his personal relations with Mao counted for much – if anything. The same applies to his relations with Liu Shaoqi and Zhou Enlai, who had by now emerged, in that order, as the most important of Mao's lieutenants.

CHAPTER 8

The Hundred Flowers, 1952–7

Deng Xiaoping was a month short of his forty-eighth birthday when he was transferred to Peking. There were now lines round his mouth and on his forehead, so that he no longer looked young. At intervals during the previous five years he had grown a moustache, but this had gone by the time he left Sichuan. Curiously, however, his head was shaved as closely as his face – a practice associated by all Chinese with Chiang Kaishek – which emphasized the sloping line of his brow and the very strong set of his jaw, and it was not until he had been in Peking for at least two years that he allowed his hair to grow again. His general state of health was good, though he had taken to wearing spectacles when reading aloud from long texts. By the end of the 1950s, he had become quite deaf, especially in his right ear, although there is no sign in photographs taken of him during his first years in Peking that he had begun to wear hearing aids by then. His style was forthright and his manners were plain. Even in the 1980s, when he received scores of foreign visitors, it was his habit on all but the most formal occasions to clear his throat and spit when speaking.

Deng was accompanied or soon followed to Peking by his wife, Zhuo Lin,* their five children – the youngest of whom, a second son, had been born in 1952 – and (probably) his stepmother Xia Bogen. He and his family were given quarters in the Zhongnanhai, the lakeside park to the west of the Forbidden City where the

* She substituted Zhuo Lin for Qiongying, the name given her by her parents, soon after reaching Yan'an in 1937. After marrying Deng, she dropped her surname, Pu, presumably because it linked her with a capitalist father.

party and the government had their headquarters and where most of their leaders lived.

Mao Zedong lived with his family in a house built on the spit of land which separates the two lakes in the park. The house, which is now empty and is sometimes shown to visitors, Chinese and foreign, consists of single-storey pavilions built round courtyards. Mao used one of its largest rooms as a library; and it is said that he often dined alone in this room with a book at his elbow.[1] To judge from the furniture and hangings, he and his family lived in only modest comfort. The house was only a few hundred yards from the buildings, most of them ancient and ornate, in which the party had its offices and not much further from the offices of the government and – a matter of importance for Mao, who enjoyed swimming – a swimming pool which had been built for public use in 1933. It was even nearer to several large pavilions on the island – a jewel of Chinese landscape and architecture – to which the empress-dowager Cixi had banished the Guangxu emperor for most of the last twelve years of his (and her) life.* He was thus within easy reach of his colleagues and of places in which he could call groups of people together.

Mao's degree of authority within the party was greater than ever. It had been reinforced by the triumphant success of his political and military strategy before and during the civil war and by his election in September 1949 as chairman of the central government council of the People's Republic. He was at the height of his powers and full of confidence. It was his style to stand back from the day-to-day operations of politics and to reserve his time for the preparation of speeches and instructions on matters of strategy. But he was jealous of his powers as chairman of the central committee – also the source of his authority as the chairman of both the politburo and the secretariat – as

---

* Cixi, the emperor's aunt, was the most powerful figure at court from the death of her husband, the Xianfeng emperor, in 1861 down to her own death in 1908. She banished her nephew because he had favoured thoroughgoing constitutional reform.

shown by this note he sent to Liu Shaoqi in May 1953: 'From now on, all documents and telegrams sent out in the name of the central committee can be dispatched only after I have gone over them. Otherwise they are invalid. Please take note.'[2]

It was not his habit, even at this time, to acquiesce in decisions by other leaders which he disliked, and he was ready to use his own fiat to get them reversed. He did not, however, work to set his colleagues against one another, as Stalin had done, or seek to damage the public standing of those among them he had criticized or overruled. It was enough for him to get his way.

Mao apart, the secretariat consisted in 1952 of Zhu De, Liu Shaoqi and Zhou Enlai. Zhu, the old soldier, was inevitably less to the fore than he had been during the years of civil war and war against Japan. Neither now, however, nor later did he become politically inactive. He expressed views on foreign policy and defence at the eighth party congress in 1956 and often spoke at central committee meetings. Besides, he remained the commander-in-chief of the People's Liberation Army and a vice-chairman, under Mao, of the party's military commission; as such he played an important part in planning the enormous effort needed to keep upwards of half a million Chinese troops in the field in Korea from October 1950 until June 1953, when the Korean War ended in truce. He was a popular figure in the party and the army, known for his straightforward dealing. He represented the homespun – and the most attractive – strand in the Yan'an tradition of purposeful activity and plain living.

Liu Shaoqi was junior to Zhu De in the secretariat until 1956, but had emerged by the late 1940s as Mao's principal political lieutenant and the manager of the day-to-day work of the party. In almost every way, he was Mao's antithesis. Industrious, deliberate and rather solemn, he was, in the striking phrase of Professor Roderick MacFarquhar, a man who was truly grey in his eminence.[3] But he was not without vanity and he could be stubborn. Nor was he frightened of giving instructions or express-ing views on matters of policy without reference to Mao. As shown, Mao reproved him in 1953 for the way in which he had issued central committee documents on his own authority; and in 1951 he described the ideas of the Shanxi provincial party committee on the collectivization of agriculture as an 'erroneous, dangerous and utopian notion of agrarian socialism' in a note which he circulated widely on his own authority.[4] Neither this independence, however, nor his cautious attitude towards social change throughout the early 1950s made Mao want at this time to downgrade him or to discourage the developing assumption in the party and the country that he regarded Liu as the person best qualified to be his own successor.

Liu, the son of a poor peasant, had become Mao's closest political associate in Yan'an, although the full story of why and how this came to be the case has yet to be told. Perhaps Mao turned to Liu because he felt more at ease with him than with the intellectuals who surrounded him in the secretariat. He and Liu both came from Hunan, were both of rural stock and were both home-grown communists (though Liu had spent a year, not altogether happily, at the University of the Toilers of the East in Moscow in the early 1920s). Liu, for his part, may have judged that he could hope to rise in the party more rapidly by actively helping Mao to become its leader than by any other means. Several of his utterances during the 1940s certainly indicate that there was more calculation than hero-worship in his contemporary attitude towards Mao. In 1942, he remarked to some colleagues: 'What is a chairman? I have never heard people in the Soviet Union calling Lenin Chairman Lenin,'* and in 1947 he declared at a conference: 'There is no perfect leader in the world. This was true of the past as it is of the present, in China and in other countries. If there is one, he only pretends to be such, like a pig inserting scallions in his nose to make himself look like an elephant.'[5]

Liu's counterpart in the government was Zhou Enlai, who had

---

* At the time, Mao was not yet chairman of any party body. But there was already talk about the possibility of his becoming chairman of the politburo, as he did in 1943.

been appointed premier of the government administration council, holding executive authority under the largely honorific central people's government council, and also foreign minister, in 1949. Quick-witted, shrewd and articulate, Zhou is famous for his gifts as a diplomat and advocate. But he was also a man of convictions. He never doubted that China needed to undergo first a bourgeois democratic and then a socialist revolution, as stages on the way to the creation of a powerful modern state and of a united national society. Unlike Mao, however, he did not see revolution as a desirable state in itself. Still less did he rejoice, as Mao came to do, in the poverty and ignorance of the Chinese people; he wanted, instead, to abolish them as quickly as possible. He was not keen, as Mao was, on mass movements and he was free from Mao's suspicion of China's intellectuals – the class of four or five million people who had enjoyed a full secondary or university education.

Zhou, at least as industrious as Liu, was fastidious about manners, dress and speech and was considerate in his treatment of people who worked for him. There are many stories of how he went out of his way to be kind to orderlies, drivers and cooks and how he was never too busy to visit the sick or to arrange for their better treatment. During the Cultural Revolution, he became a hero to millions of ordinary people, coming to represent for them sanity and compassion in a world which had been turned upside down.

By the time Deng reached Peking in the middle of 1952, the new national leadership had achieved most of its original objectives, as set out in the Common Programme and the early statements of its members. Politically, it had established its authority over the whole territory of nationalist China, with the exception of Taiwan and some offshore islands. The dictatorial element in this process had been a nationwide purge of counter-revolutionaries, a category which embraced groups as various as nationalist officials with records of hostility to communism, pro-nationalist trade-union organizers, urban gangsters and rural bandits (including the son of one of the two bandit leaders who had collaborated with Mao

Zedong on Jinggangshan in 1927). The features of the campaign, which began in February 1951 and lasted until the spring of 1953, were its relentlessness and its reliance on popular action under party control to identify victims and determine their fate. It was not organized by the army or by the government. The number of those executed ran into hundreds of thousands and very many more were imprisoned. Its effects were to shatter what was left of the urban constituency of the nationalists – much reduced by the flight of hundreds of thousands of civilians to Taiwan – to put an end to the endemic lawlessness which had prevailed in both the cities and the countryside under the nationalists and to generate both fear of and respect for the communists throughout society.

Socially, the leadership had achieved almost the whole programme of New Democracy. In the countryside, land reform was complete except in areas where non-Han people were in the majority. In the industrial cities, the bureaucrat-capitalists – nationalist officials installed to run industrial concerns confiscated from Japanese owners – had been turned out and many foreign-owned enterprises taken over, sometimes by outright expropria-tion, but as often by putting pressure on them to accept settlements under which they surrendered their assets in return for the cancella-tion of accumulated financial liabilities (which could be run up without limit by local authorities). The foreign economic presence, for a hundred years dominant in the modern sector of the national economy, had been brought to the brink of extinction.

Going beyond New Democracy, the leadership had begun to move against the national bourgeoisie, one of the classes in the four-class bloc which was in theory in political power. In a confidential note of June 1952, Mao wrote that the 'contradiction between the working class and the national bourgeoisie' had now become the principal contradiction in China. This verdict was not published. But by midsummer no one could be in any doubt that the national bourgeoisie and capitalism were both under siege. For four months, the owners of factories and shops had been the targets of a campaign against the 'five evils' of bribery, tax evasion, theft of state property, cheating on government contracts and theft of classified economic information. As in the campaign against counter-revolutionaries, control of this campaign, which soon became known as the five antis movement, was vested in the party and popular participation was encouraged. Hundreds of businessmen killed themselves and thousands were compelled to pay heavy fines or large arrears of tax.

In the countryside, the leadership had likewise moved beyond New Democracy. As soon as land reform was over, rural branches began to encourage peasants who had little land, or were short of draught animals and agricultural implements, to band together in mutual aid teams. To begin with, such teams were small, having perhaps a dozen or two members, and seasonal; but no effort was made to conceal the party's intention to bring on these 'sprouts of socialism'.

Economically, the country had done well. Inflation had been brought under control and a policy of 'resistance, stabilization and construction', under which central government expenditure on development was restrained in order to make room for additional spending on military programmes, had kept it under control after China's entry into the Korean War. In spite of land reform, the five antis movement and the end of most trade between China and the West, agricultural and industrial output rose in 1952 to levels above those of their best years before the Japanese invasion (and far above those of 1949). This performance owed a good deal to natural rebound in conditions of domestic peace, and more than a little to the acquisition of the Japanese-built industrial base in Manchuria, but was nevertheless impressive.

In 1952, when Deng Xiaoping reached Peking, there was agreement at the top of the party that China should embark on a programme of rapid economic development as soon as the constraints of the Korean War had been removed and that this programme should be modelled on Stalin's in the Soviet Union. Its key features were to be a very high rate of investment, the allocation of the lion's share of investment to industry and its allocation within industry to large-scale, capital-intensive projects. No one in the leadership seems to have asked at this time whether agriculture, itself to receive little from central investment, would be able to sustain such a programme by providing food for a rapidly expanding urban population. Nor does anyone seem to have asked whether light industry, which would need to provide clothing and other consumer goods for this urban population and which could generate quicker and greater returns on investment, should not receive more than the 10 per cent share of central investment which was ultimately allocated to it. Soviet institutions and procedures were copied wholesale. The institutions included a state planning commission, a state statistical bureau and a set of industrial ministries, each with control over all factories, old and new, within its sphere. The key procedure was material balance planning, under which output targets and distribution tables were drawn up for all important industrial products.

On the other hand, there was no consensus at the top on social policy. Having decided that the national bourgeoisie was now a hostile class, Mao wanted to press on with the 'socialist transformation' of agriculture, handicrafts and industry and commerce. But several others, Liu Shaoqi certainly and Zhou Enlai almost certainly among them, wanted to stabilize the economic forms of New Democracy – the private ownership of land and of factories and shops – and to keep them in being, in parallel with socialist forms, for a long time. Mao criticized the proponents of this line at a politburo meeting in June 1953, saying that he disliked the slogans of 'firmly establish the new-democratic social order', 'move from New Democracy towards socialism' (without specifying any time limit) and 'sustain private property' which they had proposed, and again at a party conference in August on financial and economic work. He prevailed; and a general line for a period of transition to socialism, which made clear that the forms of New Democracy were to undergo progressive attenuation, was made public in October.

On his arrival in Peking, Deng Xiaoping was appointed a

vice-premier and a vice-chairman of the financial and economic commission and therefore to government rather than party posts. In these, Zhou Enlai and Chen Yun, a vice-premier and chairman of the commission, became his chiefs and closest associates. His executive responsibility was for land and sea communications.[6] In September 1953, the accent in his work became more strictly financial, when he was appointed to succeed Bo Yibo, a northerner he had come to know well in the base areas of the 129th division during the war against Japan, as minister of finance (Bo was compelled to resign because he had introduced a tax system at the end of 1952 which imposed no greater burden on privately owned business than on state-owned enterprise and had then been criticized by Mao at the August conference for having made a mistake which was a 'manifestation of bourgeois ideas').

Deng must have expected that he would stay in his new post – a sensitive and important one – for much longer than the nine months for which he in fact held it. In June 1954, however, he was appointed to the new post of secretary-general of the central committee, moving from government to party work and to a job which brought him into much closer contact with Mao and Lui Shaoqi and made him the chief link between them and the party's apparatus in the country at large.

The background to this second move was the failure of a plot by Gao Gang, a member of the politburo and chairman of the state planning commission, and Rao Shushi, the director of the party's organization department, to drive Liu Shaoqi and Zhou Enlai from high office. Gao and Rao, moved more by personal ambition than principle, tried to discredit Liu and Zhou by attacking (unnamed) doubters about the soundness of the new general line at party conferences in 1953; and they tried to stir up resentment against them by circulating a confidential (and, according to Mao, unauthorized) list of candidates for future membership of the politburo which short-changed several senior military figures. They linked the list with Liu by pointing out that it had been drawn up by a close associate of his at party headquarters. Their plot ramified until the end of the year, but then came suddenly to grief; Deng Xiaoping and Chen Yun, who had both been approached by Gao, decided – apparently separately – that his behaviour was unprincipled and reported it to Mao.

In December 1953, Mao trapped Gao at a politburo meeting into making proposals about party and government appointments which revealed his animus against Liu and then gave Liu the chance to take his revenge by naming him to preside over a forthcoming central committee meeting. Liu seized his opportunity; he attacked Gao and Rao as anti-party conspirators and persuaded the meeting to agree that the activities of the two men should be investigated by separate ad hoc commissions. There is a story that Gao threatened to shoot himself on the spot and so frustrated immediate action against him. Whether or not this is true, the meeting marked the end of the conspiracy. Gao and Rao soon lost their posts in the party and the government and Gao at least was imprisoned. Sometime during the summer of 1954, he killed himself in gaol.

Besides being made secretary-general, Deng was appointed to succeed Rao as director of the organization department and chosen to make the formal report on the conspiracy at a party conference in March 1955. A month later, he was elected to the politburo, in the thirteenth (and last) position, but ahead of many who had outranked him in the central committee. At the very least, the plot had given him opportunities which would not otherwise have come his way.

At the conference which passed judgement on the plot of Gao and Rao, Mao announced that the central committee (meaning the party's leadership) had decided to convene a party congress, the first to be held since 1945, in the second half of 1956. He outlined its formal agenda, spoke about the need for the party to take a 'big step forward' in all fields 'within a year', and declared that the criticism of party members by others at the congress ought to be sharp.

Mao thus set a timetable of eighteen months for the preparation of the congress. This ought to have been ample for Deng

Xiaoping, the secretary-general, and his assistants to draft documents and make detailed arrangements. As it turned out, however, there was a last-minute rush. There were no doubt particular reasons for this. But a general reason was that developments at home and abroad had changed the political landscape. At home, China had moved on from New Democracy to full-blooded socialism; abroad, Khrushchev had denounced Stalin and his 'cult of personality' and proposed new strategies for the international communist movement.

In China, 'socialist transformation' was set off by Mao's victory in a dispute between himself and most of the rest of the party's leadership over the right way to react to a crisis in agriculture. In 1953, the government found that it was short of grain to feed the urban population. A system of compulsory procurement, under which private transactions in grain were forbidden in rural markets until the agents of the state, often millers, had bought up fixed quotas of grain at low prices, was therefore introduced. This change relieved the situation in the towns. But, in the absence of any rapid growth in output, it produced severe shortages in the countryside. Mao's response was to demand the rapid collectivization of agriculture – the replacement of privately owned farms by agricultural-producer cooperatives, to begin with of a kind in which members would be remunerated in part for their contributions of land, draught animals and tools, but quite soon at a 'higher stage', where members would be rewarded only for their labour.

It was Mao's belief that collectivization would lead to increased output, through the achievement of economies of scale from the creation of larger farms, and also make it easier for the government to procure the grain it needed to feed the country's urban population. But he was influenced at least as much by his fear that the pattern of ownership created by land reform would soon produce a high degree of economic and social polarization in the countryside – that the richer peasants would accumulate more land and other assets, that the poorer peasants would be forced to sell or mortgage their land and that the levelling effects of land reform would therefore be undone.

At the end of April 1955, a national conference called by the party's rural work department decided, under the slogan of 'halt, shrink and develop', that collectivization should go ahead in some parts of China, but be halted or reversed in others. Mao reacted angrily. He told a meeting of provincial party secretaries that he regarded 'develop' as the keyword in the official slogan, rounded on the director of the rural-work department and engaged in a 'violent dispute' with him, and then demanded a complete change in policy at a further meeting of provincial secretaries. He began his speech to this second meeting with words which quickly became famous:

An upsurge in the new, socialist mass movement is imminent throughout the countryside. But some of our comrades, tottering along like a woman with bound feet, are complaining all the time: 'you're going too fast, much too fast'. Too much carping, unwarranted complaints, boundless anxiety and countless taboos – all this they take as the right policy to guide the socialist mass movement in the rural areas.

No, this is not the right policy; it is the wrong one.[7]

He went on to declare that most peasants wanted collectivization, that it was the job of the party to lead them towards it, and that Soviet experience did not suggest that China's target, which he now set as complete collectivization in eighteen years from 1949, was too ambitious.

Mao's behaviour produced a bandwagon. Believing their reputations and careers to be at stake, the provincial secretaries set to work to make a reality of his 'upsurge' – and to such effect that the collectivization of agriculture, which brought about 110 million rural households into rather more than 300,000 higher-stage cooperatives, was complete by the end of 1956, eleven years ahead of his target date. This enormous transformation was accomplished without the widespread use of violence against landowning peasants or the severe drop in agricultural output which had marked collectivization in the Soviet Union. But it did not solve the economic problems which Mao had expected it to solve; and Mao's reaction to this was to bring in policies which led to at least as much misery in China as collectivization itself in the Soviet Union.

The movement in the countryside gave rise to a parallel movement in the towns and cities. Beating drums and clashing cymbals in an orgy of factitious enthusiasm, the owners of factories, workshops and stores asked that their property should be turned over to joint state and private ownership. Their demand was accepted, and they became salaried managers and/or the recipients of dividends at a fixed rate (normally 5 per cent) on the assessed value of their former property. By the end of 1956, Chinese capitalism had all but disappeared.

Mao Zedong was unhappy from the outset about Khrushchev's denunciation of Stalin at the twentieth congress of the soviet party in February 1956. In a statement to the politburo at the end of April, he declared:

In the Soviet Union, those who once extolled Stalin to the skies have now in one sweep condemned him to purgatory. Here in China some people are following their example. It is the opinion of the central committee that Stalin's mistakes amounted to only thirty per cent of the whole and his achievements to seventy per cent, and that all things considered Stalin was on balance a great Marxist.[8]

As the consequences of Khrushchev's action unfolded, first in riots in Poland and then in the collapse of Stalinist rule in Hungary, Mao came to the conclusion that Khrushchev had been in ideological error, as well as imprudent and unjust, to attack Stalin in the way he had. He also concluded that Khrushchev had jettisoned a large part of Leninism by talking in another speech at the congress about the possibility of a parliamentary road to state power for communist parties. He used one of the most vivid of all his metaphors to express his views at a central committee meeting in November 1956.

I think there are two swords: one is Lenin and the other Stalin. The sword of Stalin has now been discarded by the Russians and Gomułka [in

Poland] and some people in Hungary have picked it up to stab at the Soviet Union and oppose so-called Stalinism. As for the sword of Lenin, hasn't it too been discarded to some extent by some Soviet leaders . . .? Is the October Revolution still valid? Can it still serve as the example for all countries? Khrushchev's report says that it is possible to seize state power by the parliamentary road . . . Once this gate is opened, by and large Leninism is thrown away.[9]

At the eighth congress of the Chinese party, ultimately held in September 1956, there were four platform speakers: Mao Zedong, who gave a short opening address, Liu Shaoqi, Zhou Enlai and Deng Xiaoping. Liu delivered the central committee's political report and Zhou made a long report about the second five-year plan, due to be launched in 1958. Deng, who spoke on the second day, covered the state of Chinese society and the tasks of the party in a very long report on a revised party constitution. As his report differed markedly in style and to some extent in substance from the speeches of the other three, it can be read as a personal political testament – valuable not only as a statement of his contemporary political views but as a standard by which to measure their whole subsequent development.

Deng dealt with three key political issues: the state of class relations in China, the manner in which party members ought to conduct themselves and the role of the leader in a Marxist party. On the first of these, he committed himself without qualification to the view that China was well on its way to becoming a classless society (in the sense of a society with only one class, not one in which class itself had melted away). Making a comparison between the situation in which the party had been in 1945 and the one in which it found itself in 1956, he declared:

Now the situation in our country is entirely changed. Under the leadership of our party, the people's revolution won nationwide victory in 1949, and an unprecedented national unification was realized. Except in a few border areas, we have not only completed the tasks set for the stage of bourgeois-democratic revolution but in the main carried out the tasks for the stage of socialist revolution. Moreover, in the past seven years we have scored tremendous achievements in all spheres of our socialist construction. All this has brought about a fundamental change in China's class relationships. The working class has become the leading class in the state; the peasantry has changed from individual farming to cooperative farming; and the bourgeoisie as a class is on its way to extinction.[10]

In a later passage, he said:

Both before the seventh congress and for a considerable period after-wards, it was essential to have different procedures of admission for applicants of different social origin ... But in recent years the situation has drastically changed. The difference between workers and office employees is now only a matter of a division of labour within the same class ... The vast majority of our intellectuals have now come over politically to the side of the working class ... Every year, large numbers of peasants and students become workers, large numbers of workers, peasants and their sons and daughters join the ranks of the intellectuals and office-workers, large numbers of peasants, students, workers and office-workers join the army and become revolutionary soldiers, while large numbers of revolutionary soldiers return to civilian life as peasants, students, workers or office-workers. What is the point, then, of classify-ing these social strata into two different categories? And even if we were to try and devise a classification, how could we make it neat and clear-cut?[11]

The implications for the role of the party and for policy of what he had said were spelled out in the congress's political resolution, which declared that the 'principal contradiction' in China was no longer the 'contradiction between the working class and the bourgeoisie', but the contradiction between the 'demand of the people for rapid economic and cultural development' and the existing state of economic and cultural conditions, and stated that the 'chief task confronting the whole nation' was to 'concentrate all efforts on developing the productive forces, industrializing the country and gradually meeting the people's incessantly growing material and cultural needs'.

In speaking about the conduct of party members, Deng developed two themes to which he was often to return: the baneful character of bureaucracy as a style of work and the need for the party to cooperate with non-communists. In a bravura passage about bureaucracy, he condemned the habits of following instructions 'mechanically and blindly', spending too much time 'dealing with official papers and telegrams and attending too many unnecessary meetings', passing on problems 'to those on a lower rung of the departmental ladder, who in turn pass them on to others on a still lower rung', giving way to 'swollen conceit and self-satisfaction' and resorting to orders 'to get things done'. The conclusion he drew was that many party members were behaving in ways at variance with the party's 'mass line'. He went on to prescribe remedial measures and to declare that it was of 'vital importance' in the struggle to 'carry out the mass line and combat bureaucracy' for party members to 'cooperate still more closely with non-party people and to draw as many of them as possible into the struggle'. The party's policy of cooperation with 'democratic parties and with democratic personages having no party affiliation' was, he said, a long-term one, which had been taken further since 1949; although 'struggles' existed in this kind of cooperation, 'democratic personages' could 'provide a kind of supervision over our party' which could not easily be provided by itself.

On the role of the (not 'a') leader in a Marxist party, Deng skilfully balanced the need to take account of Mao's standing and views and the need to show that the Chinese party had neither accepted what Khrushchev had said about Stalin nor treated it lightly. He began by saying that Marxism did not deny the role played by 'outstanding individuals' in history or in political parties. But he went on to distinguish between 'leaders of the exploiting classes' and 'leaders of the working-class party'; unlike the former, the latter did not 'stand above the masses, but in their midst, nor above the party, but within it'. For this reason, it was incumbent on them to maintain close contact with the masses, to obey party organizations and to observe party discipline. For the led, 'love for the leader' was essentially an expression of 'love for the interests of the party, the class and the people', and not the 'deification of the individual'.

Deng then turned to the particular. Soviet experience had shown that serious consequences could follow from the deification of the individual. The Chinese party, for its part, had always held that no party or individual was 'free from flaws and mistakes'. For this reason, it abhorred deification and, on Mao's proposal, had taken measures, such as the prohibition of birthday celebrations for party leaders, to check the 'glorification and exaltation of individuals'. The 'cult of personality' was nevertheless a 'social phenomenon with a long history' and was therefore bound to 'find certain reflections in our party and public life'. It was therefore the task of the party to 'observe faithfully' the central committee's principle of opposition to the 'elevation and glorification of the individual' and to achieve a 'genuine consolidation of the ties between the leaders and the masses'.[12]

No one in Deng's audience, Chinese or foreign, could have objected to his statement of principles. Nor could anyone have objected to his brief and value-free reference to Soviet experience. Nor, again, could they have objected to the pitch of what he had said about the attitudes and practice of the Chinese party; he had avoided any hint either of apology or of complacency. Most adroit of all, he had defended Mao against the charge of encouraging a cult of his own personality by identifying him as the author of proposals adopted by the party to prevent the 'glorification and exaltation' of any individual.

On one crucial matter, however, Deng had nothing to say. This was the party's decision that the two references to the thought of Mao Zedong in the existing party constitution should be dropped. It is not hard to see why. Anything he said would have been bound to make it seem either that Mao had yielded to pressure, internal or external, to agree to the change or that he had to some extent lost faith in himself, or both. The delegates of course became aware of the change as soon as they were given copies of the revised text and wanted to know why it had been made. The line taken with them in briefings by senior party officials was that there was no longer any need to be explicit about something – the guiding role of Mao's thought – which was now taken for granted. But, given that Deng had stressed the need for the provisions of the new constitution to be complete and precise, this cannot have persuaded many.

The story of how the change in fact came to be made is still unclear. But there are two certainties. One is that the change was originally proposed by Peng Dehuai, the minister of defence (and a man who had never treated Mao with more than respect). The other is that the change could not have been made without Mao's concurrence. Many more years may have to go by before it becomes known who approached him with Peng's proposal, how it was described to him and how he reacted. Until then the safest assumption about Deng's role is that he simply waited for instructions, both as chairman of the group responsible for drafting the revised constitution and as a speaker.

The last act of the congress was to elect a new central committee. The new committee itself met as soon as the congress was over and, working from an official slate, proceeded to elect its own officers (a chairman, four vice-chairmen and a general secretary), a new politburo and a politburo standing committee. The post of general secretary was a revival from the party's past, although with altered status. Whereas the general secretary had been the party's leader in the 1920s and 1930s, he was now to be its chief of staff. The new standing committee of the politburo replaced the old secretariat, with unchanged responsibilities.

Deng was elected general secretary and a member of the standing committee. He thus became a policy-maker, as well as the party official chiefly responsible for implementing policy. As general secretary, he was given a staff, called the secretariat, of very senior party officials. Within the politburo, he jumped in rank from thirteenth to sixth place, overtaking Lin Biao and six others, including Peng Dehuai and Luo Fu, who had been members of that body for far longer.

These moves ended a sequence of promotions which took Deng

in four years from being a regional chief outside the politburo to being one of the six most powerful men in China. In the words of his official biography, he became 'one of the chief leaders of the Chinese Communist Party'.[13] His ascent may have owed something to luck. But it certainly owed as much to energy, efficiency and a sure touch in handling difficult tasks, such as coordinating the revision of the party constitution. There is direct evidence, from Khrushchev's pen, that Mao had formed a very high opinion of him. In 1954, Mao pointed him out to Khrushchev, at a meeting in Peking, as a person of outstanding ability.[14]

No older Chinese writer, artist or professional will ever forget 1957, the year of the hundred flowers. For the country's intellectuals, it began in doubt, continued in hope and ended in despair.

Mao Zedong himself was responsible for encouraging the flowers to bloom. He was in a mood for economic progress and he wanted to turn the country's non-communist intellectuals into enthusiastic participants. He believed that the party needed to undergo a new rectification campaign and that such a campaign would be more effective if non-communists were encouraged to join in. And he had concluded that the best way to inoculate China against the disorders which had swept Eastern Europe in 1956 was to shift the political balance between dictatorship and democracy in favour of the second. As had become his habit, he theorized before acting, and on 27 February 1957 he expounded to the supreme state conference – a non-party body – his famous theory of 'contradictions among the people'.

The heart of the theory is that there are two kinds of contradiction in society: antagonistic and non-antagonistic. Antagonistic contradictions exist between 'the people' (a category which varies in composition) and their enemies; non-antagonistic contradictions exist within the 'ranks of the people'. The former cannot be resolved by peaceful means; the latter can and should be. His operational conclusions for China were that the bounds within which non-communist politicians could criticize the behaviour of the party and its members, and within which intellectuals could write and speak in pursuit of their interests, should both be widened. He then called for action by these two groups under the slogans of 'let a hundred flowers blossom, let a hundred schools of thought contend' and 'long-term coexistence and mutual supervision'. That the end result was to restrict rather than widen these bounds was due neither to bad faith on Mao's part (though he was later readier to lay himself open to a charge of bad faith than to admit miscalculation) nor to sabotage on the part of his colleagues (though some among them were wholly opposed to exposing the party to criticism from without). It was due to the development of a great surge of criticism of the whole political and social system, and not only of deviant behaviour by party members, once criticism had officially been called for by the party, as it was at the beginning of May.

To begin with, criticism was muted. But it became livelier when the party's united-front work department, directed by Deng's old colleague and antagonist Li Weihan, began to hold meetings for intellectuals and non-party officials in government departments. It became livelier still when writers, artists and university students started to hold meetings of their own. At Peking University, the students, heirs to a long tradition of political action, created a 'democracy plaza' and a 'democracy wall', which they soon covered with posters. Some newspapers reported these activities, with the result that students in other parts of China began to speak out. Some students merely criticized the way in which the party had behaved towards particular individuals (such as the writer Hu Feng, who had been condemned as a counter-revolutionary in 1955) and social groups. But others denounced party leadership as a principle and a matter of political fact, saying that rectification could not cure its vices because these were intrinsic. There was a strong anti-Soviet overtone in much of what they said. Non-communist politicians were on the whole more cautious, though quite a few of them made it clear that they saw a wide gap between what the party had said about 'mutual supervision' and the way in which party members in fact treated non-communists.

The period of criticism – 'blooming and contending' – lasted for just over five weeks. Then, on 8 June, an editorial in the *People's Daily* declared that many acts and utterances had shown that class struggle was not extinct in China, and described as 'right-wing elements' all those people who had been 'misusing' the rectification movement to turn the clock back and to attack the Communist Party, the working class and the socialist cause. Five more editorials followed in the next six days. On 19 June, the *People's Daily* published Mao's original speech about contradictions, accompanied by a note to say that its author had been over the verbatim record and had made some 'corrections and additions'. The text included six criteria for distinguishing between 'fragrant flowers' and 'poisonous weeds'. Very many people knew that the criteria were an interpolation (over 1,800 had heard Mao speak in February): everyone knew that their appearance in print with attribution to Mao meant that a counter-attack was about to begin.

This attack started a day or two later and soon became a national purge, extending to many people who had said nothing during the period of blooming and contending, out of prudence or through lack of opportunity, but whose social origins were suspect, and to thousands more who had transgressed in the party's eyes for other reasons at other times. It first swept into its net many of the leaders of the small non-communist parties, two of whom were named and denounced as organizers of an anti-communist conspiracy, and then brought in writers, journalists and artists, professors and students. By the early autumn, workers, peasants and provincial party officials had become targets. Some organizations were given quotas to meet. In government offices, enormous pressure to confess and recant was brought to bear on pre-selected victims, including many who had been named by informers as people of unsound views. Sentencing followed, though sometimes only after an interval of weeks or even months. Many of the sentences were harsh, a common type being exile for an indefinite period to a state farm in a distant part of the country. Some of the heavier sentences were imposed on party members. Ding Ling, a woman writer who had a national reputation, but who had fallen foul of the deputy director for literature in the party's propaganda department, was sent to a labour camp in the far north-east; and Wang Meng, a young writer who had written a story about bureaucracy and inertia in the organization department of a party branch, and who was one day to be made minister of culture by Deng, was exiled to Sinkiang. Neither was allowed to return to Peking for more than twenty years.

The consequences for the country of the blooming and wilting of the hundred flowers were wholly negative. It led to an enormous waste of talent. It finally brought to an end an epoch of experiment in literature and the arts which had lasted for over forty years. And it persuaded Mao that the intellectuals of China had treated him with contempt. He reacted in two ways: by concluding that China's economic development must henceforth be by means which did not depend on them; and by deciding that the eighth congress had been wrong to resolve that the principal contradiction in China had become the contradiction between the 'advanced socialist system and the backward social productive forces'. Instead, the principal contradiction was still the contradiction between 'the socialist road and the capitalist road', which meant that class warfare must remain at the top of the political agenda.

Deng Xiaoping was as active as any of the party's leaders both during the period when Mao was preparing to launch his experiment and during the campaign against 'right-wing elements'.

In the preparatory period Deng, clearly relishing the opportunities given him by promotion, spoke frequently on many kinds of platform. His speeches show that he was enthusiastically in favour of liberalization, and that he differed clearly from Mao on only one issue: 'big democracy'. In a speech to a party meeting, Mao had said that he was happy to tolerate big democracy – spontaneous demonstrations and even strikes – as a way for ordinary people to show that they wanted change in the party's methods. Deng, however, took a different line. In a speech to party activists in Xian in April 1957, he said:

Today, isn't it true that trouble is brewing in some places? Aren't there some people who are talking about big democracy? Some young people always believe that big democracy can solve problems. We don't agree with the practice of big democracy ... we definitely do not advocate big democracy; it is not good to go in for big democracy. Hungary practised big democracy and will take several years to recover ... Poland also went in for big democracy and will take quite a long time to recuperate.[15]

As to his behaviour during the purge, Deng had, and still has, the reputation among many Chinese intellectuals for having been among the most zealous of the enemies of the rightists. Many years later, his own verdict on the campaign against them was that a 'resolute counter-attack' against 'a handful of bourgeois rightists' had been 'entirely correct and necessary', but that its scope had been made 'far too broad'.[14] But was this his contemporary attitude? The only evidence is circumstantial. In a report to the central committee in September 1957 on the whole course of party rectification, he described the anti-rightist struggle as only one phase, the second, in the rectification movement and forecast that this phase would soon be over. He was wrong about that. Yet the implication is that he wanted the struggle to be limited in time and, because time was needed to organize any struggle in places distant from the larger cities, in space as well. Besides, he based his report closely on an article in which Mao had said that the contradiction between 'the people' and 'the bourgeois rightists' was an antagonistic contradiction, but that the latter should not be treated too harshly. This is not enough to redeem his reputation. But it is perhaps enough to earn him an open verdict.

CHAPTER 9

Looking after Leaping, 1957–65

Deng Xiaoping was at the centre of affairs throughout the ten years from his promotion in September 1956 to the onset of the Cultural Revolution in 1966. His membership of the standing committee of the politburo and his office as general secretary of the party – formally of the central committee – placed him there. It was also in his nature to be up and doing and to take the lead whenever he had identified a problem to be tackled. He was not a man to wait for his moment, as was Zhou Enlai at times, or to withdraw when his proposals were criticized or rejected, as was Chen Yun. When he could not get his way by persuasion, or judged that an attempt to persuade would fail, he was ready to act first and report later, as Mao had encouraged his commanders to do in their dealings with nationalist officers during the war against Japan, or even to act and make no report. It was this just as much as his political views which Mao complained of during the Cultural Revolution.

As general secretary, Deng was the chief executive of the Communist Party, the institution which controlled all the other institutions of the state (though the control of the party over the armed forces was exercised more by one man, Mao Zedong, than by the party as such). The instrument through which he worked was the secretariat, which was very strongly staffed from the start. It became even more so in May 1958, when three members of the politburo, besides Deng himself and his deputy Peng Zhen, were added to it. As time went by, moreover, it acquired additional authority from other institutions, outside and inside the party. During the Great Leap Forward, it took over from the state council, the highest government body, general responsibility for making and implementing economic policy, because it could organize a campaign of mass mobilization in a way which the state council could not; and it kept a good deal of this when emergency action was needed to rescue the country from the consequences of the leap. Thereafter when Mao drew apart from the other members of the politburo standing committee except for Lin Biao on almost all kinds of policy, it made many decisions of its own. It took over much of the work which would normally have been done by the politburo and its standing committee, because these bodies could only issue documents in the name of the central committee and therefore only after they had been approved by Mao personally, whereas it was not so constrained. Deng, strongly supported by Peng Zhen, was very much in charge; and there was more than a little justice in Mao's later assertion that he had created an 'independent kingdom'.

From 1958 to 1962, Chinese politics were dominated by the turbulent course and disastrous consequences of the Great Leap Forward, Mao Zedong's attempt to launch China on a path of very rapid economic development. The leap was unique among Mao's great campaigns in that it was not intended to deprive any section of society of property or status or to purge or remould the party. Yet it led to more deaths and greater suffering than any of the others.

The leap followed the period of the first five-year plan, which ended in December 1957. In some ways, the national economy had done well under the plan. China's industrial base had expanded and the rate of growth of industrial output, at nearly 20 per cent per year, had been impressive (and above target). Several thousand miles of new track had been added to the national railway network. In other ways, however, performance had been disappointing. In particular, the rate of growth of agricultural output, at barely 4 per cent, had been low (and well below target). This had constrained the development of light industry and had confronted the party with the choice between squeezing the rural population in order to feed a rapidly expanding urban population and squeezing the urban population in order to maintain rural well-being. In the end, it had been forced to squeeze both.

In the spring of 1956, the party's leaders had agreed that the second five-year plan would have to differ in its priorities and methods from the first. Mao himself had expressed the consensus in a long speech to an enlarged politburo meeting. He proposed that rates of investment in agriculture and light industry should be increased, relatively and absolutely, that greater authority to make investment and other economic decisions should be given to provincial and local authorities, and that fewer new factories should be built in remote parts of the country, a long way from their markets and sources of supply. He said that the Soviet model for development had proved not to be suited in several respects to China's capacities and needs, and he even criticized 'defects and errors' in the Soviet use of the model. But he did not say that the model was misconceived or that there was anything fundamentally wrong with the system of material balance planning. Yet within eighteen months he had decided that China should abandon the model altogether and adopt a development strategy which was based on quite different assumptions about human nature and was to depend mechanically on different ways of using resources and setting targets.

What lay behind this change? Was it simply an alteration in Mao's mood or was it a change in his nature? It is tempting to argue from the patterns of Mao's behaviour before and after the winter of 1957–8 that he became a different man at this time, surrendering almost altogether to the urge for rapid and heroic achievement which had always been strong in him, but had hitherto been held in check by respect for 'objective conditions'. But there is no clinching evidence; and, without it, one can only point to influences which certainly affected him.

One influence was the completion, years ahead of all target dates and expectations before 1955, of the collectivization of agriculture and the nationalization of industry and commerce. For Mao, this demonstrated (yet again) what could be achieved by mass mobilization and the bold approach. It also opened the way in his scheme of things for the use of energies which feudal and capitalist 'exploitation' had bottled up before. During the winter of 1955–6 he therefore demanded that administrative procedures should be streamlined and that plans of all kinds, in public health and education as well as in industry and agriculture, should be made to 'balance upward', making the performance of the best units the standard for all. This produced a surge of activity. But it also produced bottlenecks, inflation and a great deal of confusion and waste. In April 1956, Zhou Enlai proposed to Mao that this drive should be brought to a halt. Mao agreed, but only reluctantly and with a sense of grievance; and this was increased by a series of editorials in the *People's Daily*, approved by Zhou, which criticized haste and over-ambition and described the spirit of the drive as one of 'reckless advance'. This made Mao all the more determined to show that he had more right on his side than the faint-hearts around him.

Another influence was the behaviour of the intellectuals during the blooming of the hundred flowers. This had been restrained. But Mao had not seen it as such and had concluded that many of them were hostile to socialism, party leadership and himself. This strengthened his (already very strong) prejudice against them and by extension forms of activity, such as planning on the Soviet model, which could only be undertaken by educated people. He swung over, or back, to the view that success in any important undertaking was chiefly a matter of stimulation by leaders, competence in basic skills among the led and ideological commitment in both. He began to speak of the intellectuals with brutal contempt and to say that there was no reason why China could not make rapid economic progress without them. As early as July 1957, when the period of blooming and contending had only just been brought to an end, he declared:

Intellectuals are teachers employed by the working class and the labouring people to teach their children. If they go against the wishes of their masters and insist on teaching their own set of subjects, teaching stereotyped writing, the Confucian classics or capitalist rubbish ... the working class will sack them.[1]

A third influence was the success of the Soviet Union in 1957 in putting earth satellites into orbit and in launching a long-range ballistic missile. This encouraged Mao to think that world socialism was overtaking capitalism, and that it was time for socialist China to contribute to a general advance. The paradox is that it was a Soviet achievement which reinforced Mao's inclination, already strong by the autumn of 1957, to make a break with Soviet methods.

The key slogans of the Great Leap Forward were 'politics in command' and 'walking on two legs'.

'Politics in command' expressed Mao's conviction that normative, or non-material, incentives could produce results in the economic field as striking as those in political campaigns. Experience was to show that he was wrong. But it was also to show that the slogan could be turned against the very pursuit of material prosperity. The simple line of argument was that, if prosperity could not be obtained by the use of non-material incentives, then it was not worth having. A more sophisticated line of argument was that the achievement of prosperity might well weaken attachment to socialist values, even if it had been achieved through an appeal to these values, and was therefore not to be seen as an unqualified good, or even as a good at all. This eventually produced the view that wealth and virtue were mutually exclusive and that poverty was therefore desirable.

Mao himself never took this view. But it came to be held by some of the radicals who worked closely with Jiang Qing, his wife, towards the end of the Cultural Revolution, and perhaps by Jiang Qing herself. Its most famous saying was that a socialist train which ran late was better than a capitalist train which ran to time. It was a view with which Deng Xiaoping was to take bitter issue.

'Walking on two legs' meant the simultaneous development of a capital-intensive, high-technology industrial sector in the cities and a labour-intensive low-technology sector (covering industry as well as agriculture) in the countryside. This was not irrational. There were large unused, and under-used, resources, including some simpler industrial skills, in the rural areas, and much could have been achieved by their intelligent use. As it turned out, however, the use of resources was far from intelligent. One mistake was to make the peasants and members of their families work on non-agricultural tasks at times of the year when their labour was needed in the fields. Another was to start up industrial projects which were beyond the technical competence of the peasants. Both had very heavy costs.

The charter of the leap was a document which cobbled together a set of beliefs expressed, and decisions made, at party conferences held outside Peking in January and February 1958. Called *Sixty Points on Working Methods*, it covered subjects as ill-assorte as a new theory of Mao's on the nature of revolution, the transfer of responsibility for national economic management from the government to the party, the devolution of a good deal of power over resource allocation from the centre to the provinces, the introduction of a new style of planning and the merits of particular farming methods. The passage on revolution shows how far Mao had moved from the orthodox Marxist view that the completion of socialist transformation – the liquidation of the private ownership of land and capital – completed the socialist revolution. It also reflects the mood of impatience and exaltation in which the events of 1956 and 1957 had left him. He was quoted as having said:

Our revolutions follow each other, one after another. Beginning with the seizure of power on a nationwide scale in 1949, there followed the anti-feudal land reform. As soon as land reform was completed, the collectivization of agriculture was begun. The three great socialist transformations [of agriculture, industry and commerce] . . . were basically completed in 1956. Last year, we carried out the socialist revolution on the political and ideological fronts . . . We must now have a technical revolution.[2]

It was the passages on planning which signalled the sharpest break with the past. Material balance planning was to be replaced by a scheme in which two sets of targets for the output of all important products were to be set at every administrative level. The higher set at each level matched the lower set on the next level down. In this way, the targets ultimately set for factories, mines and agricultural cooperatives added up to several times the national targets for their products at the centre. The new scheme worked for a while, but led quite soon to all sorts of abuses. At the lowest level, it drove local managers to demand so much from the workers and peasants that they became exhausted and demoralized. At the middle levels, it encouraged dishonesty in reporting as soon as gaps appeared between actual performance and what managers had said could be achieved. At the centre, it produced a completely false picture of the state of the economy. Politically, the purpose of the new style had been to 'integrate the leadership with the masses'. In operation, however, it had precisely the opposite effect; it created several layers of ignorant and frightened officials between Mao and his colleagues at the centre and the workers and peasants toiling in the factories and fields.

The great institutional innovation of the leap was the people's commune. The communes had their origin in the grouping together of agricultural producer cooperatives to provide labour for a large-scale campaign to build canals, dams and other water-conservancy projects during the winter of 1957/8. Grouping together led on to amalgamation; amalgamation led on to the creation of a new tier of administration; and the creation of this tier led on to the transfer to it of responsibilities which had hitherto been widely scattered among cooperatives and units of local government. As during the drive to collective agriculture two and a half years before, a bandwagon soon began to roll – so much so that over 99 per cent of rural households had joined communes by the end of 1958.

The communes existed for twenty-five years. During this time they changed several times in nature. In their original form, which lasted for less than three years, they were organizations after Mao's heart. Their large size appealed to Mao because, although he was in favour of administrative decentralization, he liked organizations at the lowest level which had populations large enough to mobilize. They were responsible for a very wide range of political, economic, cultural and military activities. This matched Mao's dislike of specialization. They tended to organize life as well as work on collective lines, encouraging all their members to eat in communal dining-rooms and wives to leave their children in nurseries when they went out to work in the fields. They equalized income, both across activities and across the brigades and teams into which their members were divided. This too appealed to Mao, because he saw equalization as a way of choking off enthusiasm for personal gain, and also because he believed that it paved the way for a system of reward under the communist principle of 'to each according to his needs'.

The leap was launched officially in May 1958, at a second session of the eighth party congress. As at the first session, twenty months before, Liu Shaoqi gave the principal report. His earlier report had been a model of sobriety; his report now was visionary. Mao himself, who had spoken only once, and then briefly and almost perfunctorily, at the first session, made no fewer than five speeches. Excited himself, he set out to excite his listeners. He criticized Stalin for his cold and bureaucratic approach to development and declared that it was the task of the whole party to 'lift the lid, break down superstition [about the possibility of overcoming difficulties] and allow the initiative and creativity of the working people to explode'. The session ended by adopting a general line for socialist construction: to work for 'more, faster, better and more economical results'. The several thousand delegates returned to their posts in the belief that their careers would depend on how ardently and effectively they were seen to be in putting it into effect.

For the next six months, the whole nation, 700 million people, was gripped by fever. One movement followed another. First the communes were formed. Then the word went round that a communist world was within reach. In this 'communist wind', many communes introduced a system of free supply – the provision on demand of as much food as members asked for. In answer to Mao's call, made in January 1958, that the countryside should aim to make the value of its industrial output match the value of its agricultural output within a few years, the communes built or expanded thousands of small factories and workshops, equipping them as best they could with recommissioned or locally designed machinery. Finally, when the shortage of iron and steel in the countryside became a bottleneck in supplying these factories, the communes turned to their production.

The movement to make iron and steel was the climax of the leap. By the end of 1958, several hundred thousand iron smelters and blast furnaces had been built in China's rural areas. Some communes had dozens. One estimate is that 60 million people were drawn into the movement, either to mine or transport iron ore or to operate smelters and furnaces. Under very heavy pressure from their leaders, many commune members were induced to surrender their pots and pans and otherwise to strip their houses of metal. But because the movement got under way at the time of the autumn harvest in north China, it led to a shortage of labour in the fields at a crucial time, to the point where some crops had to be left unharvested. Nor did this have any useful counterpart; because the skills needed to make serviceable iron – let alone steel – simply did not exist in the countryside, millions of hours were spent on the production of millions of tons of valueless metal.

In spite of all this, the grain harvest of 1958, at 200 million tons, was the largest in China's history. But Mao and his colleagues, fed on reports from the provinces about enormous increases in output, allowed themselves to believe that it was much larger still. In August, Tan Zhenlin, the director of the party's rural work department, told a work conference that the harvest could turn out to be as large as 300 million tons, and in December the central committee announced that it had amounted to 375 million tons, a figure almost twice as large as the figure for 1957.

During the winter of 1958/9, Mao and his colleagues, becoming aware that there was a good deal of rural discontent and that the leap had led to the production of many goods which could not be transported to users, or which were literally useless, worked to modify some of the policies they had favoured earlier. At a work conference in February and March 1959, Mao himself condemned the excessive equalization of peasant incomes, the use of forced labour in many communes and the premature calling in of loans to the communes by the state banking system. He also turned for advice to Chen Yun, who had earlier wanted to make many changes in development strategy but had made plain his conviction that no good could come from the substitution of mobilization for organization as the motor of economic growth. Chen argued that the steel output target for 1959 should be reduced from 30 to 13 million tons and urged that the national economy should be regarded as a 'single chequerboard', pointing out that the encouragement of local or provincial self-sufficiency in all lines of production would restrict rather than enlarge the capacity of the national economy as a whole.

All the same, Mao and the others failed to undo several decisions they had taken under the misapprehension that the 1958 harvest was overwhelmingly large. The most important were that the amount of grain to be procured by the state should be increased in 1959 from the very large amount it had procured in 1958, that the total sown area should be reduced, and that the proportion of land sown to grain within this reduced area should also be reduced. It was these decisions which turned the leap into a calamity. What was needed at the end of 1958 was the relief of pressure on the peasants, who had worked without respite for two summers, one winter and part of another, coupled with sensible use of the land, whose fertility had suffered in many areas from the side-effects of close planting and deep ploughing, two methods Mao had favoured. These needs were not met.

There are many gaps in the published record of what Deng said and did in 1958 (no speeches he made at this time appear in his selected works). But the record is full enough to show that he

1. Deng Xiaoping (right) and his uncle Deng Shaosheng in March 1921. Deng was sixteen at the time and his uncle nineteen. The photograph was taken during the last month of the short spell the two spent at the Collège de Bayeux at the beginning of their time in France.

2. Mao Zedong in 1933, aged thirty-nine. Slim and tall, he was strikingly good-looking as a young man.

3. A romantic studio portrait of Zhou Enlai and his wife Deng Yingchao. It was taken in Shantou (Swatow) in 1926, a year after their marriage.

4. Deng Xiaoping and his wife Zhuo Lin in the Taihang base area in 1939, after their marriage in Yan'an in that year.

5. Deng Xiaoping speaking at a meeting of the military and political committee of south-west China, of which he was a vice-chairman, in July 1950. Note his shaved head.

6. Deng Xiaoping and Peng Dehuai, minister of defence, in August 1958. Peng was disgraced and dismissed a year later.

7. All members of the standing committee of the politburo except Zhu De and Lin Biao at a work conference in January 1962. Zhou Enlai is on the left and Lin Shaoqi in the centre. Chen Yun has his back to the camera.

8. Zhuo Lin, Deng Xiaoping and Deng's former secretary Wang Ruilin in the garden of the house where Deng and Zhou Lin lived in exile in Jiangxi from October 1969 to February 1973.

9. Zhou Enlai saying goodbye to Deng Xiaoping at Peking airport before Deng's visit to New York in April 1974. Zhou was already a very sick man.

10. Mao Zedong and Deng Xiaoping after Deng's return from Jiangxi.
Mao, unrecognizable as the slim young man of 1933 (plate 2), was a
victim of Parkinson's disease and had suffered a stroke or heart attack.

11. Deng Xiaoping delivering the eulogy on behalf of the central
committee at Zhou Enlai's memorial service in January 1976. The
wreath behind Deng was sent by Mao Zedong.

12. Deng Xiaoping, Zhuo Lin and their five children, with Xia Bogen, Deng's stepmother, in August 1974. From the left, the children are Deng Pufang, Deng Zhifang, Deng Nan, Deng Rong and Deng Lin.

13. Chen Yun and Deng Xiaoping at the meeting of the central committee in December 1978 which put 'socialist modernization' at the top of the party's agenda. Born only a year before Deng, Chen looks a lot older.

14. Deng Xiaoping at the thirteenth national congress of the Chinese Communist Party in October 1987. He had turned eighty-three two months before.

sided with Mao, and against Zhou Enlai and Chen Yun, during the debates about whether the party should or should not launch the leap, and also that he supported its methods. In March, he said at a conference that those who opposed a drive were 'in error' and he spoke several times in the summer about the spectacular results the leap had already achieved and the almost limitless prospects it had opened up. He said at one commune he visited that 'we can have as much [grain] as we want',[3] and later that meat and spirits would soon be available for everyone and that women could look forward to the day when they would all be able to afford lipstick and high-heeled shoes. According to one of Mao's personal secretaries at the time, Mao used him to brief party officials all over the country about the meaning of the leap.

Nevertheless, Deng's voice was not just an echo of Mao's. He did not use Mao's (or Liu's) exalted language and he said little, if anything, about politics in command or about the regenerative ideological and social effects which Mao saw as an important object of the leap. He expressed doubts, too, about the likely efficiency of rural iron smelters and blast furnaces, saying during a tour of the countryside in October that they would benefit from an infusion of imported technology. And he declared himself against free supply when the whole subject of rewards and incentives was discussed at a special conference, convened at Mao's bidding, at the end of 1958.

In 1959 Deng's role changed. He became the coordinator of an effort by Zhou Enlai and Chen Yun to establish the facts about conditions in industry and agriculture and to deal with targets for steel output (which were already known to be impossibly ambitious). The secretariat held a conference to hear reports about the functioning of the communes and another to review targets for steel. This second conference sent instructions to the central group for economics and finance, a small ad hoc committee of very senior party members formed at the time of Mao's decision to turn back to Chen Yun for advice. As some of its members were senior to Deng, it looks as if the secretariat itself changed in character, becoming a committee under the informal presidency of Zhou

Enlai, the most senior member of the central group. Whatever the precise institutional pattern, machinery was created to bring the leap under control; and Deng himself again began to work closely with Zhou and Chen.

The year 1959 ought to have been one in which a reunited party leadership worked to prevent a growing crisis in the countryside from plunging the whole economy into depression. It began promisingly. But then a confrontation between Mao and Peng Dehuai, since 1954 the minister of defence, shattered unity and created an atmosphere in which to counsel caution was to invite persecution.

Peng was a bluff, uncomplicated man, popular in the army and with his colleagues in the party. His memoirs, written in prison during the Cultural Revolution, make clear that he was no theorist, but that he cared passionately about improving the lot of China's 500 million peasants. He was a firm believer in party and military discipline, but also believed that senior members of the party should deal with one another openly and treat Mao with no more than the respect due to the first among equals. His own relations with Mao had often been troubled. In 1959, too, he was at odds with Mao on a matter of high policy: the character of the armed forces. Mao wanted a nuclear strike force, backed by lightly armed ground forces trained to wage 'people's war'; Peng wanted armed forces on the Soviet model, capable of waging conventional as well as nuclear war with the most up-to-date weapons and equipment.

Peng visited country districts in several parts of China during the autumn of 1958 and the spring of 1959 and insisted on talking to the peasants as well as local leaders. He concluded that the leap was leading to economic disaster and that local leaders could not be relied on to tell the truth in reporting to their party superiors (or to visiting national leaders like himself). But he did not say a great deal about his conclusions to other members of the leadership or at party conferences. In May, he visited several countries in Eastern Europe, calling on Khrushchev in Moscow before returning to Peking in the middle of June.

At the beginning of July, Peng went to Lushan, a mountain resort in Jiangxi, for an enlarged meeting of the politburo, and on the fourteenth wrote a long letter to Mao about the leap. He certainly expected that Mao would respond to it personally, probably by calling him in for a talk. Instead, Mao circulated copies to everyone at Lushan, under the formal title of 'Peng Dehuai's Letter of Opinion', and then described it in a long and sarcastic speech as an unprincipled attack both on himself and on the party leadership as a whole. He insisted to his listeners that they had joined in making the policies which Peng had criticized, that he had himself led the criticism of many of these policies, and that Peng had remained silent when he could have spoken up at party meetings in the spring. He implied that Peng had conspired with Khrushchev and demanded that each member of the audience should consider where he stood in relation to Peng's 'opportunist' attack.

Peng had some active supporters, who had spoken up at preparatory meetings, and more than a few sympathizers. But once Mao had made the issue one of loyalty, he could only have been saved from disgrace if two or three of the most senior members of the party had been willing and able to force Mao to back down. They were not ready even to try. Mao was therefore free to orchestrate a general attack on Peng at a meeting of the central committee that followed immediately, and then get the committee to adopt a resolution which described Peng and three others (including Luo Fu, Mao's old adversary in Jiangxi) as members of an 'anti-party group'. Except for Zhu De, Peng's military chief for twenty-five years, none of the speakers tried to defend him. Liu Shaoqi, who had succeeded Mao as chairman of the People's Republic four months before, and who had as great an interest as anyone in stopping Mao from getting away with 'patriarchal' behaviour*, attacked Peng particularly strongly.

Peng's humiliation was completed at a meeting of the party's

---

* Deng Xiaoping used the word 'patriarchal' to describe Mao's attitude to his colleagues in speaking to the Italian writer Oriana Fallaci in 1980.

military commission in September. He was violently attacked by Lin Biao and others for having made himself the head of a 'military club' and dismissed as minister of defence. He kept his membership of the politburo, but was subsequently prevented from attending its meetings and those of the central committee. He lost his house in the Zhongnanhai and was offered nothing better in return than an empty house in a derelict suburban compound.

Lin Biao became minister of defence in Peng's place and soon began to turn the army into an instrument he could use for his own political aggrandizement. He reorganized it on lines which he knew would appeal to Mao and then set out to convert it into a stronghold of revolutionary virtue. In the autumn of 1960, he persuaded the military commission to agree that Mao's thought (alone) should be the curriculum for political instruction in the army, and in 1962 he published and circulated the selection of quotations from Mao's speeches and writings which later became world-famous as the *Little Red Book*. Mao reacted as Lin hoped he would. In December 1963, he called on the whole nation to 'learn from the People's Liberation Army' and in 1964 he directed that political departments on the military model should be formed in government departments and party offices. This allowed Lin to begin to reverse the traditional relationship between the party and the army, under which the party had controlled 'the gun'. The army started to infiltrate the party (and the government) and to detach itself from party supervision at every level.

Economically, Lushan gave the Great Leap Forward a new lease of life. This was because Mao had insisted on a national campaign against 'right opportunism'. This soon turned into a purge of all party officials who had been lukewarm about the leap or who had taken the lead in responding to Mao's own earlier calls for prudence and restraint. It became impossible for an official to say that the use of forced labour should cease or that the peasants should be rewarded according to the quantity and quality of their work. In policy caution was abandoned. Early in 1960, a drive to create urban communes was launched. Targets for output were raised, not lowered, and Mao made known his support for a system of industrial management which put politics in command.

A whole year passed before Mao, in the end shocked into sobriety by a Soviet decision to suspend all forms of aid to China, was willing to bring in a new general line of 'readjustment, consolidation, filling out and raising standards' and allow action against local officials who had driven the peasants hardest. Only in November 1960 did it become possible for those who had long known that the leap was leading to disaster to tackle it at the root. Then, at last, Zhou Enlai was able to issue an emergency twelve-point programme which allowed the peasants to live and work as they had before the leap began.

By this time, however, the countryside was in the grip of famine. In 1959, the rural population had been able to retain 122 million tons of grain. In 1960, this amount dwindled to 113 million tons, leaving each person in the countryside with an average of only 150 kilograms on which to live for a year. The state procured less for the urban population in 1960 than it had in 1959, but the harvest was much smaller – indeed smaller than in any year since 1949. The death rate in the countryside rose from 12.5 per thousand in 1958 to more than 14 per thousand in 1959 and nearly 29 per thousand in 1960. The birth rate fell as sharply as the death rate rose. In 1960, there were more deaths than births in the country as a whole, whereas there had been between two and a half and three times as many births as deaths all through the period from 1950 to 1958. The famine continued into 1961; and by the end of that year it had claimed over 20 million victims.

This famine caused more deaths, from outright starvation and disease, than any other famine in the twentieth century, in China or anywhere else. Its toll was far greater than that of the famine which followed the collectivization of Soviet agriculture. In the early 1960s, it became clear to the outside world from refugee reports that food was extremely short in some parts of China. But it was not until the early 1980s, when official figures about birth – and death – rates and grain output and procurement were finally published, that the fact of famine, let alone its scale, was revealed.

Even now, it is seldom referred to in official documents, or even in novels and short stories. The Cultural Revolution produced a whole literature of pain and anger; not so the Great Leap Forward.

Because he had broken his leg,*[4] Deng Xiaoping missed the politburo and central committee meetings at Lushan. But he was almost certainly at the meeting of the military commission (of which, Mao apart, he was the only civilian member) which completed Peng Dehuai's disgrace. Although he had never been particularly close to Peng, he must have been deeply worried about his fate – and about Mao's behaviour. His view of Mao, which was on the record, was that, although he was an outstanding leader, he was not infallible. Courageously, he was now prepared to reiterate it. In a speech to a party audience in Tientsin in March 1960, he spoke out against the growing tendency of party members to attribute all their achievements to inspiration from Mao's thought, saying that this was not detached from, and even less a substitute for, Marxism–Leninism. As leader of the party, Mao differed from the 'ordinary members' of its collective leadership. But he nevertheless belonged to this leadership, and could not be distinguished from it. On the consequences of Lushan, his later verdict was wholly unfavourable: 'Politically, this struggle [against Peng and his associates] undermined inner-party democracy from the central level down to the grass roots; economically, it cut short the process of the rectification of "left" errors, thus prolonging their influence.'[5]

As general secretary, Deng would not have found it easy to avoid association with Mao's campaign against 'right opportunism' or the second leap. But he was not among the leaders who made keynote speeches about either and there is a hint in his speech in Tientsin that he spent a good deal of time during the spring of

---

* Deng broke his right leg when playing billiards in 1958. Photographs show that he walked with a stick at least until April 1961. His injury was therefore very slow to heal.

1960 outside Peking. It is likely, too, that Sino-Soviet relations claimed a good deal of his time, perhaps giving him an excuse to leave domestic affairs largely to others. He was certainly present at conferences which Mao called in January, February and March 1960 to plot China's response to a growing crisis in these relations.

The great quarrel between the Soviet Union and China of the 1950s and 1960s was unexpected, inside and outside the communist world, cumulative and worldwide in its effects. It made a dead letter of the 1950 treaty of alliance between the two countries, destroyed the 'socialist camp', split the international communist movement and affected the world balance of power. It also led Mao Zedong to conclusions about Soviet society which had a lot to do with his decision to plunge China into the Cultural Revolution.

The quarrel began in 1958, after a spell when relations between the two states and parties were better than they had been for some time. The Chinese had drawn two principal conclusions from the turbulent events of 1956 in Poland and Hungary: that the Russians had woken up to the dangers of destalinization and that they themselves must be extremely cautious about showing sympathy for communist parties which wanted to stake out positions of greater independence from Moscow. They had come round to the view that manifestation of such sympathy could encourage 'revisionism', and through revisionism counter-revolution, and so have the same consequences as Khrushchev's original theses about Stalin and a parliamentary road to power. Accordingly, Mao was ready to state in Moscow in 1957, at a conference of party leaders to mark the fortieth anniversary of the October Revolution, that the socialist camp and the international communist movement both needed to have heads, and that those heads had to be the Soviet Union and the Soviet party.

Mao also said that the success of the Soviet Union in putting two earth satellites – the original sputniks – into orbit, and in launching an intercontinental ballistic missile showed that the 'east wind' had come to prevail over the 'west wind'. He argued that the international communist movement would do well to follow the example of the Chinese communists in their wars against Chiang Kaishek of respecting the enemy tactically, but slighting him strategically, and so be unyielding in its general posture. He spoke, too, of the likely consequences of nuclear war, declaring that the human race would not be destroyed in such a war and that a brave new communist world would arise from the 'ashes of imperialism'. But he did not foreshadow any action by China itself which could face the Soviet Union with uncomfortable political or military choices.

The Russians certainly found Mao's views on nuclear war unsettling. But they had already decided that they could afford to meet a Chinese request for help in setting up facilities to make and test nuclear weapons. A secret agreement had been signed in Moscow in mid-October, before Mao's arrival. This ought to have set the seal on a relationship of trust and cooperation between the two states. Instead, however, it marked a high point in relations between the two states and parties which was never again attained.

The issues which soon troubled relations were Taiwan, India and the Great Leap Forward. On Taiwan, China's position was quite clear-cut: Taiwan was unredeemed Chinese territory and China was entitled to use any and every means to recover it. The Soviet Union did not dispute this position, publicly or in private. But it was Khrushchev's view that, given the existence of a formal commitment by the United States to help the nationalists defend Taiwan and the importance for the Soviet Union of its relations with the United States, the Chinese ought at the minimum to forewarn the Russians about any intention on their part to use force in the Taiwan Strait. This, however, is just what the Chinese were unwilling to do. They did not want to have any hand in making Taiwan more of an international issue than it already was. When, therefore, the Chinese opened a heavy bombardment of the nationalist-held island of Quemoy, only a few miles from the mainland, at the end of August 1958, and went on to attack nationalist supply ships, there followed a crisis in Sino-Soviet as well as Sino-American relations. In due course, Khrushchev wrote to President Eisenhower to say that an attack on the People's

Republic would be an attack on the Soviet Union and that, 'loyal to its duty', the latter would do everything necessary to defend it. But he was very angry that Mao had said precisely nothing about the impending bombardment when he had had long talks with him in Peking at the beginning of August.

India became an issue because the Soviet Union was cultivating a close relationship with that country at a time when there had begun to be clashes between Chinese and Indian troops both east and west of the bloc of territory formed by Nepal, Sikkim and Bhutan. In the east, the clashes had occurred because both refugees and guerrillas were moving between Tibet and India in the aftermath of a revolt in Tibet in the spring of 1959 (and the subsequent flight to India of the Dalai Lama); and in the west because the Chinese had built a highway through territory claimed by India and occasionally penetrated by Indian patrols. China objected to the refusal of the Soviet Union to take China's side in public statements, claiming that its proclaimed neutrality in fact worked in India's favour. Khrushchev and his Chinese hosts wrangled about this when he visited Peking for the tenth anniversary of the People's Republic in October 1959. Four months later, the Soviet party (not government) told the Chinese party in a message that China's behaviour had been the expression of a 'narrow nationalist attitude'. The inner message was that the Russians wanted the Chinese to subordinate national interest to an international interest of which they saw themselves as the custodians.

These two issues might have risen between any two sovereign states. The third issue, the Great Leap Forward, could only have risen between states which shared an ideology. Ideologically and politically, the Russians had strong reasons for disliking the leap. It represented a repudiation of their own model for development and had led to claims that China, where socialism was only three years old, was advancing towards communism faster than the Soviet Union and was likely to reach it sooner. At the practical level, it had put immense strain on the Soviet agencies responsible for delivering goods to China and had produced almost intolerable working conditions for the 1,500 Soviet advisers and technicians who were working in China.

All the same, the behaviour of the Russians, and of Khrushchev in particular, was outstandingly crude and intemperate. From the autumn of 1958, Khrushchev began to speak scornfully of the leap to visitors, including Western visitors, to Moscow. In the summer of 1959, he first cancelled the agreement of October 1957 on military technology and then began to criticize the leap in public. All this was bound to suggest to the Chinese that, like the Comintern in the 1920s and 1930s, Khrushchev was keen to punish the Chinese party for going its own ideological and political way. What is more, Khrushchev's first open attack coincided almost to the day with Peng Dehuai's letter to Mao at Lushan about the communes. Mao concluded that Khrushchev and Peng had been in collusion, and that Khrushchev was quite ready to conspire with senior members of the Chinese party about Chinese affairs. There is in fact no hard evidence of conspiracy, and it would not have been in Peng's nature to plot with a foreigner. Indeed, if Peng is to be believed, he had not wanted to go to Lushan and only decided to write to Mao after he had been there for some time. But it was inevitable that Mao, a practised conspirator, should see the matter otherwise; and in due course it became the official line that Peng's intervention had enjoyed the support of the 'Khrushchev revisionist clique'.

Once these issues had arisen, they reignited debate about the issues of principle which had been raised by Khrushchev's speeches to the twentieth congress in 1956. It was the Chinese who took the initiative. In April 1960, they published four highly polemical articles in the *People's Daily* and *Red Flag*, the central committee's theoretical magazine, to coincide with Lenin's ninetieth birthday. Their general claim, implicit in the title of the first article, 'Long Live Leninism', was that they were more faithful Leninists than the Russians. To back it, they accused the Russians of having discarded Leninism in their new positions on peaceful coexistence, the non-inevitability of war and the possible existence of peaceful roads to power for communist parties in non-communist countries.

This put the Russians on the defensive; they were compelled to argue that the world had changed since Lenin's day, making necessary modifications of some of his doctrines, but they had not abandoned Leninism in spirit. So did the fact that the Chinese had opened the offensive; they had to explain themselves before being able to counter-attack.

During the summer of 1960, the Chinese and the Russians clashed at a trade-union meeting in Peking and at a congress of the Romanian party in Bucharest. In Bucharest, Khrushchev attacked Mao personally, calling him an 'ultra-leftist' and a 'left revisionist' and comparing him with Stalin for egoism, which provoked an equally offensive, but better argued, response from Peng Zhen, leader of the Chinese delegation. This exchange caused enormous consternation among third-country delegates and led to pressure from their parties on both sides to make a determined effort to reach agreement. This had an effect and it was eventually settled that three meetings should be held in Moscow in the autumn: a bilateral meeting between the Russians and the Chinese, a meeting of representatives of twenty-six parties and a summit meeting of the leaders of eighty-one parties.

At all three meetings, Deng Xiaoping was the chief Chinese spokesman. The texts of his (many) statements and speeches have not been published. But it is known from quotations and references that he argued very strongly for the positions set out in the Lenin anniversary articles. His line on peaceful coexistence was that this did not and could not amount to more than a state of armed truce between socialism and capitalism–imperialism; on war, that a new world war was unlikely (because the possession of nuclear weapons by the Soviet Union would deter the United States from launching or provoking one), but that local wars were inevitable; and on roads to socialism, that violent revolutions were bound to occur in capitalist countries and their colonies. Operationally, he argued that the socialist camp must remain vigilant and well armed, that it was right (and safe) for the camp and individual socialist countries to give active support to national liberation movements, and that it was wrong to encourage communist parties outside the camp to become less militant. It cannot be documented that Deng ever took Mao's line on the likely consequences of global nuclear war – that, in this worst case, it was imperialism, and not the human race, which would be destroyed. On the face of it, he would have found it difficult to avoid the issue during eight weeks of argument. Yet it is unlikely that he would have escaped quotation on the issue – as he did – if he had spoken about it. Nor is he on the record at any other time for having followed Mao on this issue. It would seem fair to give him the benefit of the doubt.

The third summit meeting ultimately produced a declaration which covered all subjects at issue and was subscribed to by all participants. In the words of Professor Donald Zagoria, the first Western scholar to study the Sino-Soviet conflict and to reveal its intensity and extent, it amounted to a victory on points for the Russians.[6] But it was full of qualifications of fundamental Soviet positions, and of obscurities and ambiguities. It only emerged at all because Mao, overseeing operations from Peking,* decided on the advice of Liu Shaoqi, the largely silent leader of the Chinese delegation, that the choice lay between compromise and breakdown. But, as subsequent events were to show, Liu's signature on the declaration in no way caused Mao to modify his views or to qualify his judgement that Khrushchev – and many others, inside and outside the Soviet Union – had become 'modern revisionists'.

In July 1963, Deng made another and, as it turned out, final visit to Moscow. He led a small party delegation in talks with the Soviet party represented by Suslov, an expert on ideology, to go over all the theoretical issues covered in the Moscow declaration, but since reopened, and about the ways in which each side had behaved badly in the eyes of the other, both before and after 1960. The Chinese had two particular bones to pick with the Russians: the latter's tolerance of the flight of over 50,000 people from Sinkiang to Soviet territory during the winter of 1961/2, and

---

* He and Kim Il Sung of North Korea were the only two leaders of communist parties to stay away from the conference.

Khrushchev's public criticism of China's attitudes before and after the Sino-Indian border war of 1962. The Russians, for their part, were extremely angry about the public Chinese description of their behaviour during the Cuban missile crisis of October 1962 – as 'adventurism' to start with and 'capitulationism' later on. Before the talks started, both sides set out their positions, fully and polemically, in long published documents. This augured badly. The Russians, too, made it clear that the talks with Deng's delegation loomed less large for them than simultaneous negotiations, also in Moscow, with the Americans and the British about a partial nuclear-test-ban treaty (in itself a subject provocative to the Chinese). Khrushchev himself did give a dinner party for Deng and his team, but only after five days of talks had shown that neither side was prepared to modify its positions. No date was set for a further meeting. This signalled breakdown and, as it turned out, marked the end of formal contact between the two parties for twenty-six years.

During the Cultural Revolution, the story was put about that Mao rejected Deng's draft for the document which the Chinese published before the meeting. There is probably substance in this. But, even if there is, Mao's action does not mean that he had ceased to have confidence in Deng. Mao was often dissatisfied with the drafts of others and it is most unlikely that he would have sent Deng to take on Suslov, and perhaps Khrushchev himself, if he had had any doubts about his ability to give as good as he got. In any case, he showed after the event that he was pleased by Deng's performance. Most unusually, he went to the airport to meet Deng on his return to Peking, and soon afterwards made him head of a writing group set up to prepare a detailed public account of the origins and course of the conflict. This appeared in nine instalments between September 1963 and July 1964 and lacked nothing in force of argument.

At home, there were two spheres in which Deng was particularly active from 1961 to 1965: planning a programme of economic recovery and organizing a campaign to deal with the corruption, poor discipline and low morale which pervaded the party in the aftermath of the leap.

The recovery programme was chiefly the work of four men: Liu Shaoqi, Zhou Enlai, Chen Yun and Deng himself. Its principal elements were to unwind most of the institutional innovations of the leap, to substitute year-by-year for five-year planning and to shift the emphasis in investment from heavy to light industry and agriculture (thereby giving effect to one of the most important of the proposals which Mao himself had made in the spring of 1956).

Deng contributed a good deal to the substance, especially over agriculture and industry, but at least as much as a coordinator. It seems that he made the arrangements under which a senior member of the party supervised the preparation of a policy document for every sphere of economic and educational activity; and he coordinated the work of three committees set up to conduct general policy reviews.

By the end of 1961, these people and committees had produced eight important policy documents and several sets of draft regulations. Mao convened a series of work conferences to consider them, which went smoothly on the whole. At one of them, however, Mao clashed with Deng. According to one story, he criticized a set of documents Deng had prepared after visiting several communes in the outskirts of Peking. According to another, he objected to the way in which the 'arrangements' for the conference had been made by Deng as general secretary.* In any case, he became very angry and demanded to know what 'emperor' had decided matters beyond his competence. Deng, however, was not shunted aside or made to criticize himself; and Mao must have been impressed by his efficiency in getting ad hoc machinery to produce a comprehensive long-term programme in just a few months.

The programme revoked almost all the policies of the leap. In the countryside, the communes remained in being as geographical

---

* One version is that Deng had put approval of one or more documents on the agenda before Mao had had a chance to consider them.

units, but were shorn of most of their powers. The key economic unit became the production team, of about thirty peasant households (compared with an average of about 4,000 households in the original communes). Land ownership was vested in the team, which was made responsible for managing the work of its members and for rewarding them. The unpopular equalization of incomes on a commune-wide basis thus disappeared. Individual householders were again allowed to own small plots of land. Under a regime which became popular in some parts of the country, and which was a pointer to the route by which agriculture eventually emerged from collectivization, the team was allowed to make contracts with its members for the performance of non-farming tasks. By 1965, the national grain harvest was back, at 195 million tons, to the level it had reached in 1957, the year before the launch of the leap.

In industry, the system of industrial management Mao had backed in 1960 was jettisoned. Bo Yibo prepared a set of sixty articles, which Deng turned into detailed regulations, to reintroduce hierarchy and specialization, and to re-establish wage differentials. The rate of investment in industry was cut back and many loss-making plants were closed. Many of the millions of workers who became unemployed in consequence were moved, or moved back, to the countryside, which had the important effect of reducing substantially the amount of grain which the government needed to procure for urban consumption. Industry went into depression later than agriculture – its worst year was 1961 – but then recovered much more rapidly. By 1965, levels of output for most industrial products were more than double the levels of 1957, and a number of new industries, several of them fed by a rapidly expanding output of crude oil, had come into being.

Deng's own views about development underwent fundamental change between 1958 and 1962. As late as October 1959, he had written enthusiastically about mass movements as a way of getting results:

Our basic method of work is . . . to integrate the leadership with the masses, to pursue the mass line in all fields of work, to mobilize the masses boldly, to develop energetic mass movements under the guidance of the [party] leadership, to sum up the views and pool the wisdom of the masses and rely on the strength of the masses to carry out the policies of the party . . . It is obviously an erroneous view to ignore the initiative of the masses, to maintain that it is no longer necessary to organize mass movements because everything can be done from above . . . or to consider mass movements necessary in revolution but maintain that matters are different in construction.[7]

In July 1962, however, he spoke on quite different lines to a congress of the Communist Youth League:

When it comes to ways of optimizing the relations of production, I rather think that we should take this attitude: to adopt whatever pattern will restore and develop agricultural output in each locality quickly and easily. If the masses want a particular pattern, then we should adopt that pattern, if necessary making legal what is now illegal . . . Liu Bocheng often used to quote a Sichuanese saying: 'Whether white or black, a cat is a good cat so long as it catches the rat.' He was talking about war. The reason why we were able to defeat Chiang Kaishek was that we did not use conventional methods . . . and always took account of circumstances . . . In present conditions, both in industry and agriculture, we cannot advance without taking a step back. Do you not see this? Isn't agriculture going backwards? Are the communes not in retreat? The first step now must be to restore grain production. The second step must be to restore the production of other crops and to replenish the stocks of agricultural implements and draught animals . . . In the past, we had too many movements. We had movements all the time and all those movements were national movements. This clearly didn't work.[8]

This change created a gulf between him and Mao. Mao had always taken the view that the 'forces of production' would not give of their best except under socialist 'relations of production'; and from 1958 he had believed that socialist relations of production extended beyond state and collective ownership to systems of management, meaning participation by the workers and peasants, and systems of reward, meaning great reliance on non-material incentives and equalized rates of pay. Deng had come to disagree with him on both points.

Deng also differed from Mao over reinvigorating the party. They agreed that the demoralization produced by the leap and its consequences had to be tackled. But they disagreed about the causes of demoralization and therefore about the right means to deal with it. Mao believed that the root of the trouble lay in a weak commitment to socialist values among many party members; Deng believed that it lay in poor discipline and morale, brought on by an enormous political and economic defeat. Mao wanted to indoctrinate party officials by making them do manual labour and accept criticism, even orders, from the peasants. Deng thought that the peasants had a part to play, but only after local officials had been examined, and if necessary punished, by work teams sent down from above. He also thought that party officials at the levels of the county and above should themselves undergo rectification before they became rectifiers.

A socialist education movement in the countryside was launched in May 1963, on the basis of a document, later to become known as the *Early Ten Points*, which reflected Mao's views. But it soon became clear that local party officials were unwilling to form peasant associations to supervise themselves. In September, therefore, the secretariat issued a second document (the *Later Ten Points*) which shifted the emphasis from rectification from below to rectification from above. Mao does not seem to have complained at the time. But he continued to see the movement as a course of education in socialist values and to look forward to the day when peasant associations would become its principal instrument.

At this point, Liu Shaoqi took a hand. His wife Wang Guangmei had spent five months at a commune near Tientsin and Liu himself had spent a fortnight at a commune in Henan; and both had concluded that most local officials were corrupt and that the peasants, who were no better, could never be relied on to correct them. Liu therefore prepared a third document (the *Revised Later*

Ten Points), which was issued in the name of the central committee in September 1964. Reflecting pessimistic views on the likely impact of education on either the leaders or the led, the document ordered a strong-handed investigation of the vices of local officials by large work teams sent down from the cities. This led to detailed investigation of commune management in many rural areas, which in turn led to the purge of many thousands of officials.

The *Revised Later Ten Points* remained in force for only four months. Then, after angry debate at a central work conference in December 1964 and January 1965, Mao insisted that they should be superseded by yet another document, the *Twenty-Three Articles*. This went back to the *Early Ten Points*, adding the ominous statements that the movement should be seen as a 'struggle between the two roads of socialism and capitalism' and that its target was 'people in the communes . . . and even in provincial and central committee departments who oppose socialism'. Mao thus signalled that he had begun to smell revisionists and class enemies even among his colleagues.

CHAPTER 10

Capitalist Roader, 1965–73

The Great Proletarian Cultural Revolution would not have occurred if Mao Zedong had died before 1966. Mao planned it,
launched it and had a greater hand in directing it than anyone
else.

In Mao's view, the Cultural Revolution lasted from 1966 to
1969, when the changes it had brought about were approved by a
party congress (the ninth) and registered in a revised party constitution. In the modern view of the party, it lasted for a full ten years,
a decade of political conflict and social disorder which only ended
when the Gang of Four, Mao's most radical associates, were
arrested. In the latter perspective, it was a protean movement,
constantly changing in character. Even before 1969, it had a triple
character. It was a super-revolution, intended to create attitudes
and modes of behaviour which Lenin would have tended to
associate with left-wing socialism (which he had called an 'infantile
disorder'). It was a counter-revolution, intended to break down
and re-create many institutions established under the new
democratic and socialist revolutions of the 1950s. It was also a
revolution for the sake of revolution, a process which Mao saw as
having its own redemptive value.

Among Mao's purposes in launching the revolution, three are
clear. One was to take much further the process of indoctrinating
society in what he saw as socialist values, and creating structures
to correspond with them, which had been under way since 1950.
Among these values four stand out: equality, community, simplicity and struggle. Struggle was a value for Mao because he believed
that nothing worthwhile could be achieved without struggle, but
also because he held – or came to hold – that socialism was not a

steady state, which only needed protection once it had been achieved, but an unstable condition, in which regeneration was necessary if degeneration was not to set in.

Mao was an egalitarian and had no time for qualified forms of equality, such as equality of opportunity. In his picture of the good society, its members would resemble one another in outlook, level of education and standard of living. With this went his love of community. This had at least two sources: a conviction that a mass of people, properly stimulated and led, could achieve heroic results in any undertaking and a very strong distaste for individualism, which he tended to equate with selfishness.

Mao had a very deep grudge against the educated class of the old China, disliking their scholasticism and their contempt for the common people. Conversely, he admired the simplicity of the peasants. He associated their strength with freedom from corruption; and he wanted to preserve from corruption the peasant-soldiers who had fought and worked in the wilderness for small rations and very little pay when they 'entered the cities'. In the mid-1960s, he also became concerned about the moral nature of the youth of China, who had not experienced war. He told several foreign visitors that he was particularly worried about the way in which the sons and daughters of old revolutionaries had become selfish and pampered.

In the light of all this, Mao favoured non-hierarchical institutional arrangements. In industry, he wanted the workers to play a part in management and to have an important say in decisions about targets and the use of technology. In agriculture, he wanted all activity to be organized on collective lines. In public health, he wanted a high proportion of the best-trained doctors to work in the countryside and a corps of less well-trained health workers – 'barefoot doctors' – to be stationed there permanently. In education generally, and especially in higher education, he wanted undemanding entrance examinations and courses with a large practical content. In literature and the arts, he wanted the clear projection of socialist values, in language and symbols which the less well educated would have no difficulty in understanding. More generally, he wanted to narrow the cultural and material gap between the cities and the countryside and to get rid of the distinction between mental and manual labour.

Mao's second purpose was to recover the political power he felt was slipping from his grasp. By the beginning of 1965, he had become angry about the extent to which the party's central apparatus, under the control of Deng Xiaoping and supervised by Liu Shaoqi in the name of the politburo and its standing committee, had taken policy-making into its own hands. It was at about this time that he called Deng Xiaoping's secretariat – or, according to Jiang Qing, his wife, Deng himself – an 'independent kingdom'.

Mao's third purpose was to train up 'revolutionary successors'. He had become steadily more preoccupied about his own mortality as the 1960s went by – he became seventy in 1963 – and steadily more worried about what he saw as the lack of commitment to revolution in his colleagues. He was himself developing ideas which he ultimately put together in a general theory of 'continued revolution under the dictatorship of the proletariat', but saw no enthusiasm for continued revolution around him. He saw it perhaps least of all in Liu Shaoqi, who the world assumed would one day succeed him as chairman of the party. The only one of the other members of the politburo standing committee he had not clashed with since the mid-1950s was Lin Biao, and Lin had patent weaknesses. He had no presence, he was a valetudinarian, he was unpopular and he lacked experience of non-military affairs. All the same, he began to see Lin as a better bet than any of the rest, including Zhou Enlai, who had been a member of the politburo when Lin was only a platoon commander and had never crossed the line between open and underhand opposition to himself. Zhou, however, had made it quite clear ever since the failure of the Great Leap Forward that he saw the continued pursuit of revolution as a very low priority, if a priority at all, and that weighed heavily against him.

As he drew away, politically and personally, from the other members of the old Yan'an leadership, Mao began to turn for advice, encouragement and active support to Jiang Qing, his wife, and to Kang Sheng and Chen Boda, two men he had known for thirty years, but who had not been prominent politically.

Jiang Qing was Mao's third wife. His first wife, Yang Kaihui, by whom he had three children and who to judge by his poetry was the love of his life, had been shot by the nationalists in Changsha in 1930. His second wife, He Zizhen, whom he had met at about that time, bore him six children, all but one of whom were either given to peasant families in Jiangxi or died when young. She was wounded by bomb splinters during the Long March, soon after giving birth to a child, and was sent to Moscow for medical – and perhaps psychiatric – treatment in 1938. Jiang Qing, an actress, arrived in Yan'an in that year and soon became Mao's mistress. In 1939, she married Mao and subsequently bore him two daughters. Mao's colleagues were opposed to the marriage – because Jiang was clearly a schemer and had arrived in Yan'an with a reputation for both sexual and political inconstancy – and he was only able to overcome their opposition by giving an undertaking that Jiang would keep out of politics.

Mao abided by this undertaking all through the 1950s, and Jiang may have been content that he should. Her health at the time was poor – she was sent to Moscow for medical treatment at least twice – and she had children, including a child of He Zizhen's, to look after. But she was vain, ambitions and contemptuous of the way in which the wives of most party leaders were ready to confine themselves to work in women's organizations, and it was therefore always likely that she would one day want an active political role. In the early 1960s her health improved and her children became less of a tie; and this change in her circumstances coincided with a new inclination on Mao's part to consult her, and listen to her unsolicited views, about politics. By 1963, she had become an important figure, working to purge the theatre of all influences which she judged that Mao would regard as unhealthy. This brought her into contact, and conflict, with the party's cultural establishment. She was able to get this establishment to allow eight 'revolutionary' operas and ballets which had been written under her auspices to be performed, but not to get it to move farther in the direction of a revolution in culture and the arts.

Born into a landowning family in Shandong in about 1900, Kang Sheng had spent time in Shanghai in the 1920s, in the workers' movement there and on the fringe of the artistic world, where he knew Jiang Qing. When party headquarters left Shanghai in 1933, he went to Moscow, where he was trained by the Russians in police and intelligence work. Although a full member of the politburo from 1934 to 1956, he seldom appeared in public during this time, presumably because his work in building up a police apparatus on Soviet lines, first within the party and then in the state, did not require him to. Mao and he clashed during the rectification movement in Yan'an – he wanted 'dogmatists' and others under criticism to suffer physical punishment – and he took a knock after Khrushchev's condemnation of Stalin, losing his full membership of the politburo. During the early 1960s, however, his standing improved; he became a member of Deng's secretariat and of the small group of people with whom Mao enjoyed talking about Marxist theory and philosophy. Slight in build and ferret-faced, he became a byword during the Cultural Revolution for bloodless inhumanity.

Chen Boda, bulky and moon-faced, had been a university lecturer. He became Mao's political secretary in Yan'an, learning to write in Mao's style. He was very much Mao's man and had no political constituency beyond a group of radical journalists he had assembled to work for *Red Flag*, the theoretical magazine of which he was editor. As malevolent as Jiang Qing or Kang Sheng, he was less skilful politically; he lost his footing in 1970, by throwing in his lot with Lin Biao at a time when he should have known from the omens that Lin's career had passed its zenith.

The start of the Cultural Revolution is now officially dated to an enlarged meeting of the politburo in May 1966. But the drama had really begun in the autumn before, when Mao started to plot against the party secretariat.

Mao turned to plotting after suffering a political defeat. For two years, he had been agitating for a revolution in the arts, to purge them of traditional themes and the projection of 'feudal' values, and for a complete overhaul of the nation's system of higher education. He had also been pressing for the condemnation of plays and newspaper articles which he interpreted as veiled attacks on himself. He particularly objected to a play by Wu Han, a vice-mayor of Peking, about a Ming dynasty magistrate who had been dismissed from office by the emperor because of local complaints over his correction of local injustices, seeing in it a paradigm of his own dismissal of Peng Dehuai in 1959. In a series of statements, he let fly at the party's cultural and educational establishment – represented by the propaganda department and the ministries of culture and education – and at the intellectuals in general. At the beginning of 1964, he declared:

In the field of culture, particularly in the sphere of drama, feudal and backward things predominate and socialist things are negligible ... If nothing is done, the ministry of culture will have to be renamed the ministry of emperors, kings, generals, ministers, scholars and beauties, or the ministry of foreign things and the dead.[1]

But nothing much was done. Wu Han's play was banned, but neither Wu nor the play was publicly criticized. Some writers and artists were sent to the countryside to do short stints of manual labour, but no action was taken against historians who were writing that China's history could not be interpreted exclusively in terms of class struggle or against journalists who were attributing social and economic problems in China's villages to the Great Leap Forward. Mao grew steadily more restive, finally deciding to put the whole subject of cultural reform on the agenda of a conference of politburo members and regional party secretaries.

The conference lasted for the best part of two months in the autumn of 1965. Documents about the proceedings are sparse. It is clear, though, that Peng Zhen, mayor of Peking and therefore Wu Han's official superior and head of a Cultural Revolution group which had existed for a year at party headquarters, opposed Mao head on. He declared that 'everyone was equal in the face of truth', and that even Mao should be criticized when he was in error. Deng Xiaoping made a speech in which he came out flatly against the need for thoroughgoing reform. Mao asked rhetorically what ought to be done if the leadership of the party sank into revisionism, replying that the provinces would then be entitled to take action against it, but was forced to close the conference without getting any decisions of the kind he wanted. Never since the Long March had he been so badly thwarted.

Mao's reaction was to withdraw to Shanghai, where he and Jiang Qing had good political connections and where his activities would be hard for the party leaders in Peking to follow. Once there, he took his own aim at Wu Han.

Mao's method was to prompt an article which bitterly attacked both Wu and his play, describing the latter as a 'poisonous weed' (using the language of the campaign against the rightists of 1957) in Shanghai's principal newspaper. It was published under the name of Yao Wenyuan, a local literary critic well known for his malice, but had been through Mao's hands several times in draft. At Lin Biao's instance it was promptly reproduced in the army's national newspaper, which presented party headquarters in Peking with the choice between defying the chairman and giving in to him. As Deng Xiaoping was away on a tour of inspection, it fell to Peng Zhen as his deputy in the secretariat to decide what to do. He tried to compromise, arranging for the article to appear on the science page of the *People's Daily* and in the *Peking Daily* under a note which described it as a contribution to current academic debate. Mao's response was to summon Peng to Shanghai, where he told him roundly that he saw the hero and the villain in Wu's play as Peng Dehuai and himself and that he now wanted an open campaign against Wu. Peng, however, was not to be browbeaten. Back in Peking, he called a meeting of his Cultural Revolution group and put to it a draft 'outline report' on 'current academic discussion'. The report argued against the abusive naming of names in public and, quoting the formula Peng had used in front of Mao in the autumn, stated that 'all men are equal before the truth'. It was approved, endorsed at a wider meeting called by Liu

Shaoqi, and then circulated to the whole party as a central committee document.

Precisely how this happened is still a mystery. Mao was consulted – to his face and by Deng Xiaoping among others – before the report was circulated. He may have spoken ambiguously, knowing that he would be in a very strong constitutional position if the report went out without his explicit approval. Or Deng and the others may have wanted to challenge him, believing that a majority in the politburo standing committee would back Liu's decision when it came to a showdown. Perhaps there was an element of deception on both sides.

Whatever the truth about this, it was Mao who won the contest which followed. Having decided that Peng must go, as he did by mid-March at the latest, he sent Kang Sheng to Peking with instructions to isolate Peng and then bring him under attack. Kang succeeded in his mission. On 2 April, Zhou Enlai, the senior party member in the capital (Liu Shaoqi was abroad), told Mao by telephone or telegram that he agreed with Kang's instructions, and a few days later Peng found himself in the dock at a meeting of the secretariat. Deng Xiaoping presided, but Zhou, Kang and Chen Boda were also present. The first round won, Mao called a meeting of the standing committee in Hangzhou (Hangchow) and got it to agree that Peng should be disgraced.

Action followed at an enlarged politburo meeting in Peking. Liu Shaoqi, now back in China, presided, but was either disinclined or unable to stop Kang Sheng from acting on another set of instructions from Mao.[2] On 16 May, the meeting approved an internal party circular which gave the chairman everything he wanted. It damned Peng's report, denounced Peng himself, dissolved his group, replacing it by an eighteen-strong Cultural Revolution group under the central committee (not the secretariat), and threatened further action against 'representatives of the bourgeoisie who have sneaked into the party, the government, the army and various cultural spheres'.

Mao therefore carried the day. But it was Lin Biao who created a stir at the meeting itself. Just before it ended he accused Lu

Dingyi, the head of the party's propaganda department, and Yang Shangkun, a member of the secretariat, of having plotted a 'counter-revolutionary *coup d'état*' and called for a thorough investigation of their behaviour. He announced that, in order to frustrate their scheme, he had obtained Mao's agreement to send troops into radio stations and 'public security systems' in the capital. In a letter to Jiang Qing a few months later, Mao said that he had been taken aback by what Lin had said. Taken aback he may have been; but this did not save Lu and Yang from almost immediate arrest.

It would have been logical for Mao, now victorious over Peng and the secretariat, to return to Peking at this point. But he decided to stay on in Hangzhou, leaving it to Liu Shaoqi and Deng Xiaoping to launch the Cultural Revolution which neither of them had wanted but which was now prescribed. Whether he wanted to give them a chance to redeem themselves, or simply rope to hang themselves, is another mystery; and one which may never be resolved. If they were seeking redemption, their judgement failed them. Instead of trying to please Mao, they planned and put into operation a strategy which was almost a carbon copy of Liu's strategy under the *Revised Later Ten Points* in the socialist education campaign. They sent several hundred work teams to schools and universities in Peking, with orders to set up Cultural Revolution committees and to guide these committees in ferreting out evidence of revisionism in the records and current attitudes of teachers and administrators. The masses were not to be brought in.

This strategy was sabotaged from the start by Lin Biao, Kang Sheng and Chen Boda. Working through army officers in the political departments of civilian institutions and agitators in schools and universities, these three set out to convert a party-controlled purge from above into an attack on people in authority from below. They mobilized the students to demonstrate against their seniors and to demand that 'ghosts and monsters' should be brought under attack, even in the upper reaches of the party. By the beginning of June, bands of Red Guards, formed at this stage from students of 'good' (non-bourgeois) class background, had come into being all over the capital and were beginning to clash with work teams. Behind the scenes, too, Lin and his associates were extremely active. They reconstituted the Peking municipal party committee and sent military propagandists to take control of the *People's Daily*.

Liu and Deng soon realized that they faced an insurgency organized by Mao's closest associates. They therefore went to see Mao, still in Hangzhou, and asked for his guidance. He, however, brushed them off, advising them not to rely too much on work teams as an instrument of revolution, but otherwise leaving them to their own devices. They reacted in the only way possible other than refusal to take further responsibility (which would have meant breaking with all the norms of party discipline in which they had been brought up): they returned to Peking and declared war on the Red Guards. Two of their directives banned secret meetings of teachers and students and made all Red Guard organizations illegal. This had its effect; greatly heartened, the work teams fought back and were able to prevent the Red Guards from taking to the streets. But with the control of the army in other hands, Liu and Deng were unable to suppress them.

In this situation, Mao at last returned to Peking. On the way, he swam across the Yangtse at Wuhan, where the river is nearly a mile wide. Even if he paddled rather than swam, as photographs suggest, the exploit was remarkable for a man of seventy-two; and it was represented as superhuman in the blaze of publicity which followed. The cult of Mao Zedong, assiduously developed for years by Chen Boda and his propagandists, reached its climax. He began to be credited with miraculous powers and to be represented in art as a figure who was physically larger than the people around him. He became the 'red red sun' in the hearts of his people.

On his way north, Mao had decided exactly what he wanted and now moved quickly to achieve it. A day or two after his arrival in the capital on 18 July, he told the party's official leaders that they would have to steel themselves for severe trials as they moved 'to cross the pass into socialism' and then issued this solemn warning to another group: 'If you don't make revolution, the revolution will be directed against you.' Having insisted on the dissolution of Liu's and Deng's work teams, he sent this message to a particularly militant group of Red Guards:

[Your] two big-character posters [a favourite medium of expression among the radicals] ... express your anger about, and denunciation of, all landlords, bourgeois, imperialists, revisionists, and their running dogs, who exploit and oppress the workers, peasants, revolutionary intellectuals and revolutionary parties and groupings. You say it is right to rebel against reactionaries. I enthusiastically support you.[3]

In the spring, Mao had won victories at meetings of the secretariat, the politburo standing committee and the politburo itself.* He now wanted a victory in the central committee (which had not met for four years). He achieved it, but only by packing the meeting with 'representatives of revolutionary teachers and students from institutions of higher learning', under orders to cheer him and Lin Biao and jeer at speakers brave enough to question or contradict them. One of their victims was Deng Xiaoping, who insisted that there was no substance in Lin's charge, which he had repeated, that Peng Zhen and others had been plotting a *coup d'état*. At the end of twelve days of tense and often angry debate, the meeting adopted a sixteen-point Decision on the Cultural Revolution. Vague about procedures, which gave Jiang Qing and others many openings which they were later able to exploit, the decision was quite explicit that the revolution's political target was 'those within the party who are in authority and are taking the capitalist road'.[4] Culturally, it called for an all-out assault on the 'four olds': old culture, old ideas, old customs and old habits. Other decisions, not announced at the time, turned the standing committee upside-down. Lin Biao was promoted from seventh to second place and Liu Shaoqi was demoted from

* He had himself been present only at the meeting of the politburo standing committee.

second place to eighth. Chen Boda and Kang Sheng became members, above Zhu De and Chen Yun as well as Liu. Deng held his sixth place and remained general secretary. But his only friend in a higher position was now Zhou Enlai; and the meeting had shown that Zhou, though not himself under attack, was not ready to defend the way in which Liu and Deng had handled events during the preceding two months.

On 5 August, in the middle of the meeting, Mao took the extraordinary step of issuing a big-character poster of his own. Headlined 'Bombard the Headquarters', it made clearer than anything he had said or written before whom he wanted the Red Guards to see as their enemies. He wrote:

Some leading comrades from the centre down to local party levels have enforced a bourgeois dictatorship and have struck down the surging movement of the great proletarian cultural revolution. They have ... suppressed revolutionaries, stifled opinions different from their own, imposed a white terror and felt very pleased with themselves ... How poisonous![5]

Five days later, he spoke to a crowd outside the conference building, telling it that it should be concerned about the 'national crisis', and on 18 August he presided with Lin Biao, Zhou Enlai and Chen Boda over the first of eight giant rallies of Red Guards in Tiananmen Square.*

The rally raised the curtain on a two-year period during which almost no one of high rank or reputation was immune from attack

---

* Tiananmen Square is a rectangular space of ninety-eight acres at the intersection of the main east–west thoroughfare in Peking and the city's north–south axis. It is flanked on the west by the Great Hall of the People, built in 1958, and on the east by two museums. It takes its name from the Tiananmen, Gate of Heavenly Peace, which stands in the centre of its northern boundary. The gate is the southernmost in a line of gates on a ceremonial way from the square to the Forbidden City. There is room for more than a hundred people to stand on the platform of the gate, in the spaces between its balustrades and a central pavilion, now a museum.

by Red Guards or Revolutionary Rebels, their counterpart among the industrial workers. There are no official figures for the numbers of people killed or injured, or inventories of the damage done to public monuments and publicly owned works of art and literature, let alone to private property. The death toll in street violence alone ran into tens of thousands. Many of the deaths occurred in battles between rival groups of Red Guards and many more in operations by military units to support the Red Guards or (ultimately) to disarm the Red Guards and to restore civil order. Most of the violence occurred in 1967 and 1968, after the Red Guards had seized or been given weapons. But the climate for its systematic use was created in August and September 1966, when the Red Guards were incited to wage war on the four olds and, responding with a will, broke into private houses to maltreat writers, artists and musicians and to smash or burn their books, pictures and instruments. The first deaths occurred at this time. Lao She, one of China's best-known playwrights, killed himself after being beaten up, and so did Fu Lei, a translator of French literature and the father of the famous pianist Fu Zong.

Deng Xiaoping appeared on the balcony of the Tiananmen with Mao, Lin, Zhou and the others on 18 August. Still in authority, his subsequent actions show that his top priority was now to prevent the Red Guards from disrupting the party. His situation was not hopeless. He had allies outside Peking: at least two of the secretaries of the party's regional bureaux had spoken out against a revolution from below to the central committee – and he could argue that the committee's decision had said nothing about the Red Guards (it had spoken only of Cultural Revolution committees) and had called for reasoned debate with people whose political attitudes were under investigation. The secretariat had been purged, but only one of its new members, Tao Zhu, was firmly in the Maoist camp (and he quite soon abandoned it). And his enemies were busy briefing the millions of Red Guards from the provinces who flooded into Peking throughout the late summer.

By the end of September, however, Mao had become aware

that, far from welcoming Red Guard activity, most provincial party officials had refused to have anything to do with the guards. Some had even recruited armed bands to confront them. Very angry, he reacted by convening a conference of provincial officials in Peking. Used by now to getting his way, he seems to have thought that he would be able to overawe the visitors quite quickly. But he found that he was up against stubborn resistance, and the conference lasted for nearly a month before he was able to break it.

Deng was at the centre of the storm. On 16 October, he made a report about progress in the Cultural Revolution which provoked bitter criticism from Chen Boda and several others. Chen complained that it was harder to have a discussion with Deng as an equal than to 'put a ladder against heaven', and said that he was the 'spearhead' of an 'erroneous revisionist line'.[6] He asserted that the 'thought and style' of Liu and Deng were precisely the opposite of Mao's, that Liu and Deng would not admit their errors and were still 'thinking of attempting attacks', and that Deng was the more obstinate of the two. Lin Biao again revived the story that Peng Zhen had plotted a *coup d'état*, this time suggesting that Deng might have been an accomplice. But the delegates showed that their sympathies were more with Liu and Deng than Chen and Lin, and it seemed for a day or two that the conference might be escaping from Mao's control. His response was to demand that both Liu and Deng should make statements of 'self-examination', his calculation no doubt being that the resistance of the provincial officials would crumble once they had seen the surrender of the two men who had controlled party headquarters. It is not known who applied the pressure, or by what means. But it was effective, and Mao was able to turn a dangerous corner.

Deng's self-examination, made just a week after his report, makes melancholy reading. Having decided that he must give in, he moved all the way from defiance to abject self-condemnation. He said that he accepted without reservation the instructions of Mao Zedong and Lin Biao about the Cultural Revolution and all the charges made against him by Chen Boda. The purpose of the conference was to eliminate the influence of the 'false bourgeois line', represented by Liu Shaoqi and himself, from the direction of the Cultural Revolution; the popular movement now under way had brought to a head the struggle between this line and the 'correct proletarian line'. Liu and he must accept full responsibility for errors made in applying the central committee's decisions of August.

Deng said that the roots of his 'grave errors' lay in his way of thought and his style of work. He had been altogether perfunctory about studying, propagating and applying Mao's ideas. He had shown himself to be a bourgeois 'petty intellectual' and a man whose 'world view' had not been transformed. He had sabotaged Mao's strategy for the socialist education movement, failed to report to Mao as he should have done as general secretary and ignored Mao's warning that his politics had become those of an 'independent kingdom'. It followed that the party and the people would suffer if he continued to work at party headquarters with his old way of thought, style of work and political outlook, and that his only path to redemption lay in learning from Lin Biao, who had schooled himself best in Mao Zedong thought and was 'unsurpassed' in giving effect to Mao's ideas. 'This', he ended, 'is the only route I can take if I am to correct my errors and hereafter accomplish something of value for the party and the people.'[7]

The very extravagance of Deng's language must have told all his listeners, both enemies and friends, that he did not mean what he said. Indeed, he may have chosen his words – or chosen them from among the words offered to him – precisely in order to make clear that he was acting under duress. All the same, the experience must have been acutely painful. He had made a humiliating political surrender; he had announced to many who had looked to him for support that he was no longer able to help them; he had put on the record his repudiation of all he had worked for over the years; and he had given his enemies a whole armoury of weapons for future use against him. He had also destroyed his authority as general secretary.

Once Deng (and Liu) had spoken, Mao put on a show of

magnanimity. He told the delegates that Liu and Deng were not exclusively to blame for mistakes made in the past. But he made clear how much he resented the way in which they – and Deng especially – had treated him personally:

I deliberately relinquished [supreme authority]. They then set up independent kingdoms ... From 1959 to the present, Deng Xiaoping has not consulted me about anything ... [In 1958] I was not satisfied with the Wuchang Conference* ... so I went to Peking to hold [another] conference. But though you people had met for six days, you wouldn't let me hold a meeting for even a single day. It's not so bad that I am not allowed to complete my work. But I do object to being treated like a dead ancestor.[8]

He also said that Liu and Deng should be given a chance to show whether they had really reformed. Even if he meant this, the power now enjoyed by their enemies in his circle meant that this chance was never offered them.

Liu and Deng made a number of public appearances in November and December. But then they disappeared from view, in Liu's case for ever and in Deng's for over six years. At the time, the world knew practically nothing about what had happened to them. Only during the 1980s did it become possible to reconstruct their stories.

From January to August 1967, Liu and Deng were still in theory free men. All the same, it was no longer safe for them to go beyond the walls of the Zhongnanhai, and they were harassed even there (the servants of Liu and his wife, Wang Guangmei, conducted a 'struggle meeting' against them in their own house as early as December 1966). In the streets, Red Guards demonstrated against them and both the official and the Red Guard press carried frequent defamatory articles. Liu was the prime target and was named as 'China's Khrushchev' and 'China's number one

---

* A work conference which reduced some of the more ambitious targets of the Great Leap Forward.

capitalist-roader'. Deng was called the 'number two capitalist-roader' in the Red Guard (but not the official) press.

The campaign against Liu and Deng was managed by Jiang Qing, Kang Sheng, Chen Boda and Zhang Chunqiao, an old associate of Jiang's from Shanghai. There was little to choose among them for malevolence. Zhang, who organized the first large demonstration explicitly aimed at the two men, ordered his marchers to 'flog the curs which have fallen in the water' and to 'make their very names stink'.⁹ Jiang listed 'ten crimes' of Deng's in a speech to a Red Guard rally in April. The intensity of the campaign rose and fell, varying with the course of power struggles which broke out early in 1967 and racked the party and the army for the rest of the year. Whenever the radicals felt threatened – as they did in March, after they had been attacked to their faces at party meetings, presided over by Zhou Enlai, by a group of vice-premiers and old marshals – or wholly free to go for their enemies – as they did in July, when Mao left Peking for the south – the campaign became more intense. Mao's role remains uncertain. From the spring on, he certainly favoured the complete destruction of Liu's reputation, seeing in Liu a potentially danger-ous alternative focus of party and national loyalty. But his attitude to Deng was less extreme, because Deng had never been his heir-apparent and because he liked Deng's combative nature, even in opposition. Years later, Deng himself claimed that Lin Biao and Jiang Qing would have killed him if he had not enjoyed Mao's protection.¹⁰

Deng's 'crimes' as listed by Jiang Qing in fact boiled down to four: that Deng had treated Mao with contempt; that he had opposed the reform of higher education, literature and the arts; that he had wanted to undo the collectivization of agriculture; and that he had practised 'bourgeois dictatorship' and white terror in the summer of 1966. The quotations from Deng's speeches and remarks she chose to back her allegations were not all intelligently selected. Some readers certainly enjoyed this description of Jiang Qing herself when her speech was published in the Red Guard press:

There are people who aim to make a name for themselves by criticizing others and to clamber on to the stage on the shoulders of others. They don't care about the real nature of these others. All they care about is finding shortcomings [literally, short pigtails] to exploit in seeking to get ahead themselves.[11]

The organized campaign against Liu and Deng reached its peak in the summer of 1967. In July, thousands of Red Guards were first allowed to lay siege to the Zhongnanhai and then to conduct 'struggle meetings' against Liu, Deng and Tao Zhu and their wives, with their children forced to look on, at their houses. At one meeting, Deng was forced to kneel with his arms stretched out above his back, in what the Red Guards called the 'airplane position', while his tormentors demanded that he should be paraded through the streets in a dunce's cap. At this moment, he must have feared the worst: that he would be dragged out of the Zhongnanhai, abused – perhaps physically – at a rally and thrown into prison, suffering the fate which had overtaken Peng Zhen and the other leaders disgraced in 1966.

Yet Deng escaped this fate. He was taken from his official residence and put under house arrest in a smaller house. The three children who had been living with him were sent away. But Zhuo Lin and Xia Bogen, his stepmother, were allowed to stay with him; and by degrees the campaign against him in the press died away.

Liu Shaoqi's fate was far worse. As early as May 1967, a group to investigate his 'special case' had been set up, at the minimum with Mao's acquiescence, and it soon came under the control of Jiang Qing and Kang Sheng. In October 1968, the group's report, describing him as a 'renegade, hidden traitor and scab' was accepted by a (packed) meeting of the central committee, and Liu was dismissed from all his posts and expelled from the party. Just over a year later, deprived of medicine and medical care, he died of pneumonia on the floor of a provincial prison. His wife Wang Guangmei was sent to gaol in 1968 and stayed a prisoner for eight years.

At the same central committee meeting, Deng was stripped of all his party and government posts, but was allowed to keep his ordinary party membership. Mao certainly intervened to save him from greater punishment. The blow was bad enough, however, and it came on top of another. In September, Deng Pufang, his elder son, had been very badly injured when he fell from the roof of a building at Peking University, where he was a physics student. There are several accounts of precisely what happened. But they agree on two points: that Pufang was being tormented by a pack of Red Guards, and that he was refused admission to the university's clinic when rescuers ultimately dared to move him from the concrete path on to which he had fallen. By the time he was finally given a bed in an orthopaedic clinic, it was too late to save him from paralysis from the waist down. He was discharged from the clinic and sent to subsist in a home for the handicapped in the suburbs of the capital. There he remained, weaving baskets made from wire while lying on his back, until the summer of 1971.

On 20 October 1969, after two full years in limbo, Deng Xiaoping, Zhuo Lin and Xia Bogen were suddenly moved out of the Zhongnanhai and sent under military escort to Nanchang, the capital of Jiangxi. This was part of an operation by Lin Biao to move many of the senior victims of the Cultural Revolution, and several of the old marshals, to places a long way from Peking.

Lin's operation was closely connected with an order which his chief of staff, Huang Yongsheng, had issued on 18 October. This proclaimed a state of national emergency and put the armed forces on the highest level of alert. Huang certainly acted on Lin's instructions; but Lin had not consulted Mao, and when he told Mao about the order by telephone on 19 October, the latter said that it should be 'burned'. Mao objected to Lin's taking of the law into his own hands, and in any case did not want any military incident at a time when talks were about to begin in Peking between Zhou Enlai and Kosygin, the Soviet premier, about the very tense situation on the Sino-Soviet border (there had been incidents all along it since a violent clash on a river island in

Manchuria in March). Mao's reaction shook Lin, but did not lead to the reversal of plans to move Deng and the other old soldiers and politicians from the capital. The post-Cultural Revolution verdict on Lin's behaviour is that he was rehearsing plans for a *coup d'état* or testing his ability to make important political and military moves unilaterally.[12]

Zhou Enlai would have been the first to suffer if a border incident had in fact occurred. And it was Zhou who was responsible for making the conditions of Deng's exile much better than they would have been if the arrangements had all been handled by Lin's lieutenants. Now junior to Lin in the party, he could not countermand Lin's evacuation order. But he telephoned party officials in Jiangxi and asked them to find a place of exile for Deng and the two women which was near Nanchang, and not in a mountainous area as planned. By getting them to work with local military men who were not close to Lin, he was able to arrange a soft landing; and it was almost certainly thanks to him that Deng was able to take a small library with him when he flew south.[13]

In Jiangxi, Deng, Zhuo Lin and Xia lived in four rooms of a building which had once been the residence of the commandant of an infantry training school. They were supplied with food and fuel, but otherwise had to fend for themselves. Most of the cooking was done by Xia. Deng chopped wood and broke up coal for the kitchen stove, which was the only source of heating, and did a good deal of the housework. Zhuo Lin was unwell to begin with and could not do a great deal to help until her health improved with the arrival of warm weather. She then took over some of the work which Deng and Xia had been doing and, with Deng, began to grow vegetables on a plot in the building's large garden. At about the same time, Deng and she both began to work part-time at a tractor-repair plant about a mile from their house.

Life was spartan for the three exiles. But they were left in peace by their guards, and Deng had the great solace of access to books. According to his official biography, he read 'a great number of Marxist–Leninist works and many other books, both Chinese and foreign, ancient and modern'[14] during his three years in Jiangxi. The speeches he made after his return to Peking suggest that he profited from this experience; they are full of nuggets about Chinese and foreign history in a way uncharacteristic of his speeches before the Cultural Revolution.

The guards who lived in the same building as the exiles must have known who they were. The manager of the tractor-repair plant certainly did. But the workers there seem to have been in the dark to begin with. Quite soon, though, they must have realized that the old man (Deng was now sixty-five) and the middle-aged woman (Zhuo Lin was fifty-three) who arrived for work under guard at about eight o'clock every morning and left the plant, again under guard, at noon were the party's former general secretary and his wife. The ordinary people of China, discreet about themselves, are relentlessly inquisitive about strangers and seldom fail to find out what they want to know about people who come to live or work with them. In any case, it is improbable that Deng and Zhuo Lin would have found it possible, even if they had wanted to, to stick to any cover story they might have been told to use.

In the summer of 1971, Deng Pufang was allowed to leave Peking and to join his parents. They had not seen him since his disablement and must have been appalled by his state. Thereafter, they and Xia shared the burden of looking after a heavy young man who had to be lifted out of his wheelchair to be washed, seated on the lavatory or put to bed. Soon after Pufang's arrival, Deng and Zhuo Lin were visited by their youngest daughter, Deng Rong (known in the family as Maomao), and their younger son, Deng Zhifang, who had been working on a commune in the north-west. Zhifang had to leave again quite soon, but Maomao was allowed to stay with them.

In the meantime, the Cultural Revolution was beginning to devour its children.

As early as the summer of 1969, only a few months after Lin Biao had become Mao's designated successor at the ninth party congress, Mao began to lose patience with him – over his lack of enthusiasm for rebuilding the party and government, by which Mao now set great store, his ambition to succeed Liu Shaoqi as head of state (Mao wanted the post to lapse) and his wish to intervene in foreign affairs (where Mao and Zhou Enlai were now planning the opening to the United States which led to President Nixon's visit to Peking in February 1972). Mao decided to cut Lin down to size and as a first step launched a campaign to destroy Chen Boda, who had been incautious enough to make himself the manager of Lin's moves to secure the chairmanship of the People's Republic. He then took measures he described as 'throwing stones', 'mixing in sand' and 'digging up the cornerstone'. These involved forcing Lin's military supporters in the politburo to criticize themselves for having worked closely with Chen, diluting Lin's support in several important political and military committees and reorganizing the command structure of the Peking Military Region.

Lin reacted to these moves by asking his son, a staff officer in the air force, to work out a plan to assassinate Mao. Action on the plan (code-named 571 because the Chinese for these three numerals sounds very like the term for an armed uprising) was to be taken by a group of senior, but not top-ranking, officers, most of them in the air force. It was never given away. Yet a decision in principle to put it into effect led not to Mao's death, but – through a series of conspiratorial moves and countermoves by Lin and members of his family on the one hand and by Mao and Zhou Enlai on the other – to Lin's. In the early hours of 13 September 1971, he was killed when a military aircraft he had boarded a few hours before crashed in the desert in Outer Mongolia. His wife, Ye Qun, his son and the seven other people on board perished with him.

In Jiangxi, Deng Xiaoping realized that the country was in crisis when he heard that there had been no parade in Peking on 1 October 1971, the national day, and that neither Mao nor Lin had made any public appearance. Then, on 5 November, he and Zhuo Lin were told at a political briefing that Lin was dead. The implications for himself must have been clear in a flash. His principal political enemy had been removed; Zhou Enlai, his chief friend, could only have been strengthened; and Mao, still the source of all high political patronage, would have to make new plans for the future. Quite soon, he wrote to Mao and the central committee – through Wang Dongxing, a former bodyguard of Mao's who had become a member of the politburo and the commander of unit 8341, the special force responsible for protecting party leaders – asking to be allowed to return to Peking and given work there.

The conditions in which Deng and his family were living soon improved markedly. The armed guards, members of unit 8341 who had lived in their house and accompanied them whenever they left it were replaced by unarmed watchmen. In April 1972, permission was given for Pufang to enter a well-equipped military hospital in Peking; and Maomao, who had escorted her brother to the capital, was allowed to enrol at a school of medicine in Nanchang on her return to Jiangxi. Yet Deng received no reply to his letter. In August 1972, therefore, he wrote to Mao and the central committee a second time, renewing his request for work. He stated that he supported the Cultural Revolution, on the (ingenious) ground that it had exposed the true nature of people like Lin Biao and Chen Boda, gave an account of his dealings with Lin and Chen over the years, and spoke of his own chastened frame of mind. The letter certainly reached Mao, who 'began to consider letting Deng resume his work'.[15] From Mao's point of view, such a move could have several advantages. It would add administrative experience to a team which badly lacked it, it would be popular in the party, which Mao was trying to build up again, and it would give Zhou Enlai, who was even keener to rebuild, an able and loyal lieutenant. Zhou himself certainly lobbied in Deng's favour. But there is no reason to doubt Deng's own later assertion that it was Mao, and Mao alone, who decided that he should be allowed to return.

Deng finally left Jiangxi in February 1973. In Peking, he, Zhuo

Lin, Xia Bogen and Maomao moved into a house outside the Zhongnanhai, but quite close to it,* which had been found by friends, and he resumed work almost at once. He had been appointed a vice-premier, finding himself in the same rank – and under the same chief, Zhou Enlai – as when he was transferred from Sichuan to Peking twenty-one years before.

* In a lane in the north-eastern quarter of the city.

CHAPTER 11

Against the Gang, 1973–6

The political scene to which Deng Xiaoping returned differed in several important respects from the one which had existed at the time of his banishment. Liu Shaoqi was dead, though this was a state secret. Lin Biao was dead too, and his principal supporters, including Chen Boda, were in prison. Over ten million former Red Guards, sent to the countryside during the winter of 1968/9, were coming to terms as best they could with the realization that their rustication was to be permanent and that they would never complete their formal education. But the scene was no less troubled.

Mao Zedong's health had now begun to fail. He was suffering from Parkinson's disease and he had had a stroke or heart attack in 1972. Intellectually, he had ceased to be able to prepare the long speeches, full of argument and counter-argument, but always clear in thrust, on which he had relied to put his stamp on proceedings at party meetings. He could still frame theories and make phrases. But his stamina had gone and he had fallen into the old man's habits of dwelling on the remoter past and of repeating his stories and instances. Psychologically, he had become moody. Socially, he had ceased to see much of his colleagues or of members of his family (Jiang Qing had moved out of his house, taking his children with her). He now liked to be surrounded by young women, one of whom, Zhang Yufeng, was becoming his confidante, his nurse and the mistress of his household.

Yet Mao still dominated Chinese politics. Such was his prestige that his word was enough to set or change a policy or to make or break a political career. This meant that his endorsement was a condition for the success of any initiative by another leader and that his support was vital to the achievement and retention of political power. It also meant that he had much the greatest say in determining who would hold what office after his own death.

Zhou Enlai's health was also failing. It had been discovered during a routine medical check in May 1972 that he was suffering from stomach cancer. He was still vigorous in the spring of 1973, but neither Mao nor anyone else could now assume that he would outlive the chairman or that, if he did, he would be capable of exercising effective political power. Zhou himself had always been careful to disparage suggestions that he was the person best qualified to lead China after Mao's death – perhaps because he realized that the position of heir-apparent was a vulnerable one – but it is improbable that he would have rejected the chairmanship of the party if it had come to him by acclaim.

Zhou had asserted himself strongly in 1972. He had planned and supervised a programme to brief party officials and military officers about Lin Biao's treachery and death, organized a purge of Lin's known supporters in the armed forces, and worked to restore the structures of the early 1960s in agriculture, industry and education. He had also brought back into office many people who had been disgraced between 1966 and 1969. In all this he had worked closely with two men who had survived the purges of the Cultural Revolution and who were destined to provide the only continuity in leadership between the 1960s and the 1980s: Ye Jianying, an old marshal who had been chief of staff of the eighth route army throughout the war against Japan; and Li Xiannian, Deng Xiaoping's companion in the Dabie mountains and finance minister for many years after 1954. Ye had been in charge of the day-to-day work of the central military commission since Lin's death; under Zhou, Li had presided over what was left of the apparatus of government during the years of greatest disorder.

Zhou had acted under the slogan of opposing the 'ultraleft'. Mao, badly shaken by Lin's treachery and damaged politically by his flight and death, did not object. But there could be no guarantee that he would continue to acquiesce. He was, and perceived himself to be, a man of the left, so that Zhou's slogan was bound to make him uncomfortable. He was proud too of the Cultural Revolution and its 'newborn socialist things'. Most important of all, Lin's treachery had not caused him to lose faith in Jiang Qing, Zhang Chunqiao and Yao Wenyuan. Indeed, it seems to have increased his inclination to rely on them. They, for their part, had been rather in eclipse during the period of Lin's ascendancy and welcomed the greater political space which his disappearance had given them.

In these circumstances, Deng's own position was bound to be insecure. Mao had agreed to bring him back from exile and had said of him in 1972 that he was a man of rare talent, who had 'rendered service' in battle and fought robustly against Soviet revisionism. But the record showed – glaringly – that he could not rely on Mao for consistent support. Zhou Enlai, his strongest supporter, was weaker both physically and politically than he had been when Deng's rehabilitation was under discussion. Ye Jianying and Li Xiannian were friends, but also men who had survived the earlier stages of the Cultural Revolution by remaining in tune with Mao's varying wishes. Kang Sheng and Jiang Qing were as much enemies as ever, and there were many other beneficiaries of the Cultural Revolution who must have doubted whether Deng would deal with them tenderly if he ever became leader of the country. Formally, too, his position was weak. As a vice-premier, he was entitled to attend meetings of the state council, give instructions to ministries and to keep in day-to-day touch with Zhou. But, as an ordinary member of the party, he lacked the right to attend the meetings of any senior party body.

It so happened, too, that Deng's return to Peking coincided with an unfavourable turn in the political tide. A set of decisions made by Mao in late 1972 and early 1973 allowed the radicals to gain control of the political agenda and embark on a political campaign to destroy the authority and reputation of Zhou Enlai.

One decision concerned the succession. Liu Shaoqi and Lin Biao had both failed Mao and he could see no one who was likely to be both reliable ideologically and durable politically among those nearest to him. Zhou was ruled out by his state of health –

and in any case was probably more suspect politically in Mao's eyes than he had been at any time since the early 1960s. Among the radicals, Kang Sheng was old, ill and unpopular, and none among the trio of Jiang Qing, Zhang Chunqiao and Yao Wenyuan had shown talent for much except party infighting. In his youth, Mao had been an ardent champion of women's rights (his concern had been reflected in the Marriage Law of 1950, which gave women equal status with men in relation to property and divorce). But he knew that prejudice against women rulers was very strong in the Chinese political culture; and he knew, too, that Jiang Qing was ideologically weak, uninterested in administration and generally unpopular. Zhang Chunqiao had shown signs of administrative ability as chairman of the Shanghai revolutionary committee, but had otherwise behaved as a cat's-paw of Jiang Qing's. So had Yao Wenyuan.

Instead, however, of looking for a candidate, or candidates, for promotion and testing among the remaining members of the politburo, or just outside it, Mao made a move which showed just how far his behaviour was now governed by caprice. He brought Wang Hongwen, a radical agitator from Shanghai, who at thirty-eight was less than half his own age and who was hardly known outside his native city, into his circle. He made it known that he would like Wang to give the report on the party constitution at the party congress which was then being planned, and to be elected a vice-chairman of the central committee. There is a story that he installed Wang in his own household for a while, to instruct him in the ways of politics at the top. If he did, Wang did not learn a great deal. He emerges from party documents circulated after his arrest in 1976 as a slow-witted and malleable young man. He was fond of fishing and shooting and the perquisites of high party office. But he had few ideas of his own and always agreed with Jiang Qing when she asked for his comments on her views. He was out of his political depth.

Another decision was to reverse the political verdict on Lin Biao. Mao suddenly ordained that Lin had been a representative of the 'ultra-right' and not of the 'ultra-left'. This switch gave him a double bonus. One was to increase the political distance between Lin and himself. The other was to break the association, which was strong in the minds of most people, between Lin's behaviour from 1966 to the time of his death and the programmes and style of the Cultural Revolution. In policy, Mao wanted above all to preserve the fruits of the revolution, including practical instruction, political indoctrination and manual labour in education and the barefoot doctors in public health. And he had come to suspect that Zhou Enlai was working to throw out the baby of newborn socialist things with the bath water of Lin's reputation.

Quick to spot the opportunities for themselves in Mao's reclassification, the radicals began to press Mao to allow them to launch a public campaign against Zhou's programme and Zhou himself. Mao demurred, saying that Zhou was immensely popular and that a campaign would only rebound on its authors. But he agreed to their launching a campaign to criticize Lin Biao and Confucius.

A campaign by such a name could only have occurred in a country where the distant past looms large in high and popular culture and where there is a tradition of using surrogates from history and literature for living political figures. Organized by Jiang Qing and Wang Hongwen, teams of writers from Peking's two best-known universities, Peking University and Qinghua, wrote articles to criticize Confucius and the Duke of Zhou, a ruler of the twelfth century BC whom Confucius had held up as a model, and to commend as political leaders the conqueror who united China and became its first emperor and women rulers of later dynasties. Readers were quick to spot that the contemporary analogues of these figures were Zhou Enlai, Mao Zedong and Jiang Qing. But many among them, communists as well as non-communists, were shocked by claims that the first emperor, who had put to death the Confucian scholars of his day and burned their books, was a 'progressive' ruler and that several women rulers who had behaved tyrannically were also progressive. For all who hoped that the death of Lin Biao had at last opened the way to a period of political and social peace, it was dismaying to read that these figures were progressive because they had been resolute about the use of 'revolutionary violence'. And for all who had welcomed the rehabilitation of Deng Xiaoping it was discouraging to read that the Duke of Zhou had been in error to 'revive states that had been extinguished, restore families whose lines of succession have been broken and call to office those who had retired to obscurity'.[1]

Zhou was not brought down by the campaign. But it compelled him to devote time and energy he could ill spare to protecting himself. There are several stories of how he intervened with newspaper editors to stop them from publishing particularly far-fetched or malicious articles. The campaign seems finally to have convinced him that he must treat Jiang Qing, to whom he had often been kind when she was a person of no political importance (for instance, by going to see her in a sanatorium some way from Moscow during one of his visits to the Soviet Union in the 1950s) and with whom he had tried to maintain good relations during the most turbulent years of the Cultural Revolution, as an enemy, never to be conciliated.

Deng Xiaoping was a target at one remove in the campaign. Paradoxically, however, the period of the campaign, the summer of 1973 to the summer of 1974, coincided with a period when his political fortunes flourished.

The tenth party congress, held in secret over a period of five days in August 1973, was a triumph for the radicals. Zhou Enlai gave the political report, filling the shoes of Mao Zedong in 1945, Liu Shaoqi in 1956 and Lin Biao in 1969, but showed that he was aware of the vulnerability of his position by using much of a text prepared for him by a group under Wang Hongwen. Wang introduced a revised party constitution which enshrined a whole set of radical themes, including the need for repeated revolutions on the lines of the Cultural Revolution, the need to persist in the criticism of revisionism and, reflecting the populist element in Mao's way of thought, the unacceptability of the suppression of criticism by the masses. Immediately after the congress, Wang became a vice-chairman of the central committee, as Mao had wished, and Zhang Chunqiao and Jiang Qing both became members of the politburo standing committee.

Deng was a delegate to the congress and was elected to its presiding committee. At its end, he was re-elected to the central committee, in company with many other members of the eighth (1956) committee who had been dropped in 1959. He thus took his first step back towards senior party rank. He did not, however, go further when the new central committee elected a new politburo. He would have known when the committee met that his name was not on the slate. It is unlikely that he was surprised by this at a time of radical ascendancy. Nor was he necessarily disappointed; membership of the politburo could have brought him face to face with the radicals before he had had time to win Mao's active favour.

In the autumn Mao sent Deng and Wang Hongwen out of Peking on a joint tour of inspection. His motives for throwing the two men together were presumably to test them against one another and to discover whether they were willing and able to work together. Unfortunately, it is not known how they got on. But Deng's later view of Wang and his abilities emerges from his coining of a new verb, to helicopter, to describe the way in which Wang had been promoted. When the tour was over, Mao asked the two what they thought would happen in China after he had died. Wang replied that the country would continue to apply the chairman's 'revolutionary line' and would achieve unity on this basis. Deng, shrewder or more honest, said that warlords would emerge and the whole country would sink into chaos. Mao thought Deng's answer the better.

Having moved to burnish his own reputation and to preserve the fruits of the Cultural Revolution, Mao now acted to loosen the grip which the army had established over the political life of the country. In the provinces, party committees were taking back most of the powers they had lost to revolutionary committees before and after the ninth congress in 1969. But the military men who had dominated the latter had not in consequence given up their authority; they had become members in large numbers of the reconstituted party committees and party secretaries in many provinces. Mao wanted to replace serving officers with civilians as senior party officials and greatly to reduce military representation in committees at all levels. He also wanted to break the local power which the commanders of China's eleven military regions had built up over the years. He perhaps had in mind Deng's prognostication that warlords would emerge after his death; in any case, he was well aware that, outside Peking, 'the gun' now controlled the party.

Mao took action in December 1973. He told a meeting of the politburo that he wanted a reshuffle of regional commanders and repeated his demand at a meeting of the military commission, telling that body that it had ceased to deal with military affairs as it should. To integrate himself with its members he admitted that he had been hoodwinked by Lin Biao about the records and political attitudes of many 'revolutionary heroes', including Zhu De. And, in order to calm fears that acceptance of the reshuffle would mean that the army sacrificed regional military power in return for nothing, he proposed that Deng Xiaoping, an authentic military hero, should rejoin the commission. His tactics were successful; the eight commanders left their regional headquarters without complaint or delay when ordered formally to do so.

Mao also suggested to the commission that Deng should become chief of staff of the armed forces. This suggestion was not acted on at the time. But Deng was promoted to the politburo as well as to the commission. This put him at least on level terms with the radicals. Two of them, Wang Hongwen and Zhang Chunqiao, still outranked him in the party. But none of them could now match his positions in the army and the government.

Also at the beginning of 1974 Zhou Enlai devolved to Deng day-to-day, and perhaps also general, responsibility for foreign affairs. This was a new sphere for Deng, and it soon emerged that his style was very different from Zhou's. The silken element was missing and also perhaps some of the subtlety. Zhou and Kissinger had established a relationship of mutual respect and understanding during the four visits which the latter had paid to China between

July 1971, when he had come and gone in total secrecy, and November 1973. He found it much harder to get on terms with Deng, and not easy to like him. Deng, it is true, had harsher messages to convey than Zhou in his time – for instance, that it was dangerous for the United States to suppose that it could gain anything from *détente* with the Soviet Union and that the United States had failed to deliver on earlier undertakings about Taiwan and trade. Besides, the radicals were on the alert for any sign which would allow them to assert that he was a friend of imperialism or a worshipper of foreign things.

Deng's first important task in his new role was to address the General Assembly of the United Nations, at a special session called to discuss international cooperation for development. His brief was not to give China's views on the many issues, some extremely technical, which had arisen in what was coming to be known as the North–South Dialogue, but to propound Mao's last great theoretical innovation: his theory of the three worlds.

Mao's theory reflected the sinocentrism which had always marked him and which had become more pronounced as he got older. The theory was descended not from Leninism – which it contradicted – but from his analysis of China's class structure in the 1920s and 1930s. Just as he had then seen three camps in China (revolutionary, anti-revolutionary and intermediate), he now saw three worlds in the world at large. The first world consisted of the two superpowers, which were stronger than all other countries and shared an ambition to dominate the world. Indeed, it was this rather than their economic or political strength which made them superpowers. The second world was made up of all other developed countries. China belonged to the third world. It had the potential to become as strong as the United States and the Soviet Union, but was nevertheless free from the ambition to dominate the world and so would never become a superpower. By contrast, the existing superpowers would not shed this ambition and would therefore remain each other's enemy: indeed, it was more likely than not that war would break out between them. If it did, the whole world would be engulfed in a third world war.

Deng's speech drew a large audience and was given a lot of publicity outside China. On his return to Peking he was treated very much as he had been on his return from Moscow, after five days of argument with Suslov, in 1963. Most members of the politburo, including his enemies, went to the airport to meet him and he drove into Peking in a car at the head of a long motorcade. It was made clear to the world that Mao was pleased when, three weeks later, he occupied the seat traditionally reserved for Mao's principal adviser at a meeting between the chairman and the prime minister of Pakistan, even though Zhou Enlai was also present.

His visit to New York was important for Deng in two other ways. It made him far better known internationally and it gave him his first sight of the modern Western world. Until 1974, he had been a rather shadowy figure to non-communist politicians, diplomats and journalists. A few American military men had met him during and after the war against Japan and one of these, Evans Carlson, a marine officer, had written enthusiastically about his knowledge of affairs and sharpness of mind. But only communists and fellow-travellers had been taken to meet him during his time as general secretary and references to him are sparse in the many books written by Western journalists after visits to China in the 1950s and 1960s.

There is nothing in the published record about what Deng thought of New York. But he would have been unique if he had not been impressed. Nothing in his experience of Paris in the early 1920s, or of Moscow in the 1950s and 1960s, could have prepared him for its skyline, its opulence and its bustle. Four days in Manhattan would have brought home to him more forcefully than any amount of reading how far China had to go before it could claim to be a modern country.

Two weeks after appearing with (but below) Deng Xiaoping at Mao's meeting with the prime minister of Pakistan, Zhou Enlai left the Zhongnanhai and moved into a suite of rooms in the Capital Hospital nearby. There may have been a tactical element in this, in that a move to hospital would make him freer from oversight by the radicals. But he was by now a very sick man. A photograph taken of him with Deng at the airport in April 1974 brings out the contrast in the health of the two men. Deng, only six years his junior, is round-faced and clear-skinned. Zhou is hollow-cheeked and has dark patches on his face from his temples to his chin. His jacket appears to hang on him.

Zhou's chief remaining ambitions were to complete the reconstruction of the party and government (especially the latter) and to launch an economic strategy with rapid modernization as its explicit purpose. He faced formidable obstacles. Ideologically, the concept of modernization was suspect in Mao's eyes – he regarded it as a substitute for class warfare – and was seen by the radicals as a challenge and a threat. Organizationally, party headquarters no longer consisted of a coordinating agency, the secretariat, and a set of functional departments, but only of a general office and a propaganda department, both controlled by beneficiaries of the Cultural Revolution. In the government, many ministries were short-staffed and a large number of ministerial posts were vacant. Zhou's scheme was to convene the national people's congress – a body which, in spite of its sovereign status had not met since the winter of 1964/5 – and present to it a long list of candidates for government office and a twenty-year development programme. He also planned a central committee meeting, so that those he had chosen for government office could be given the backing of high party rank. Fearing sabotage by the radicals, and in any case determined to give them as few posts as possible, he left them out of his preparations. He restricted consultation to a small circle of confidants – led by Deng Xiaoping, Ye Jianying and Li Xiannian – all the time making sure that Mao approved generally of what he had in mind. Long practised by the radicals, the politics of conspiracy became Zhou's politics too.

Zhou and his allies were helped by a shift in Mao's attitude towards the radicals, especially Jiang Qing. As early as March 1974, Mao had told Jiang that it would be better if he and she ceased to see one another, saying that she had ignored his instructions for years and failed to study the books by Marx, Lenin and himself which he had given her. At a politburo meeting in July, he described her and her three allies to their faces as a Gang of Four, coining the label of opprobrium which was to stick to them for good. At about the same time, he told some visitors that she had 'wild ambitions' and that she was not entitled to speak in his name. This shift gave Zhou the chance to tighten his control over the media, where the gang had been strong, and to bring the campaign against Confucius to an end. He managed, too, to get Mao to accept a central-committee directive which commended the radical slogan of 'going against the tide', but went on to condemn behaviour like rebelling against local party leadership and refusing to work for managers in industry and commerce on political grounds.

Zhou was probably helped, too, by Mao's decision, made in July 1974, to leave Peking for a period of rest in the south. Mao was becoming more and more of a recluse, in spite of his appearances at party meetings in the summer. He was distressed by a sharp deterioration in his eyesight and seems to have found the company of all his political associates increasingly burdensome. Mao's absence meant that Zhou had the power to decide when the politburo should meet, and what it should discuss, as well as to direct the government. It also meant that the gang could only keep in touch with Mao by going through Zhou or by making special expeditions to see him.

In October, Mao let it be known from Changsha that he would like to see Deng Xiaoping appointed first vice-premier by the National People's Congress. The gang were appalled. The news could only mean that Mao saw Deng as the person best qualified to succeed Zhou as premier and, because Zhou's successor could not appropriately be outranked in the party by anyone except Mao himself, as his own presumptive successor. After a politburo meeting at which Jiang Qing exchanged angry words with Deng, the gang sent Wang Hongwen to put it to Mao that Deng was disqualified for the post and that it ought to go to Zhang Chunqiao. By now Mao had decided that Wang was a broken reed. The gang's choice of emissary was therefore unhappy and they did themselves, and Wang personally, additional harm by instructing him to tell the chairman that Zhou was only pretending to be ill in hospital. Mao was old and feeble. But he could still spot a lie and resent the assumption that he would believe it.

The gang's intervention rebounded on them. Mao told Wang Hongwen that he should be wary in his dealings with Jiang Qing and avoid 'ganging up' with her. He instructed a second emissary, his own cousin Wang Hairong, to tell Zhou that he wanted Zhou to stay on as premier and that he would like to see Deng made a vice-chairman of the central committee as well as first vice-premier. Worse still from the gang's point of view, he renewed his proposal that Deng should become chief of staff and added to it the suggestion that Deng should become a vice-chairman of the military commission. In December, Mao repeated these proposals to Zhou and Wang Hongwen in person, praising Deng for his outstanding ability in 'political and ideological affairs'.[2] The discomfiture of the gang was complete.

In January 1975, Deng Xiaoping was elected to all the posts which Mao wanted him to have. Wang Hongwen remained senior to him in the party, but seems to have been deprived of the day-to-day control of party headquarters which he had exercised at times in 1974. Ye Jianying stayed his senior in the military commission, but was perfectly content to allow him to make all the running in dealing with the politics of military affairs.

Deng lost no time exercising his new authority. For a man of seventy, which was what he now was, his show of energy during the next nine months was extraordinary. He convened at least ten conferences to discuss particular social and economic problems, and spoke at every one of them. He presided over many meetings of the state council, fought the gang foot-to-foot at several politburo meetings (under Mao's eye on at least two occasions), visited several distant provinces, travelled to France on a sentimental journey, and met scores of foreign visitors.

Deng began by tackling organizational problems, of which the

most serious were widespread unrest in industry and low morale
and poor discipline in many military units. Unrest was particularly
serious on the railways – the backbone of China's transport system
– and in the steel industry. He devoted three-quarters of a speech
to party secretaries responsible for industry to railway safety and
efficiency, discussing them under the headings of strengthening
'centralized and unified leadership', enforcing rules and regulations
and dealing with local trouble-makers. He revealed that there had
been 755 major railway accidents in 1974 (compared with 88 in
1964) and that one of the most important marshalling yards, at
Xuzhou in Jiangsu, was under the control of a self-appointed local
boss. He said:

Take for instance that ringleader in Xuzhou who has been creating
disturbances. He is so 'capable' that he exercises a virtual dictatorship
over the place. If we don't take action against this sort of person now,
how much longer are we going to wait? As I see it, we should only give
him one month to mend his ways . . . If he fails to do so [by then] . . .
then his misdeeds will be treated as crimes.[3]

When his warning was ignored, Deng sent troops to Xuzhou and
the local boss was arrested.

But Deng had his eye too on economic strategy. His point of
reference was Zhou Enlai's call to the national people's congress
in January for China to modernize its agriculture, industry,
national defence, and science and technology by the end of the
century. Zhou had first spoken of the 'four modernizations' in
1965, but apparently without Mao's endorsement and in any case
at a time when Mao had completely different priorities. Now he
had been careful to obtain, and announce, Mao's support. Deng
asked the party secretaries responsible for industry to look ahead:

The whole party must now give serious thought to our country's overall
interest. What is that interest? The reports on the work of the government at the first sessions of the third [1964–5] and fourth [1975] national
people's congresses both envisaged a two-stage development of our
economy. The first stage is to build an independent and relatively

comprehensive industrial and economic system by 1980. The second will be to turn China into a powerful socialist country with modern agriculture, industry, national defence, and science and technology by the end of this century ... The entire party and nation must strive for the attainment of this great objective. This constitutes the overall national interest.[4]

During the summer of 1975, Deng commissioned and set guidelines for three reports: on problems in industrial development; on the work of the Chinese Academy of Science; and – more comprehensively and more provocatively – on a general programme of work for the party and nation. One of the authors of the second report was Hu Yaobang, who had been general secretary of the Communist Youth League for many years before the Cultural Revolution. The author of the third was Deng Liqun, who had once worked as Liu Shaoqi's secretary and was to become known in the 1980s as a political conservative. Both men belonged to a group which, in the absence of any coordinating body at party headquarters on which he could rely, acted as Deng's staff.

Deng's methods were to act rapidly, to obtain Mao's prior approval for each of his principal moves (and to relate all his policies to statements made by Mao at one time or another) and to confront rather than evade his enemies. They, for their part, made two bad mistakes. They tried to sabotage the drive, begun by Zhou Enlai and carried forward by Deng, to bring back to office ministers, officials and officers disgraced since 1966 by launching a campaign to condemn 'going by the back door'. But in this they misjudged Mao. Now greatly worried about national unity, he criticized a theme which would tend to split rather than unite the country. Then, in the spring, they displeased the chairman by mishandling a call he had made for the nationwide study of the concept of the dictatorship of the proletariat. Mao had wanted to balance Zhou's appeal for economic development by reminding the party that the threat of counter-revolution continued to exist. Zhang Chunqiao and Yao Wenyuan reacted by publishing long theoretical articles on the ways in which enthusiasm for material gain and the persistence of 'bourgeois right' – a pejorative synonym for the (impeccably Marxist) principle of 'to each according to his work' – could lead first to the creation of a new capitalist class and then to its assumption of state power. Besides giving inconsistent accounts of where the new class would come from – Zhang said that it would emerge from within the party and Yao from the groups in society which were allowed to accumulate wealth – the articles offered no positive economic programme and were transparently intended to attack, and not to provide a complement to, Zhou's programme. Mao reacted angrily to what he saw as theoretical incompetence and a deliberate distortion of his purpose.

Political conflict came to a head at two politburo meetings in the spring. At the first, Deng, supported by Ye Jianying and Li Xiannian, criticized the gang for their abuse of Mao's recent instructions; at the second, Mao himself scolded them. He said that they had ignored his 'three dos and three don'ts' ('practise Marxism–Leninism, not revisionism; unite, and don't split; be open and above-board, and don't intrigue or conspire'),[5] told them to stop acting as a gang and declared that the fact they had formed one was a 'question' which the politburo ought to discuss and resolve. These strictures put the gang wholly on the defensive – to the point where Wang Hongwen retired to Shanghai and even Jiang Qing wrote a short note of self-criticism. For the rest of the summer, and into the autumn, Deng and his supporters had things very much their own way.

At the end of October or the beginning of November 1975, however, the tide turned again. The reason, quite simply, was that Mao decided that Deng's programme had begun to threaten the legacy of the Cultural Revolution. Two developments did Deng particular damage in Mao's eyes. One was Deng's use of the phrase 'key link' to describe a set of instructions by Mao which emphasized the need to promote stability and unity and to press on with economic development. This was heresy. For Mao, the 'key link' was, and could only be, class struggle.

The other development was Deng's endorsement of an attempt by the president of Qinghua University to dismiss two of the gang's most active supporters there. The two appealed to Mao; Mao supported them; and they then made public his support and called for a campaign to counter the 'right deviation of reversing correct verdicts'. Mao followed up with a statement to say that 'some leaders' had worked from July to September to spread unwarranted political rumours, to split the leadership of the party and to attack the Cultural Revolution and its fruits. At the end of November, a summary of his statement was read out at a 'notification' conference by Hua Guofeng, minister of public security and the only member of the politburo standing committee who was neither a member of the gang nor a supporter of Deng's, and then circulated to provincial party officials. According to one account, Deng was stripped then and there of all his government responsibilities except for foreign affairs. Whether or not this happened, Hua's reading out of the summary amounted to a sentence: Deng had forfeited Mao's confidence and in consequence the right to direct party and government affairs.

For Deng the next four months resembled the period between July and November 1966, when he had come under steadily fiercer attack by the radicals of the day. But he now reacted differently. In 1966, he had agreed to make a humiliating statement of self-criticism; in 1976, when put under pressure (by Mao, through Ye Jianying) to do so again, he steadfastly refused. His calculation, no doubt, was that Mao could not live for much longer and that, once he had died, no one would have the authority to get his friends to suggest to him that he should humiliate himself. He knew too that he would stand to lose in the political warfare which was bound to follow Mao's death by saying anything critical about his own behaviour since 1973. When put under pressure by the gang themselves, his tactics were to say nothing. In March 1975, they arranged for him to be attacked to his face, by themselves and by supporters brought in from outside, at an enlarged meeting of the politburo. His reaction was to turn off his hearing aids and, when challenged to respond, to declare that he had not heard a word of what had been said.

The key events of the winter and spring were the death of Zhou Enlai, the appointment of Hua Guofeng as acting premier and demonstrations by the people of Peking which made clear that they revered Zhou's memory, saw Deng as his rightful successor and detested the gang and all their works.

From August 1975, Zhou had been confined to hospital. In October, he underwent an operation, at least the third, but unsuccessfully. By December, he was often in a coma, though Deng Yingchao, his wife, Ye Jianying and Li Xiannian continued to talk to him about politics in his lucid moments. Mao, who had himself undergone an operation (for cataract) in August apparently sent him no messages of comfort or sympathy. On the contrary, he failed to insist, as he still could have done, that Zhou should be set aside from attack in the campaign against the reversal of verdicts. Thus did the chairman reward the man who had served him more loyally than anyone else over the years.

Zhou died on 8 January 1976. Although he had been in baulk politically for over two months, Deng was allowed to give the formal address on behalf of the central committee at his funeral service. Deng was careful to avoid any display of personal feeling which could be held by the gang to show that he had been close to a man Mao mistrusted. He bowed towards Mao by stating that Zhou had 'listened attentively' during the last few days of his life to an old poem of Mao's about revolution. He praised Zhou's 'fine style' – 'modest and prudent, unassuming and approachable' – and 'his conduct and manner of living in a plain and hard-working way'.[6] This was safe ground. No member of the gang could have claimed that Zhou had behaved otherwise without provoking the charge that the cap fitted.

Zhou's death meant that Mao would at last have to indicate who he wanted to be Zhou's successor. Even now he hesitated – in time and over the rank of his candidate. After a month, he told the politburo – probably through his nephew Mao Yuanxin, a serving officer who had joined his household during the autumn – that he wanted Hua Guofeng to take charge of the government, but only as acting premier.

Deng may have felt bitter that he had been passed over. But he is unlikely to have been surprised. Zhang Chunqiao, who had been immediately junior to Deng as a vice-premier, was deeply disappointed, showing that his reading of the political omens had been poor. Documents circulated within the party after the downfall of the gang show that Mao's degree of exasperation with all its members had stayed high throughout 1975 and that he had come close to saying that he considered no member of the gang fit to hold very high office. Although a compromise candidate, and a member of the politburo only since 1973, Hua himself showed no sign of doubting his ability to hold his own and win promotion. A man of phlegmatic temper but limited imagination, he may have failed to perceive that, in anything but the short term, his position was precarious. Mao's accolade was an enormous asset. But it was bound to be a wasting asset once Mao had died; and it was in the logic of the situation that he would be seen as an upstart and an impediment by the gang if they managed to triumph over Deng and his supporters, and vice versa.

Meanwhile, the gang behaved in a manner which showed that Mao had been right to mistrust them. Instead of setting out to win the confidence of Hua, who – whatever the underlying weakness of his position – was the man of the moment, they pursued their vendetta against Deng without consulting Hua and got their writing teams to suggest in the press that Hua was timid, foolish and inexperienced. Even more recklessly, they embarked on a campaign to defame the memory of Zhou Enlai. They had hated Zhou, and Zhou had come to hate them. Now, however, that he was dead, they had nothing to gain from blackening him except the gratification of a posthumous desire for revenge. Conversely, given the affection for Zhou of the population at large, and the respect in which he was held by millions of party members, they had a great deal to lose.

*

In February and March, the gang stepped up their campaign against Deng. On 26 February, the politburo decided that Deng could be attacked by name in the press and in unofficial publicity, and Jiang Qing immediately began to revile him – calling him the 'old king of counter-revolution' and even a traitor – at meetings she had convened in the margins of a national conference 'to purge cadres'. Deng's protection against complete disgrace was Mao's injunction that his case should be treated as a 'contradiction within the ranks of the people'. Jiang Qing made it clear that she chafed under this constraint. But Hua Guofeng said the leadership as a whole must abide by it; and the fact that Deng did not go into hiding, or even find an excuse for failing to attend the politburo meeting which the gang arranged in March to put him in the dock, suggests that he judged at this stage that he might be able to ride out the storm.

By the end of March, there were the makings of deadlock. The gang had failed to persuade Mao to cease to protect Deng or to cajole Hua into ignoring that protection, and there were no signs that the campaign against him had done him popular damage – if anything, rather the reverse (many foreigners were reporting that there was much smiling and nodding among the crowds which assembled to read the quotations from his speeches with which agents of the gang had covered the walls of the capital). Deng, for his part, could not make headway against the gang for as long as Hua continued to insist, as he had at a rally towards the end of February, that he had 'slandered' the Cultural Revolution, 'rejected the revolutionary line of the chairman' and committed 'grave errors'.

The deadlock was broken by a crisis in the gang's parallel campaign against Zhou Enlai. On 25 March, the Shanghai newspaper which had published Yao Wenyuan's attack on Wu Han ten years before carried an editorial which attacked 'that capitalist-roader within the party who had wanted to reinstate in power the capitalist-roader who had been overthrown and is unrepentant to this day'. Shanghai was under the control of the gang. But Nanking, a hundred miles away, was not; and demonstrations of protest, led by the city's large student population, were held on the following day. They were broken up, and the gang succeeded in blocking any mention of them in the national press. Yet news about them spread fast, carried by travellers and by messages daubed in tar on the outside of trains. In Peking, it gave enormous stimulus to a developing movement to show respect for Zhou's memory through the laying of wreaths at the foot of the monument to revolutionary heroes in Tiananmen Square. The first wreaths had been removed by the police, but later wreaths, deposited by soldiers and workers as well as students, were not.

On 4 April, the festival of the departed in the lunar calendar, enormous crowds gathered in the square. Many people arrived in marching columns, organized by factories, offices and schools. Some of the visitors left wreaths, on the plinth of the monument or on stands, and many others showed banners, made speeches and recited poems. The poems and banners were as critical of Jiang Qing as they were eulogistic of Zhou. Photographs in Deng's biography show legends which read 'when demons stir up waves, the people should rise to eliminate them' and 'premier Zhou Enlai will for ever live in our hearts'.[7] One of the poems referred to the gang as 'wolves and jackals' and another said baldly Jiang Qing 'must be mad to want to be an empress'. In the evening, the politburo met in emergency session and decided that Deng had been responsible, that the poems and slogans of the demonstrators contained direct attacks on Mao and other members of the party's leadership and that the events of the day constituted a 'counter-revolutionary incident'. Mao was consulted through his nephew Mao Yuanxin, and the police were ordered to clear the square of all wreaths and posters as soon as word came back that he agreed with the politburo's decisions. By daybreak on 5 April, every one of the memorials left in the square the day before had been removed.

The popular reaction was furious. Throughout 5 April, crowds demonstrated in the square, scuffling with the police, burning police vehicles and dealing roughly with the few supporters of the gang who dared speak disobligingly of Zhou Enlai. After dark, when most of the demonstrators had left the square, troops, militiamen and police swept through it, beating and arresting the few hundred people who remained. Meeting again, the politburo concluded that the clearance of the square had been necessary to deal with a 'counter-revolutionary riot' and asked Mao Yuanxin to report this conclusion to the chairman. Mao once again concurred, adding two instructions of his own: that Hua Guofeng should be appointed premier (instead of acting premier) and first vice-chairman of the central committee; and that Deng should be relieved of all his posts, 'inside and outside the party', although he was to be allowed to keep his ordinary party membership, 'so as to see how he behaves in the future'.[8]

The Tiananmen incident, as it quickly came to be called, reduced Deng politically to where he had been in 1969. His friends in the politburo had been silenced (Ye Jianying and Li Xiannian either had been excluded from the meeting on 4 April or had thought it prudent to stay away). Perhaps most sinister of all, the politburo had agreed, with or without Mao's approval, that his case now represented an 'antagonistic contradiction', making him open to arrest and violent treatment. He himself later claimed that the incident had weakened the gang, by turning public opinion even more strongly against them. This may have been the case. But a fact which must have loomed larger for him at the time was that the army, the militia and the police had acted without hesitation on the orders they had received. They had not turned against the gang; and the demonstrations had driven Hua and the gang to work together.

Yet if defeated, Deng was not defenceless, as he had been in 1967. Because he had made a contingency plan, or because he kept in close touch with friends as the crisis developed, or both, he was able to escape from Peking on the very day Mao decided that he should be stripped of office. He travelled to Canton by air, 'under the escort' of Xu Shiyou, the commander of the Canton military region and a member of the politburo. The operation was so well managed that Jiang Qing and the other members of the gang remained in the dark over his whereabouts all through the summer.

To begin with, Wang Hongwen believed that he had gone to Sichuan. Later, officers sympathetic to the gang sent spies to the south, to follow and report on the movements of Xu Shiyou and other local leaders who could be expected to be his supporters, in the hope of tracking him down. But they all drew a blank.

There is only one first-hand account about Deng's movements during the next six months: a speech by Zhang Pinghua, then director of the party's propaganda department in July 1978. This shows that Deng moved about from place to place and that he actively encouraged those who visited him, including Zhang himself, to make plans to overthrow the gang. At some stage in the later summer, he told Zhang and others that there would have to be a fight to the finish against them:

Either we accept the fate of being slaughtered and let the party and the country degenerate – let the country which was founded with the heart and soul of our proletarian revolutionaries of the older generation be destroyed by those four people, and let history retrogress one hundred years. Or we struggle against them as long as there is still any life in our bodies. If we win, everything can be solved. If we lose, we can take to the mountains for as long as we live or find a shield in other countries, to wait for another opportunity. At present, we can at least use the strength of the Canton military region, the Fuzhou military region and the Nanking military region to fight against them. Any procrastination and we shall risk losing this, our only capital.

Zhang described one of Deng's journeys in these terms:

To escape notice, commander Xu [Shiyou] used a paddy wagon, all the windows of which were closed. From morning till night, the wagon rattled on the bumpy road. Inside the wagon, it was hot and stuffy . . . one of the guards accompanying vice-premier Deng exhorted him earnestly to take a rest when he saw him lose his appetite, become red-eyed, cough and become increasingly thin.[9]

The circumstances of the journey apart, it is not surprising that Deng's health had begun to suffer. The danger that his where-abouts would be given away to an agent of the gang, inadvert-ently or otherwise, was ever-present. The news from Peking was not good; Hua Guofeng was clearly unable, even if willing, to overrule the gang on any important matter of policy, or to protect Deng's friends and supporters from dismissal. The campaign which the gang had launched against him in the national press was growing in its degree of intensity and in the deadliness of its charges. He had met Ye Jianying secretly during a visit which Ye had made to the south and knew from him that plotting against the gang was on foot; but he could not be sure that it would succeed. And he knew that Jiang Qing was perfectly capable of using action, or a threat of action, against members of his family as a means of forcing him out of hiding.

The fair degree of political and economic order which Deng and his supporters had succeeded in creating in 1975 gave way to renewed disorder in the summer. When Hua Guofeng convened a national planning conference in July, the gang attacked all his proposals, creating a policy vacuum. They encouraged their sup-porters in the provinces to organize strikes and demonstrations, giving millions the impression that they were willing to sacrifice everything else to the pursuit of factional advantage, or even that they favoured anarchy. Their most flagrant abuse of authority – and worst political error – was to use an official message to the surviving inhabitants of the city of Tangshan, where 250,000 people had died in an earthquake in August, to appeal to them to 'deepen and broaden' the criticism of 'Deng Xiaoping's counter-revolutionary revisionist line'.

All through the summer, the standard-bearer of resistance was Ye Jianying. He had given Deng strong support after the latter's appointment as chief of staff. He had suffered for this when Hua rather than Deng was appointed acting premier after Zhou Enlai's death; he had remained minister of defence, but had been set aside as the person in charge of the commission's day-to-day work. He was nevertheless able to visit the south without hindrance during the summer, by when he had certainly decided that the gang must be removed by direct action. But he had also decided that it would be more dangerous to make a move before Mao's death than after it, even though the gang were working hard to build up their military support in the provinces, and also that the circle of conspiracy would have to be extended to include some of those who had taken the gang's side during and after the Tiananmen incident. Hua Guofeng, Wang Dongxing, the commander of unit 8341, and Chen Xilian, who had displaced Ye on the military commission, were key figures. Yet their attitudes towards the gang would depend on how the gang behaved during the crucial weeks after Mao's death, and he could take it for granted that the gang were watching him carefully. His hand was fraught with difficulty.

Mao Zedong died a few minutes after midnight on 8 September 1976. Contemporary accounts of reactions to the news of his death speak of bewilderment and anxiety among the people, but not of great grief. For all Chinese under thirty, the great majority, he was an icon more than a man. For senior members of the party, he was a great man, but a man who had also made great mistakes, especially in his treatment of colleagues. For most military leaders, his reputation still stood high; he had turned the ragged little armies of Jiangxi and Shaanxi into the strongest and most success-ful army in modern Chinese history, creating its ethic and its strategic and tactical doctrines. These men were, and would remain, the fiercest defenders of his name.

The pattern of the future was settled at politburo meetings held in the small hours of 9 September, immediately after Mao's death, and on 19 and 29 September. The gang made it quite clear that they were not prepared to accept Hua as Mao's successor. Their demands, all turned down in formal votes or left for later decision, were that Deng Xiaoping should be expelled from the party, that Mao Yuanxin should be given custody of his uncle's personal papers and that Jiang Qing should become chairman. Their behaviour made Hua Guofeng, who had temporized when Ye Jianying first suggested to him that the gang should be arrested, come round to the view that only their arrest could stop them from continuing to fight for total political power. As a positive inducement, Ye promised that he, Li Xiannian and other survivors of the old Yan'an leadership would vote for Hua as chairman and support him in that office once the gang had been disposed of.

Hua's change of mind allowed talk about desperate measures, such as the establishment of a rival party headquarters in Canton, to be superseded by planning for a limited purge of the politburo under the direction of its senior member (Hua) and with the backing of a majority within it. It guaranteed that the army, which might otherwise have split, remained united and available to act against the militia units which supporters of the gang had been arming in Shanghai and a few other large cities. It ensured, too, that Wang Dongxing's guards regiment was available for use.

Final decisions were taken at a politburo meeting, from which the gang were excluded and of which they remained in ignorance, held at a military headquarters on 5 October. On the evening of the sixth, Zhang Chunqiao, Wang Hongwen and Yao Wenyuan were arrested by troops put in position by Wang Dongxing himself as, one by one, they entered a building in the Zhongnanhai for a meeting to which Hua had summoned them. Jiang Qing and Mao Yuanxin were arrested in their houses at about the same time. The story goes that one of Jiang's servants spat at her as she was led away, screaming at her captors.

CHAPTER 12

Mending China, 1976–81

On the day after the arrest of the Gang of Four, it was announced that the politburo had elected Hua Guofeng chairman of the central committee and its military commission and confirmed his appointment as premier. But nothing was said about the event which had made this action possible. Hua, Ye Jianying and Wang Dongxing, the three leading conspirators, wanted to keep their purge secret in order to make it easier to disarm the gang's supporters in the provinces. These latter had distributed heavier weapons to militia units in Shanghai and several other parts of the country and had been told by Wang Hongwen, who had set up a special command centre in the Zhongnanhai, to be ready to receive orders to take military action.

As it turned out, the triumvirate in Peking did not find it difficult to impose their authority in Shanghai. The gang's lieutenants there were warned in a coded telephone message ('mother's operation has been unsuccessful') that the gang had experienced a set-back, but then allowed themselves to be lured to the capital in ones and twos. There was some sporadic street fighting, but it ended in about a week. In other parts of the country, clashes between regular and militia units continued for over a year. It is not clear how much of this was due to resistance by local supporters of the gang and how much to attempts by provincial leaders to maintain their own power bases. The disturbances were widespread, especially south of the Yangtse, and the central government did not regain control of Tientsin, less than a hundred miles from Peking, until the end of 1977 or the beginning of 1978. At no time, however, was there any danger that regular army units loyal to the gang would seize power in the capital itself or in any large block of territory.

On 21 October, fifteen days after the event, widespread rumours that the gang had been arrested were officially confirmed. The news brought enormous, and this time joyful, crowds on to the streets of cities all over China. For several days on end, processions blocked most main roads in the capital and very little work was done in factories and offices. Unlike the processions of the spring, these processions were colourful and noisy; they formed up behind groups carrying banners and were accompanied by lorries carrying drummers and cymbal-players. At night, the noise of exploding firecrackers led at least one Western correspondent to report that local supporters of the gang were being executed. Large numbers of prisoners were released from the gaols attached to work units, known as cow-pens, in which they had been incarcerated. In Shanghai, ships in the harbour sounded their foghorns. All over the country, men and women who had been sent to work in communes left their places of exile and set out for home.

After Mao's death, Deng Xiaoping had returned to Peking – though advised by some to remain in comparative safety in the south – and had gone into hiding there. His protectors in Guangdong, Xu Shiyou and Wei Guoqing, the provincial governor, were both members of the politburo and so were able to keep him informed about the arguments which took place in that body in September. How much he knew of Ye's planning and plotting has never been revealed, by him or anyone else. But he certainly knew that Ye was determined to take action, and he knew too that he could best contribute to the success of Ye's plans by making sure that he himself was not tracked down and arrested.

According to one source, Ye telephoned Deng as soon as the overnight meeting of the politburo which followed the gang's arrest had finished. He certainly heard the news quickly. On 10 October, he wrote to Hua Guofeng, to say that he supported 'with all my heart' the politburo's decisions to promote Hua to the two chairmanships and to describe the arrest of the gang as a victory of the proletariat over the bourgeoisie, and of socialism over capitalism.[1] It also seems certain that Deng met Hua at the end of October, in a hospital to which they had gone (independently) to visit Liu Bocheng, Deng's former commander. Deng told Hua that he, a 'capitalist-roader', was delighted by the turn events had taken and was strong in Hua's support. In answer to Hua's request for advice, Deng said that agriculture and light industry should have priority in economic planning, although heavy industry should not be neglected. He added that consolidation of the 'dictatorship' was necessary if the 'livelihood of the people' was to receive the attention it deserved. Here, expressed in conversational language, is the key to the contradiction many outside China have seen between Deng's readiness to experiment boldly in the economic sphere and his political conservatism. Far from seeing political liberalization as a necessary condition for economic liberalization, he has seen it as a serious potential threat to social and political stability and therefore to development.

During the same conversation, Liu said he would like Deng to preside over his funeral service when he died (Liu was eighty-two and completely blind). Deng said that there could be a problem over this; he was a man who had made mistakes. In any case, Hua was extremely busy and ought not to be detained. Hua commented that Deng had not lost any of his spirit. Deng replied, artfully or otherwise, that his spirit was at the service of the politburo.

Deng was in fact determined to fight for his complete political rehabilitation. He had many supporters, led by Chen Yun, who had been 'set aside' but not persecuted during the Cultural Revolution, and Wang Zhen, a former general who had lobbied on his behalf with Mao Zedong in 1972. Hua, however, had strong reservations. Apart from the threat to his own authority which Deng's rehabilitation would pose, it could not be accomplished without at least modification of the official verdict on the Tiananmen incident; and any such modification would be hard to achieve without criticism, direct or implied, of Mao Zedong, to whom he owed all his authority.

In March 1977, Hua convened a central work conference to chart the way ahead. Deng, as an ordinary party member, was not present. But many of his supporters were, and they demanded both that the Tiananmen incident should be reassessed and that Deng should be rehabilitated. Hua had already taken, and refused to budge from, the line that the Gang of Four represented the 'ultra-right' (using the formula which Mao and they had used against Lin Biao, and for the same reasons), that the campaign against Deng and his drive to reverse the verdicts of the Cultural Revolution had been correct, and that the incident had been counter-revolutionary. He stood pat, too, on a formula about Mao and his thought which Wang Dongxing had suggested to him: 'Whatever policy chairman Mao decided on, we shall resolutely defend; whatever directives chairman Mao issued, we shall steadfastly obey.'[2] He would only concede that Deng had not been in any way responsible for the Tiananmen incident, that it had been 'reasonable' for 'the masses to go to Tiananmen Square to mourn for the late premier Zhou', and that it would be necessary to 'let comrade Deng Xiaoping resume work at an opportune moment'.

This, however, was enough to open the way to a negotiation between the two men. It is not clear which of them took the initiative or whether they ever met face to face. The first known move was made by Deng. On 10 April, three weeks after the end of the work conference, he wrote to Hua again. He said that he supported the thrust of what Hua had said at the conference, admitted that he had made errors in 1975, accepted Mao's criticism of those errors, and referred back to an earlier letter – almost certainly that of 10 October – in which he had stated his 'sincere support' for Hua in the posts to which he had been promoted after the arrest of the gang. He suggested that both his letters should be circulated within the party. This, it seems, was done. Then, towards the end of May, Deng was visited by 'two leading comrades of the general office of the central committee', one of whom was almost certainly Wang Dongxing, the head of the office. He told them that Hua's 'two whatevers' were unacceptable. If 'this principle' were correct, there could be no justification for his rehabilitation (because his disgrace had been ordered by Mao) or for 'any statement' that the activities of the masses in 1976 had been 'reasonable'. A few days later, he was visited by 'two leading comrades of the central committee',* to whom he repeated his line.[3]

This was bad news for Hua. He nevertheless decided that he could not make a sticking-point of Deng's obstinacy. At a meeting of the central committee in July, Deng was reappointed to all the offices – in the party, the army and the government – which he had held before April 1976. He made a speech to the meeting, on its last day but before any vote about his reinstatement could have been taken, in which he abstained from endorsing the two whatevers, argued that Mao's thought should be treated as an 'integral whole' and insisted that the right way in which to improve the party's style of work was to follow the mass line and to act in accordance with the principle of 'seeking truth from facts'. He rubbed it in that this principle had been central to Mao's theory of party building and that Mao had proposed 'seek truth from facts' as the motto for the central party school in Yan'an. No one who heard him could have been in doubt that he had challenged Hua on a fundamental issue.

Deng was now nearly seventy-three. He was therefore as old as Mao Zedong when he launched the Cultural Revolution. But he did not look much older than he had at fifty and was extremely fit for a man of his age. His only serious disability was his deafness. But he had long become used to wearing hearing aids and with their help could hear well enough to remain on top of proceedings even at large meetings. His voice was strong, if rather harsh, and he could deliver long speeches without any apparent fatigue. He walked quickly, his broken leg of eighteen years before having mended completely.

Deng's wife and stepmother had survived their three years of exile without serious damage to their health. Indeed, Zhuo Lin

---

* They were almost certainly Ye Jianying and Li Xiannian. Among politburo members, only they had the seniority and credentials as friends to argue with Deng.

was fitter when she returned to Peking than when she left. Xia Bogen, the ferryman's daughter, was wiry and tough, devoted to her stepson and his family and capable of prodigies of physical labour. She was still alive in 1992, the year of her eighty-ninth birthday.[4]

Among Deng's children, only Deng Pufang had come to serious harm during the Cultural Revolution. This harm, though, was grievous; by the time he was allowed to enter a well-equipped hospital in Peking in 1972, he was almost completely paralysed. In 1976, he was discharged from the hospital and given work in a television factory. He lived at home at any rate from the spring of 1977 and Deng made alterations to his house to allow his son to move freely from room to room in his wheelchair and to travel between floors in a lift. In 1980, he was sent by Deng in secrecy to Canada, where he underwent at least two operations. These allowed him to sit up again and to move his arms and neck, but not to walk. In the 1980s, he became a public figure in his own right, as the president of an organization – the Chinese National Welfare Fund for the Handicapped – which he had established to care for China's many millions of handicapped people.

Deng's eldest daughter, Deng Lin, was married and had become an artist (she had wanted to be a musician, but had not been able to move to the Peking Conservatory from the middle school attached to it because of an illness in the early 1960s). His second daughter, Deng Nan, was also married. She had met her husband when working in a commune in Shaanxi in 1971 and had subsequently moved with him and their two children to Tientsin. Deng Rong (Maomao), Deng's third daughter, was a medical student and lived at home. Of the three girls, she was the one who most resembled her father. Energetic and outspoken, she had been an enthusiastic Red Guard during the opening phase of the Cultural Revolution and had apparently criticized her eldest sister in public for defending their father at meetings. Like Deng Pufang, but unlike Deng Lin, she became a party member. She had spent more time with her parents in Jiangxi than any of the other children and was later to write a long account of their time there for the *People's Daily*.

Deng Zhifang, Deng's younger son and youngest child, had also been a Red Guard – at the age of fourteen – and like Deng Nan had been sent to Shaanxi when his parents were put under house arrest in 1967. In 1973, he had become a student of physics at Peking University and so must have witnessed the mobilization of students there to demonstrate against his father in late 1975. But he himself does not seem to have been molested. In 1980, he was sent to the University of Rochester in New York State to do postgraduate work (though it seems that few among his tutors or fellow-students knew his true identity). He returned to China in the early 1980s, with his wife and a new daughter, but did not become a party member.

The Cultural Revolution had taken its toll in Deng's wider family. His second brother, Deng Shuping, who had become a party member after being deprived of his land in Sichuan during land reform, had committed suicide in March 1967, after suffering weeks of ill-treatment by Red Guards at Wuhan. One of the charges brought against him had been that he was a close relation of China's 'number two capitalist-roader'. Zhuo Lin's eldest brother, who had done forced labour for several years after being dispossessed of his father's meat wholesaling business in the 1950s, had been reimprisoned.

Deng's reinstatement allowed him to take careful stock politically. With renewed access to official information, he could form a much more accurate picture of the state of society and the economy and conditions in the party, the army and the government than when in exile or even when negotiating his return to office.

Social order was poor. Crime and industrial absenteeism had become endemic and gangsterism was still common on the railways. Urban levels of unemployment were high, boosted by the return from the countryside of many former Red Guards. In the villages, many party officials had turned into local tyrants. Corruption was prevalent and cynicism had replaced the enthusiasm and readiness to work for the common good which had impressed many foreign visitors in the 1950s.

In a speech to a national science conference in March 1978, Deng said that the gang's sabotage of the four modernizations had brought the national economy to the brink of collapse. This was an exaggeration. Figures released during the 1980s show that the epoch of the Cultural Revolution had produced a good deal of economic dislocation, but no economic disaster. Industry was badly disrupted in 1967 and 1968, the years when the Red Guards and the Revolutionary Rebels were on the rampage. Even in these years, however, there was no slump of the kind which followed the Great Leap Forward, and the levels of output of most industrial goods in 1969 were higher than they had been in 1966; only steel, cement and chemical fertilizer continued to lag. By 1975, the output of many products, including cement and chemical fertilizer, was well over twice as great as in 1966. In industry, a feature of the whole period of the Cultural Revolution was a very high rate of investment in industry, especially heavy industry. Indeed, the entire Soviet model was applied at least as faithfully as it had been during the period of the first five-year plan (1953/7). This is perhaps the greatest paradox of a movement to purge the party and the nation of a disease, revisionism, seen by Mao Zedong to have its chief source in the Soviet Union.

In agriculture, output had grown quite rapidly. As in industry, 1968 was a poor year – mainly because of a shortage of chemical fertilizer – but the growth in grain output was thereafter steady. Output reached 285 million tons in 1975, an increase of 70 million tons over its level in 1966. The worry here was that the population had grown almost as fast. One of the consequences of the Cultural Revolution had been a baby boom in the countryside, whose influence is now being very strongly felt, twenty years on.

The party, the army and the government were all in poor shape. The party now had about 35 million members, of whom at least half had joined it since 1966. Most of these recruits were young and many were radicals. These people were not inclined to accept discipline or the humdrum life which would follow any shift from 'revolution' to 'production'. The army was suffering from factionalism, bloated staffing and 'laxity, conceit, extravagance and inertia'

(Deng's words) among its officers. In a speech to the military commission in December 1977, Deng condemned all these vices, called for the exclusion from important posts of 'bad elements' and people who had engaged in 'beating, smashing and looting' during the Cultural Revolution and said that standards of perform-ance among commanders needed immediate improvement.[5] A few months earlier, he had stated roundly that the army was 'not sufficiently capable of conducting modern warfare' and, though numerically strong, was 'of relatively poor quality'. Deng had his own reasons for contrasting a heroic past with an unsatisfactory present; but there can be no doubt that the political use of the army all through the Cultural Revolution, and the prosecution of vendettas by Lin Biao against almost all its former leaders, had left it in a slack and demoralized condition. The government was hardly better off. It was overstaffed at the top and many ministries were controlled by vested interests. So as to play safe, many officials had lapsed into the bureaucratic ways which Deng had so strongly condemned to the eighth party congress twenty years before.

From the summer of 1977 to the end of 1978, Deng was directly responsible for education, science and technology, military affairs and foreign affairs.

Deng was put in charge of education, science and technology at his own request. He had long taken a particular interest in these subjects. In 1961 he had presided over the preparation of draft regulations for work in universities and research institutes, conclud-ing in the process that a high standard of general education was a condition for progress in science and technology and that such progress was a condition for rapid economic development. He abominated the gang's view that there should be no specialization or cultivation of excellence in education. Like Deng, the gang had seen links between education and science and technology, and between science and technology and modernization. But they had argued that, precisely because modernization would mean scrap-ping their kind of education, it was a dangerous notion.

Operationally, Deng called for the restoration of streaming in China's schools and the cultivation of excellence at all levels, going for the gang in the process:

The Gang of Four made the absurd claim that, the more a person knew, the more reactionary he would become. They said they preferred labourers without culture and they praised an ignorant reactionary clown who handed in a blank examination paper as the model of a 'red expert'. On the other hand, they vilified as 'white and expert' those good comrades who studied diligently and contributed to the motherland's science and technology. For a time, this reversal of right and wrong and confounding of the people with the enemy caused deep confusion in many minds.[6]

In the army, Deng, as a vice-chairman of the military commission and chief of staff, worked to put right the moral and professional weaknesses he had condemned. Here his task was particularly difficult. As a military hero of the wars against the Japanese and Chiang Kaishek, his prestige in the armed forces was extremely high. But the people around him included several who had favoured his disgrace in April 1976, notably three military men in the politburo: Wang Dongxing, commander of unit 8341, and Chen Xilian and Li Desheng, commanders of the Peking and Shenyang (north-eastern) military regions. Politics apart, these men were bound to regard Deng's strictures about indiscipline, factionalism and low standards of professional competence as criticisms of themselves. Deng could not therefore be sure of their cooperation over his programmes for 'regularization' and the expulsion from senior posts of sympathizers with Lin Biao and the gang. The extent to which they did work with him in these early days is hard to judge. What is certain is that the poor performance of the armed forces in a two-week war with Vietnam in the spring of 1979 showed that Deng had been quite right to assert that they had become of 'relatively poor quality'.

Deng was no less active in foreign affairs, where there was just as much to be done. During 1976, there had been no policy – only a sour xenophobia. In the summer, Zhang Chunqiao had attacked the United States for maintaining formal links with Taiwan; and in the autumn, after Mao's death, Soviet overtures for improved relations had been brusquely rejected. China had therefore put itself into the posture favoured by Lin Biao, of strong and equal hostility towards each of the superpowers. Besides carrying still considerable military risks, this posture was incompatible with Deng's ambition to promote rapid economic development by importing foreign equipment and technology on a large scale.

Deng's prescription was to reopen and push forward the dialogue with the United States which had languished since his fall from grace at the end of 1975. But, given the weight of the past, he could not afford to show any disposition to compromise over Taiwan. Nor could he afford to cease chiding the United States for failing to stand up to the Soviet Union; it was the legacy of both Mao Zedong and Zhou Enlai that the United States should not, in Kissinger's words, be allowed to 'have its maotai and vodka too'.[7] He therefore took a robust line both on Taiwan and on the geopolitical balance. As it happened, the timing was good. Support was gathering in Washington for the view that the active pursuit of the 'normalization' of relations between the United States and China – entailing the recognition by the United States of the government of the People's Republic as the sole legal government of China – would tend to bridle the Soviet Union, whose behaviour had become increasingly assertive in Africa and South-East Asia, rather than provoke it. Deng helped the process forward by working hard to get Zbigniew Brzezinski, President Carter's national security adviser, who was known to favour a tilt towards China more strongly than Cyrus Vance, the Secretary of State, to visit China, and by making sure that Brzezinski was not attacked in the Chinese press after his visit (in May 1978) as Vance had been after a visit a year earlier.

Normalization was achieved in December 1978. It was accompanied by a United States government statement that it reserved the right to sell military equipment to Taiwan. But the Chinese were now more interested in deeds, especially the refusal of Washington to sanction several orders from Taiwan for military aircraft, than words. This became clear when the forces massed on the coast opposite Taiwan were thinned out for the first time in thirty years and a public appeal was made to the nationalists in Taiwan to 'adopt reasonable policies and measures in settling the question of unification'.

This was a great diplomatic success. It simultaneously opened the way to closer relations with the United States, better relations with Japan (which now ratified a treaty of peace and friendship with China which contained a clause committing both countries to oppose 'hegemonism', the code-name for the ambition of the Soviet Union to dominate beyonds its borders) and the pursuit by China of a punitive policy towards Vietnam, which had expelled many of its ethnic Chinese inhabitants.

All this was part of an overt minimum programme. But Deng had a maximum programme as well. Its goals were to get the party to repudiate the ideology, policies and purges of the Cultural Revolution, to substitute development for class warfare as the highest order of business and to allow bold economic experiment. In due course it would emerge that Mao and the gang had been right to believe that Deng wanted to wipe the slate clean of the Cultural Revolution and to draw out the implications of his judgement in 1956 that antagonistic classes had ceased to exist in China. It would also emerge that he was not prepared to accept Hua Guofeng as either Mao's or Zhou's successor, certainly to the extent that he resisted Deng's programme and almost certainly at all.

To begin with, Deng moved cautiously. At the eleventh party congress, held a few weeks after his reinstatement in July 1977, he repeated his argument that an essential feature of Mao Zedong thought was to 'seek truth from facts' and avoided praise for the Cultural Revolution. But he did not explicitly attack the two whatevers, said that it was still necessary to 'grasp the key link of class struggle' and described Hua as 'our wise leader'. Nor did he comment adversely, except perhaps in the privacy of small meetings, on a grandiose ten-year plan for development which Hua presented to the National People's Congress in February 1978, though he must have known that it had been based on no rigorous matching of ends and means. During spring and summer, he continued to speak about the importance of seeking truth from facts, now arguing that this approach represented 'the fundamental principle' of Mao Zedong thought. It was not, however, until September 1978 that he first criticized the two whatevers to an audience outside the inner circle. By then, there had been an important change in the national political mood.

Deng was certainly responsible for this change constructively – simply by being who he was and being known to want a new start in politics. But it is not clear how far he took the initiative in promoting it. He must have talked about a new start to his intimates, grumbled to Ye Jianying and Li Xiannian about the two whatevers, and criticized Hua and his supporters over particular issues at politburo and standing committee meetings. He may well have gone further. Even if he did, much of the active work was done by his allies, including Hu Qiaomu, who had become president of the (newly established) Academy of Social Sciences in March 1978 and had promptly prepared a long critique of economic policy since 1950, and Hu Yaobang, who had worked closely with him in 1976 and was now director of the party's organization department.

Like the gang, the two Hus made maximum use of the press. In early May, Hu Yaobang arranged for the *Guangming Daily*, a newspaper for the intelligentsia, to publish a long article under the headline 'Practice is the Sole Criterion of Truth'. This led on to the publication of an editorial in the *People's Daily* which argued that theory should be governed by practice, and not vice versa. Hua Guofeng and Wang Dongxing were quick to spot the threat posed to their ideological position, and therefore their legitimacy as leaders, by these articles. But they were unable to prevent their wide republication or conferences called by party and military committees to discuss them.

By late summer of 1978, the press campaign had turned into a political movement. Wall-posters and handbills were calling for many kinds of ideological and political change, including the dismissal of Wu De, the mayor of Peking and the person most closely associated in the popular mind with hostility to Deng Xiaoping and the suppression of the demonstrations of April 1976. In this atmosphere, Deng himself proposed that party headquarters should convene a work conference, to prepare for a policy-making meeting of the central committee.

Deng was abroad when the work conference met on 10 November. He may have contrived to be absent. In any case, his absence helped him; if he had been present, he would have had to listen to strong criticism of his politburo colleagues and by extension of the collective leadership to which he belonged. As it was, he was able to keep out of sight until the time had come for the leader who was most in tune with the feeling of the meeting to sum up its conclusions.

Deng's speech on 13 December, the final day of the conference, was the speech of a man who had put prevarication behind him. After expressing keen satisfaction with the way in which 'lively debate' had revived the party's 'democratic tradition', and with the resolution of 'many major issues concerning the destinies of our party and state', he developed four themes. These were the need for all party members, and especially the more senior among them, to get away from dogma and 'book worship' in tackling problems; the need for the party to practise a greater degree of 'democracy', both in internal debate and in devolving responsibility for decision-making; its need to correct the wrongs done to the victims of the Cultural Revolution and to 'evaluate' Mao Zedong as a revolutionary leader and the Cultural Revolution itself; and the need for radical change in the fields of management style, management structure and economic policy. He dwelt on the importance of seeking truth from facts, linking this with an appeal for the 'emancipation of minds', and he referred (though only in passing) to the 'debate about the criterion for testing truth'.[9]

One important decision, to reverse the verdict on the Tiananmen incident of April 1976, was announced – by the Peking party committee – before the conference ended. The others were formalized during a short subsequent meeting of the central committee.

The most important were to reject the two whatevers, to make the four modernizations the 'focus of all party work' and to abandon class struggle as the 'key link'. Taken together, the second and third of these decisions are described in Deng's official biography as a 'fundamental rectification of the political line'. This is fair. They brought to an end an epoch of action to change the character of society which had lasted ever since Mao Zedong had decided in 1957 that 'socialist transformation' had not brought China's revolutionary era to an end.

Hua remained in all the posts he had held before. But Hua's most powerful supporter, Wang Dongxing, was dislodged as director of the general office of the central committee and replaced by Hu Yaobang in the re-created post of general secretary. Chen Yun, the *éminence grise*, became (once again) a member of the politburo standing committee and three of Deng's strongest supporters Deng Yingchao, Zhou Enlai's widow, Hu Yaobang and Wang Zhen were added to the politburo itself. The resolutions of the politburo on Deng's activities in 1975 and 1976 were formally rescinded. The process of rehabilitating dead victims of the Cultural Revolution was begun: the verdicts on Peng Dehuai, who had survived in prison almost until it was over, and Tao Zhu, who had died in exile after being persecuted with Deng and Liu Shaoqi in the Zhongnanhai in 1967, were reversed. Among the living, Peng Zhen and Bo Yibo were rehabilitated.

Like the central committee meeting of August 1966, at the beginning of the Cultural Revolution, the work conference took place against a background of popular agitation. But this new agitation was different in kind. The agitators were young factory and office workers and not students from middle schools and universities; they were acting spontaneously; and they were demanding political change which, in the lexicon of the party, was right rather than left. Like the Red Guards, they were opposed to party authority, but because they wanted more social and political freedom for the individual citizen and more pluralism in formal political life, and not because they liked militant populism.

The agitation began in mid-November, in the form of open-air meetings along a stretch of wall near the principal crossroads in western Peking. The wall, which soon came to be called Democracy Wall, was quickly covered from end to end with posters – at this time a form of expression explicitly permitted in the state constitution – which criticized Mao, the Gang of Four and a 'small group of highly placed people' who wanted no reversal of the verdict on the Tiananmen incident, and praised Zhou Enlai and Deng Xiaoping. As it became known that Hua Guofeng and his allies had come under attack at the work conference, and in the absence of intervention by the army or the police, the poster-writers became bolder and the crowds round the wall a good deal denser. By the end of November, debates about democracy and human rights had become a feature and the more adventurous spirits had begun to issue broadsheets and newspapers. After the turn of the year, the movement became more militant, involving sit-ins in government offices and hunger strikes, and spread to many other large cities. The tone of its publicity towards Deng became less friendly.

To begin with, Deng undoubtedly saw some merit in the agitation. It had its antecedents in the Tiananmen incident, which he was bound to regard as a revolutionary and not counter-revolutionary event, and in the movement to promote practice as the sole criterion of truth. It had made a hero of him and villains of his enemies. And he certainly believed that it was both right in principle and sound in practice for the party to remain sensitive to popular opinion. As time went by, however, he began to perceive dangers. One was that its tolerance could damage him politically. He was dependent on a group of victims of the Cultural Revolution for his strongest political support; and the members of this group, led by Chen Yun and Peng Zhen, were acutely suspicious of political action which was not under party management. Another was that the agitation could undermine general social discipline, which he saw as essential for progress towards modernization.

Deng did not act hastily. Indeed, he did not act at all until he had worked out a complete theory of the politics of modernization. Then, but only then, he made a speech which was as important as a political testament as his report to the eighth congress in 1956. It complemented his speech to the work conference in December and set out guidelines which have since become commandments. For this reason, and because it is characteristic of Deng the advocate at his best, it deserves quotation at some length.

Deng spoke at the end of March to a meeting of party theoretical workers. Having reviewed trends since the arrest of the Gang of Four, which he described as generally favourable, and discussed the difficulties which would make the achievement of the four modernizations a 'gigantic task', Deng said that he wanted to talk about ideology and politics. He then went straight to the heart of his message:

The Central Committee maintains that, to carry out China's four modernizations, we must uphold the four cardinal principles ideologically and politically. This is the basic prerequisite for achieving modernization. The four principles are:
1. We must keep to the socialist road.
2. We must uphold the dictatorship of the proletariat.
3. We must uphold the leadership of the Communist Party.
4. We must uphold Marxism–Leninism and Mao Zedong thought.

Deng continued that the four principles had 'long been upheld by our party' and that it was necessary to 'struggle unremittingly' against 'currents of thought which throw doubt on the four cardinal principles', whether of the ultra-left (as represented by Lin Biao and the Gang of Four) or of the right. He then turned to defend the principles against criticism from this second quarter, arguing for them one by one:

Some people are now openly saying that socialism is inferior to capitalism. We must demolish this contention. In the first place, socialism and socialism alone can save China – this is the unshakeable historical conclusion that the Chinese people have drawn from their own experience in the sixty years since the 4 May Movement [of 1919]. Deviate from socialism and China will inevitably retrogress to semi-feudalism and semi-colonialism. The overwhelming majority of the Chinese people will never allow such a retrogression. In the second place, although it is a fact that socialist China lags behind the developed capitalist countries in its economy, technology and culture, this is not due to the socialist system but basically to China's historical development before Liberation; it is the result of imperialism and feudalism. The socialist revolution has greatly narrowed the gap in economic development between China and the advanced capitalist countries.

On the dictatorship of the proletariat, Deng explained why this needed to continue in a socialist epoch:

We have conducted a lot of propaganda explaining that the dictatorship of the proletariat means socialist democracy for the people, democracy enjoyed by the workers, peasants, intellectuals and other working people, the broadest democracy that has ever existed in history . . .

. . . But we must recognize that in our socialist society there are still counter-revolutionaries, enemy agents, criminals and other bad elements of all kinds who undermine socialist public order, as well as new exploiters who engage in corruption, embezzlement, speculation and profiteering. And we must also recognize that such phenomena cannot all be eliminated for a long time to come. The struggle against these individuals is different from the struggle of one class against another, which occurred in the past (these individuals cannot form a cohesive and overt class). However, it is still a special form of class struggle or a special form of the leftover, under socialist conditions, of the class struggles of past history. It is still necessary to exercise dictatorship over all these anti-socialist elements, and socialist democracy is impossible without it. This dictatorship is an internal struggle and in some cases an international struggle as well; in fact, the two aspects are inseparable. Therefore, so long as class struggle exists and so long as imperialism and hegemonism exist, it is inconceivable that the dictatorial function of the state should wither away, that the standing army, public security organs, courts and prisons should wither away.

On party leadership, Deng argued that the alternative was anarchy:

Without the Chinese Communist Party, who would organize the socialist economy, politics, military affairs and culture of China, and who would organize the four modernizations? In the China of today we can never dispense with leadership by the Party and extol the spontaneity of the masses. Party leadership, of course, is not infallible, and the problem of how the Party can maintain close links with the masses and exercise correct and effective leadership is still one that we must seriously study and try to solve. But this can never be made a pretext for demanding the weakening or liquidation of the Party's leadership. Our Party has made many errors, but each time the errors were corrected by relying on the Party organization, not by discarding it. The present Central Committee is persistent in promoting democracy in the Party and among the people and is determined to correct past errors. In these circumstances, it would be all the more intolerable to the masses of our people to demand the liquidation or even the weakening of leadership by the Party. In fact, bowing to this demand would only lead to anarchism and the disruption and ruin of the socialist cause.

In his passage about Marxism–Leninism and Mao Zedong thought, Deng drew two distinctions – between Mao the man and his thought, and between his thought as the ideas of one man and the wisdom of the Chinese communist movement as a whole – which were soon to become part of the party's official interpretation of history:

Was it not Mao Zedong thought which enabled the Chinese people – about a quarter of the world's population – to find the correct road for their revolution, achieve nationwide liberation in 1949, and basically accomplish socialist transformation by 1956? This succession of splendid victories changed not only China's destiny but the world situation as well . . .

. . . Comrade Mao, like any other man, had his defects and made errors. But how can these errors in his illustrious life be put on a par with his immortal contributions to the people? In analysing his defects and errors, we certainly should recognize his personal responsibility, but what is more important is to analyse their complicated historical background. That is the only just and scientific – that is, Marxist – way to assess history and historical figures. Anyone who departs from Marxism on so serious a question will be censured by the Party and the masses . . .

. . . The cause and the thought of Comrade Mao Zedong are not his alone: they are likewise those of his comrades-in-arms, the Party and the people. His thought is the crystallization of the experience of the Chinese people's revolutionary struggle over half a century.[9]

Action against the democracy movement followed very quickly. On 2 April, the municipal authorities in Peking banned many of its forms of activity and on the following day its best-known spokesman, Wei Jingsheng, was arrested. Six months later he was put on trial and sentenced to a prison term of fifteen years.

The most recent official history of the party, published in August 1991, states that Deng Xiaoping became the 'kernel' of the party's leadership at the central committee meeting of December 1978. But this may not have seemed to be the case either to Deng himself or to colleagues, in the spring of 1979.

According to one source, Deng by no means had things his own way at a bad-tempered meeting of the politburo in March. He found himself in a minority when he argued that the party should be cautious in reacting to the democracy movement and under criticism for the losses the army had suffered during its recent invasion of Vietnam (these had indeed been severe). It is possible that he moved as quickly as he then did to lay down the four cardinal principles precisely because he sensed that Hua Guofeng and his supporters could use the movement as a rod for his back. This is not to suggest that he did not mean what he said – only that the timing of his speech and its tone were influenced by the exigencies of inner-party struggle.

Whether or not this is right, Hua and the rest of the whatever faction had been forced back on to the defensive by the autumn of 1979. A principal reason was that Hua's ten-year development plan had by then been shown to be the stuff of dreams. It had stipulated a more than fourfold increase in oil production, but from fields which remained to be discovered, and a twofold increase in steel output, which could only be achieved by importing equipment on a scale far beyond China's means. A huge surge in investment, especially in heavy industry, had led to rapid inflation and to renewed pressure on the countryside to supply more grain to the cities. Chen Yun, chairman of a re-created financial and economic commission, presided over a three-week work conference which shelved the plan and substituted a strategy of 'readjustment, restructuring, consolidation and improvement'. History thus repeated itself. The Great Leap Forward had been followed by 'readjustment, consolidation, filling out and raising standards'; Hua's great leap outward, as it came to be called, was followed by an almost identical programme. And it was Chen who had presided over both reversals.

Deng left most of the running at the conference to others. He was wholly committed to the four modernizations and believed as strongly as Chen Yun that Hua's plan would be counter-productive. But his priority now was to use policy rather than make it. Acting deliberately, but without any relaxation of pressure, he achieved some of what he wanted at a central committee meeting in September and the rest at another in March 1980. By the time the second meeting was over, Hua's four principal supporters in the politburo, including Wang Dongxing and Wu De, had been voted off that body and Hu Yaobang had become general secretary, at the head of a secretariat which consisted almost entirely of men on whose loyalty Deng could rely.

During 1980, Deng extended his sapping and mining to the government and to Hua himself. His tactic was to propose that party veterans, himself included, should resign from their posts and be replaced in them by younger men. Hua may have put up some resistance. If so, it was rapidly overcome. It was the politburo which made decisions about senior government appointments and Hua was now isolated there. In August, he was forced to resign as premier, thus losing the first of the three posts he had won in 1976.

In name, Hua stayed on as chairman of the central committee and the military commission until June 1981. But it was only in name. In November and December 1980, he was attacked, on grounds of principle, policy and public behaviour, at a series of nine politburo meetings and – his spirit finally crushed – asked to be relieved of his party posts. No one demurred and it was agreed that Hu Yaobang and Deng Xiaoping should occupy the posts de facto until the central committee could accept his resignations. For reasons which are not clear, the committee did not meet for another seven months. Only then did the great majority of Chinese, and the world at large, learn that Mao's designated successor had been ousted. In a short coda to his political career, Hua remained a vice-chairman of the party until September 1982. But then, following the path taken by Wang Ming and Bo Gu thirty-seven years before, he sank to simple membership of the central committee. He disappeared from sight and his name ceased to appear in the press.

What is one to make of Deng Xiaoping's behaviour towards Hua Guofeng? Did he betray Hua, as Dr Harry Harding, who has made a thorough study of the politics of the period, has judged?[10] Or was he in any way justified in moving against Hua as he did?

Formally, the case against Deng rests on the unqualified professions of support for Hua in his letters of October 1976 and April 1977, and on the admission of error in 1975 in his second letter, which implied that he would not attempt to promote under Hua the policies for which Mao had criticized him then. The case for him relies on one main point: that he made it quite clear before Hua agreed to his reinstatement that he could not, and would not, accept the two whatevers. In politics, however, the formal position cannot be the whole of the picture.

In another phrase of Dr Harding's, Deng was a man with a mission,[11] set on rescuing the party and the nation from the influence of thinking which had already done them enormous damage. He was also a man who had been general secretary of the party at a time when Hua was a county party official and who was seen by most of his peers as the leader the country needed. And, if far from fastidious, his methods were a model by comparison with those which had prevailed in inner-party struggle since Peng Dehuai's disgrace in 1957. He did not prompt the press to attack Hua personally, in the way which Hua had allowed it to attack him in 1976. Nor, once he had won his battle, did he insist that Hua should make a self-examination of the kind Peng, Liu and he (among many others) had been forced to make by Mao.

All the same, the way in which Deng's letters to Hua of October 1976 and April 1977 are covered in his selected works (the first is only referred to and the account of the second is incomplete) suggests that Deng himself feels he has something to hide.

In facing up to the past, the other chief events of 1980 and 1981 were the posthumous rehabilitation of Liu Shaoqi, the trial of the Gang of Four and the adoption by the central committee of a resolution which dealt head on with the linked issues of Mao Zedong's political record, the character of Mao Zedong thought and the nature of the Cultural Revolution.

Liu Shaoqi had not been a particularly popular figure, in the party or outside. Although he had been the political commissar of the new fourth army for a time during the war against Japan, he was not regarded by many party members in the 1960s as someone well qualified to succeed Mao as chairman of the military commission, and there were some who doubted whether he would make a good chairman of the central committee. The way in which he had been treated during the Cultural Revolution was regretted rather than mourned by many of its other victims. His case, too, was sensitive in a way which the cases of, for example, Peng Dehuai (who had died) and Peng Zhen (who had survived) were not. The two Pengs could be rehabilitated without total repudiation of the Cultural Revolution or direct condemnation of Mao's role in launching it. But because of Liu's seniority, and the formal manner in which he had been expelled from the party as a 'renegade, hidden traitor and scab', Liu could not.

Deng wanted Liu to be rehabilitated precisely because he wanted to bury the Cultural Revolution. He was ready to face up to the consequences in terms of Mao's record and reputation, and he must in any case have been conscious that his own total rehabilitation would have been incomplete without Liu's to complement it. But it was not until March 1980 that he was able to get the central committee to resolve that all the charges brought against Liu had been false, and not until the following May that he could arrange a formal ceremony of rehabilitation. Hua Guofeng certainly resisted the annulment of the case against Liu, and so it seems did several senior military figures, perhaps including Ye Jianying. One consequence of these moves was that Liu's widow, Wang Guangmei, who had spent nearly ten years in prison, again began to appear in public. A woman of great intelligence and charm, her presence at official occasions seemed to herald the arrival of a less drab as well as a less frightening epoch.

The trial of the Gang of Four – and also of Chen Boda and the survivors among Lin Biao's senior supporters – was an innovation in the political practice of the party. Stalin had put his political opponents on trial, and many communist leaders in Eastern Europe had followed his example. But Mao had never sought to represent 'anti-party' or 'counter-revolutionary' activity on the part of his opponents as activity against the state, to be judged in the courts. This, perhaps, was because the party loomed so much larger for him than the state. Or it may have been because he sensed the intellectual difficulty in creating a single category of counter-revolutionary crime to cover activities as unalike as murder and robbery and inner-party conspiracy. Deng, however, did not suffer from these, or other, inhibitions. Indeed, it was very much part of his purpose to establish a clear distinction between the 'errors' committed by Mao and the 'crimes' of the gang and Lin Biao's supporters.

The trial was held from late November 1980 to late January 1981, in a former palace owned by the ministry of public security. It was a foregone conclusion that the ten defendants would be found guilty and sentenced. Only the course of proceedings and the severity of the sentences – and perhaps not even the latter –

were open. Among the accused, only Jiang Qing attempted to defend herself. Zhang Chunqiao refused to speak and the other eight spoke only to admit guilt or ascribe it to their co-defendants. Jiang Qing's principal arguments were that she had only done what Mao had wanted her to do ('I was chairman Mao's dog'), that many of her judges had been as active as herself in working to bring down Liu Shaoqi and that the law had necessarily been in suspense in a time of revolution. She succeeded in creating uproar in the court and reluctant admiration for her spirit among many who watched the trial on television. It did, however, emerge from documentary and oral evidence that many thousands had died violent deaths as the result of the gang's activities and that Jiang Qing had behaved with relentless malevolence towards all those who knew things to her moral or political discredit.

Jiang Qing and Zhang Chunqiao were given suspended death sentences (commuted two years later, when the probationary term expired, to prison sentences for life). The other defendants were all sentenced to long terms in prison, though the periods for which they had been held as prisoners before trial were set off against the amount of time they would have to stay behind bars. Chen Boda and Lin Biao's other supporters were released during the 1980s, though none of them was ever seen in public again.

It is doubtful whether Deng was altogether satisfied. Jiang Qing had rejected the existence of a distinction between her 'crimes' and Mao's 'errors', and had not been answered effectively by her judges. She had also made the whole process smell of victor's justice and personal revenge. Deng seldom referred to the trial in later talks and speeches and he must have had its course and consequences in mind when he argued in 1989 that Zhao Ziyang, disgraced as general secretary after the crushing of the democracy movement of that year, should not be put on trial.

The resolution on party history was more effective as an instrument of judgement. Prepared by a group under Hu Qiaomu, it went through several versions before Deng was finally satisfied with its length, balance and conclusions. He spoke on at least nine occasions to Hu and his colleagues or to other groups about successive drafts, concentrating above all on their assessment of Mao Zedong as a revolutionary leader. The final text is striking for its clarity, its internal consistency and the careful shading of many of its judgements. It is as easy to read as the most spirited of Mao's essays and speeches.

The earlier sections told the whole history of the Chinese communist movement from 1921 to 1979. Its central section dealt with Mao's place in history and the nature of his thought. Two of the key passages were these:

Comrade Mao Zedong was a great Marxist and a great proletarian revolutionary, strategist and theorist. It is true that he made gross mistakes during the 'cultural revolution', but if we judge his activities as a whole, his contributions to the Chinese revolution far outweigh his mistakes. His merits are primary and his errors secondary. He rendered indelible meritorious service in founding and building up our Party and the Chinese People's Liberation Army, in winning victory for the cause of liberation of the Chinese people, in founding the People's Republic of China and in advancing our socialist cause. He made major contributions to the liberation of the oppressed nations of the world and to the progress of mankind . . .

. . . Mao Zedong thought is Marxism–Leninism applied and developed in China; it constitutes a correct theory, a body of correct principles and a summary of the experiences that have been confirmed in the practice of the Chinese revolution, a crystallization of the collective wisdom of the Chinese Communist Party. Many outstanding leaders of our party made important contributions to the formation and development of Mao Zedong thought, and they are synthesized in the scientific works of comrade Mao Zedong.

The resolution was quite categorical about the Cultural Revolution: 'The "cultural revolution", which lasted from May 1966 to October 1976, was responsible for the most severe set-back and the heaviest losses suffered by the party, the state and the people since the founding of the People's Republic.' Nor did it beat about the bush in ascribing responsibility for the Cultural Revolution to

Mao personally, stating that it was 'initiated and led by comrade Mao Zedong' and that 'chief responsibility for the grave "left" error of the "cultural revolution", an error comprehensive in magnitude and protracted in duration, does indeed lie with comrade Mao Zedong'. It was, however, very careful to distinguish this 'error', whose sources it examined, from the plotting and 'sabotage' of the 'counter-revolutionary Lin Biao and Jiang Qing cliques'. It also projected Mao as a tragic figure, a victim of his own illusions and mistakes, and Zhou Enlai as another:

Comrade Zhou Enlai was utterly devoted to the party and the people and stuck to his post till his dying day. He found himself in an extremely difficult situation throughout the 'cultural revolution'. He always kept the general interest in mind, bore the heavy burden of office without complaint, racking his brains and untiringly endeavouring to keep the normal work of the Party and the state going, to minimize the damage caused by the 'cultural revolution' and to protect many Party and non-Party cadres. He waged all forms of struggle to counter sabotage by the counter-revolutionary Lin Biao and Jiang Qing cliques. His death left the whole Party and people in the most profound grief.[12]

The resolution begs many questions – above all why the rest of the party leadership was unable to stop Mao from launching the Cultural Revolution (though its responsibility for failing to do so is acknowledged) – and it says nothing about the famine which followed the Great Leap Forward. But it was at least as successful as the resolution on party history of 1945 in putting an end to party controversy about the past and in providing an interpretation of history with which the party could live comfortably. It has not proved an embarrassment since, and there are probably very few judgements in it which any of the party's present leaders would want to alter.

CHAPTER 13

National Leader, 1981–4

At no time during the 1980s could there be any doubt, either in China or abroad, that Deng Xiaoping was China's national leader. Yet he did not owe this status to his rank. He was not chairman or general secretary of the central committee or head of the government. Nor did he become president of the People's Republic when that office, replacing the chairmanship which Liu Shaoqi had once held, was created in 1983. He owed his status to his authority; and he owed his authority to his record, his qualities as a leader and, as time went by, his success as a policy-maker and as a spokesman and champion of his country.

At the end of the Cultural Revolution, Deng and Chen Yun were the only survivors of the group of seven which had made up the standing committee of the politburo from 1958 to 1966. Chen had been Deng's senior during that period (and for long before). But Chen lacked his credentials as a man who had struggled against Chen Boda and Kang Sheng during the early months of the Cultural Revolution or fought against the Gang of Four in 1975; and Chen had tended to shun the limelight, preferring to exercise influence by arguing behind closed doors, so that he was much less well known in the country at large. Among the other senior members of the party who had lived through the Cultural Revolution, Peng Zhen, Ye Jianying and Li Xiannian were men of consequence. But they all lacked Deng's battle honours and his variety of experience. Besides, Ye was seven years older than Deng, and both he and Li would have put themselves in conspicuously false positions if they had been seen to oppose Hua Guofeng after promising him unqualified support before the arrest of the gang.

Deng's style as a leader was quite unlike Mao's. Where Mao had stood aloof from his colleagues, he kept in touch with them. Where Mao had dissembled, he made his views as clear as possible. And where Mao had often dealt in abstractions, he was always concrete, even when expounding a principle. Yet his qualities as a leader went a long way beyond matters of style. He was both a man of vision and a man of action. He had, and could project, a picture of the future he wanted for China; and he much preferred to act than to wait and see when he perceived a problem taking shape before him. In his treatment of people, he was strong but not brutal. He did not organize a press campaign to destroy the whole reputation of Hua Guofeng once judgement had been passed on him by the politburo, let alone imprison him. When he insisted at the beginning of 1987 that Hu Yaobang should resign as general secretary, he allowed Hu to stay on as a member of the politburo standing committee. Conversely, he did not shrink from disciplining senior party members who had helped him in the dark days of 1976. He forced the dismissal of Wei Guoqing as director of the general political department of the army in 1982, after Wei had prompted, or tolerated, the appearance of an article in the official army newspaper which attacked 'some responsible comrades in cultural fields', and he arranged for Xu Shiyou to be dropped from the politburo after the latter had made clear his disapproval of the rehabilitation of Liu Shaoqi.

Unlike both Mao and Hua, Deng strongly discouraged the development of a cult of his own personality. Here he practised what he had consistently preached from 1956 onwards. He permitted, almost certainly encouraged, the publication of many of his speeches and statements in successive volumes of his selected works, and he allowed specialist and provincial publishing houses to issue additional texts and accounts of his military career. But he did not allow his portrait to be shown in public places or statues of himself to be put up anywhere. Nor did he allow hyperbole in written or spoken references to himself. He was always described as 'chairman Deng Xiaoping' or 'comrade Deng Xiaoping' and never as 'our wise leader', like Hua, let alone as a man with exceptional attributes as a prophet, teacher or guide, like Mao.

*

As a policy-maker, Deng had two particular strengths: he took the long view and he laid it down that all plans and proposals should be tested for feasibility. In taking the long view, he was in both the Leninist tradition and the tradition of Chinese statecraft. He was also in the mould of Mao during the first half of his career. In the 1930s, Mao had preached the need for the party and the army to see themselves as engaged in 'protracted war' against the nationalists and then the Japanese. Deng went even further. He set dates for the attainment of particular political and economic objectives which were in some cases likely and in others certain to be beyond the end of his own lifetime. He was willing to set 1997 as the target date for the transfer of government in Hong Kong from Britain to China, and he related the economic targets he set for the party and government to dates at the end of the twentieth century and the middle of the following one. He could of course afford to take a longer view than political leaders in countries with multiparty systems. But he was not bound to do so; many communist leaders did not look so far ahead. The test of feasibility was all of a piece with his attachment to the slogans he had used against Hua Guofeng: 'Seek truth from facts' and 'Practice is the sole criterion of truth'. Neither slogan meant that he had abandoned socialism. They meant only that he saw socialism (and communism) as being associated with prosperity – as had Marx – that he was ready to try a wide variety of means in the quest for prosperity, and that he was not prepared to leave method to men who worked out blueprints in their offices without reference to social or economic facts. Only in this sense was he the pragmatist he was called by a host of non-communist writers.

To a far greater extent than Mao, Deng came to owe his authority to his activities in relation to the rest of the world. In 1978, the year when his posture towards Hua Guofeng changed from wary surveillance to open challenge, he travelled abroad a good deal. He visited Burma and Nepal during the late winter, and Thailand, Malaysia and Singapore in November. He also visited Korea. In January 1979, he spent a week in the United States. While there, he demonstrated a considerable talent for public relations – for instance, by being perfectly willing to wear a ten-gallon hat at a rodeo in Texas – and achieved a very good press. At the end of the year, he went to Japan and again did well as a smiling ambassador.

After that, Deng stayed at home. But he devoted a great deal of time to receiving foreign visitors. He met visiting heads of state and heads of government as a matter of course. Yet he also received foreign politicians who were no longer in office, such as Nixon, Kissinger and Edward Heath, giving them as much time as he would have done before. In talking to his visitors, it was his method to draw them out about their own interests, but to make sure that he had time to put two or three key points to them. These points often went beyond anything he had so far said at home. Most of his visitors came away impressed by his candour and ease of manner. Some spoke of his wisdom.

During these conversations, Deng returned again and again to three themes. The first was that the turmoil of the Cultural Revolution was a thing of the past and would not recur. Another was that China wanted international peace, for the sake of its own development, and would work for its preservation. The third was that, however much China might need to learn from the rest of the world, it was determined to maintain its political and economic independence. It would never yield to external pressure or allow itself to be put in situations where it would become vulnerable to such pressure.

By making himself popular abroad, Deng made himself more popular at home. The perception grew that he had put China on the map internationally and brought it renown. He was also admired for having made progress, where Mao had made none, in the cause of national reunification (of which more below).

China was ruled during the 1980s by a leadership with two quite distinct components: a group of veteran revolutionaries who saw themselves as having the right to oversee policy-making; and a smaller group of younger men (though only by half a generation) who had been chosen by Deng for the most important executive posts. From 1982 to 1985, the politburo resembled the board of a company with a majority of non-executive directors. From 1985 onwards, this balance was reversed. But the number of non-executive directors remained high; and at the level of the standing committee they were in the majority all the way down to 1987.

Among the veterans, the men who mattered most were Chen Yun, Peng Zhen, Li Xiannian and Wang Zhen. Born in 1905 in the suburbs of Shanghai, and a typesetter by trade, Chen had joined the party in the same year (1924) as Deng. He became a member of the politburo in 1934, twenty-one years before Deng, and except during the Cultural Revolution had been right at the top from then on. During the 1980s, when the texts of many of his reports in the 1950s and 1960s were published, his degree of originality as an economic policy-maker became clear. But he was not simply an economist. He also had strong – and strongly Leninist – views about the role of the party in the state and about party discipline. Nor did he always avoid a prominent political role. In 1977, and again in 1978, it was he who took the lead in demanding at work conferences that the verdicts and policies of the Cultural Revolution should be reversed.

Chen looks lugubrious in photographs taken of him as an old man. For years it has been rumoured that his health is poor and that he lives for most of the year in the south. But he was not lugubrious, or even dour, in middle age. He often smiled and had a striking gift of phrase. In the 1950s, he compared socialist planning and the functioning of the market to a cage and a bird; if the cage was too small, the bird would die; if, on the other hand, it was removed, the bird would fly away. In 1959 he compared the national economy to a 'single chequerboard', a metaphor which showed he understood that the capacity of the national economy would be greater if each region concentrated on producing what it could produce most efficiently. In 1978, at the work conference which effectively buried Hua Guofeng's 'two whatevers' he pronounced a verdict on Mao which probably summed up the feelings of the whole of his generation:

Had chairman Mao died in 1956, there would have been no doubt that he was a great leader of the Chinese people . . . Had he died in 1966, his meritorious achievements would have been somewhat tarnished. However, his achievements were still very good. Since he actually died in 1976, there is nothing we can do about it.[1]

During the 1980s, Chen was assiduous about attending meetings of the central committee and of the central discipline inspection commission, created in 1982, of which he was chairman. As time went by, he came to be associated with a cautious approach to structural economic change, macroeconomic policy (he set great store by the control of inflation and the preservation of balance in the national budget) and social and cultural liberalization. Yet it would be wrong to see him as an opponent of the big changes of the time, such as the decollectivization of agriculture. He represented what had been mainstream party opinion, even if the total defeat of the extreme and then of the less-extreme left after Mao's death made it seem that he stood on the left. He was so senior and so closely associated with policies which Deng had favoured that, friendship apart, Deng was bound to listen to him.

With his domed head, large mouth and high colour, Peng Zhen would have been conspicuous anywhere. As in the early 1960s, he worked closely with Deng in the 1980s. To begin with, he was much more than an adviser, taking general charge within the party of security and legal work, his portfolio of twenty years before. Later, he became chairman of the standing committee of the national people's congress and so China's senior parliamentary figure. There is no sign that he bore Deng a grudge for the way in which Deng, his chief, had joined his accusers in 1966 or that he pressed for a seat on the politburo standing committee, as he would have been well entitled to do. For all his seniority, he remains a rather indistinct figure politically. He is not known for any firmly held views. Perhaps he is less a leader than the permanently efficient party servant, even if he was a lot braver than most in standing up to Mao during the months which led to the Cultural Revolution.

There was nothing indistinct about Li Xiannian or Wang Zhen. Both were tough, and tough-minded, old soldiers. As president of the People's Republic, Li met many foreigners during the 1980s, and on the whole impressed them by his bluff good nature and willingness to talk to them bluntly about China's problems. 'Under collectivization', he told one visitor, 'the peasants simply downed tools and turned their bottoms to the sun.'[2] Deng and Li had fought together in the Dabie mountains in 1948 and had been together in the party secretariat from 1958 to 1966. Yet they never seem to have been more than good colleagues. Wang, on the other hand, became one of Deng's intimates. He had lobbied strongly for Deng's rehabilitation, in 1972 and again in 1977, and Deng was therefore in his debt. But this cannot account by itself for the frequency with which Wang now appeared at Deng's elbow in public, in Peking but also on tours of inspection in the provinces. Li's health deteriorated during the second half of the 1980s and he became a deal less active politically after he had been replaced as head of state by Yang Shangkun in 1987. Wang, a vice-president of the People's Republic, continued to be influential. In 1989, the leaders of the democracy movement regarded him as one of their two or three principal enemies.

Executive responsibility was chiefly in the hands of two men. The better-known until the mid-1980s was Hu Yaobang, who was chairman of the party – replacing Hua Guofeng – for just over a year until September 1982, when the post was abolished, and then its general secretary. A tiny man, shorter even than Deng and a good deal slimmer, he was full of animation and, in a manner unusual for a Chinese, gestured a lot as he spoke. His revolutionary credentials were impeccable. He had joined Mao Zedong's ragged band on Jinggangshan at the age of fourteen and had made the Long March, during which he was wounded by bomb splinters, as secretary of the Young Communist League. A political officer in the eighth route army during the war against Japan, he served under Deng in that capacity during the civil war. He was transferred to Peking from Sichuan at about the same time as

Deng and then became general secretary of the organizations which succeeded the Young Communist League as training grounds for the party. He lost his post at the beginning of the Cultural Revolution and was sent to work in a commune. But he returned to Peking in time to become one of Deng's principal assistants in 1975. No later than 1978, Deng earmarked him to be his own successor as the party's chief executive.

Deng's choice turned out not to be a shrewd one. Hu was industrious and articulate, but also tactless and impetuous. He lacked gravity and also an instinct for caution in dealing with the party veterans. In 1985, the *People's Daily* had to publish an official correction of a statement in which he had said that Marx, a nineteenth-century thinker, had said nothing to help China solve its late-twentieth-century problems, and he embarrassed the other Chinese in his party by quoting Shelley instead of Shakespeare during a visit to Stratford-upon-Avon in 1986. He drew fire, too, for failing to visit Marx's grave in Highgate cemetery in that year. It was natural for Deng to look for a general secretary who was not a veteran; but it is puzzling that he made his choice so early, apparently without thinking hard about the claims of men in their sixties who had done well as provincial leaders or central administrators before the Cultural Revolution. Perhaps he allowed himself to be swayed too much by Hu's self-confidence and energy.

The second man was Zhao Ziyang. Born in 1919 into a land-owning family in the central province of Henan, Zhao was fifteen years younger than Deng and five years younger than Hu. He had had a good secondary education and had joined the party in 1938. By 1961, he had become the (very young) secretary of the Guangdong provincial party committee and had gained a reputation for sympathizing more with the peasants than their taskmasters in the communes. Disgraced at the beginning of the Cultural Revolution, and made to walk through the streets of Canton in a dunce's hat, he was restored to office in the early 1970s, and was one of those who protected Deng in the south in

1976. As governor of Sichuan during the next two years, he experimented in systems which allowed both factories and farms to keep or sell freely everything they produced above predetermined levels of output. He was brought to Peking and appointed premier in September 1980, to fill the vacancy created by the resignation of Hua Guofeng.

Like Hu, Zhao in the end lost Deng's confidence. But his record as premier for rather more than six years was good. He was effective both as an administrator and as a quiet, but always collected and dignified, representative of his country.

In September 1982, at the twelfth party congress, Deng set the party a three-point agenda for the 1980s: to accelerate 'socialist modernization'; to 'strive for' China's reunification; and to 'oppose hegemonism and work to safeguard world peace'. He added four domestic objectives, on a time-scale extending to the end of the century: to 'restructure the administration and the economy'; to 'build a socialist civilization which is culturally and ideologically advanced'; to crack down on crime; and to 'rectify the party's style of work'. In his political report, Hu Yaobang expanded on these themes. In particular, he set the quadrupling by the year 2000 of the 1980 value of industrial and agricultural output as a development target, and declared that China would never 'attach itself to any big power or group of powers', or 'yield to pressure from any big power'.

China's political history during the four following years is the history of action on the three points and four objectives. Deng's own general role was to guide and supervise. He also took on two particular tasks: to explain what China was trying to achieve, and how, to foreigners, and to give ideological cover to the constantly changing patterns of experiment under the headings of 'socialist modernization' and action to 'restructure the administration and the economy', which soon became subsumed under the wider heading of 'reform'.

In this second task, Deng's first step had been to set 'socialist modernization' as China's goal of goals. His next move, which he made in 1982, was to introduce the concept of 'socialism with Chinese characteristics', which he justified in terms of the need to 'proceed from Chinese realities' and described as a requirement for the country and party 'to blaze a path of our own'. The appeal to patriotism was characteristic and very clear. His third step, which he took in 1983, was to bring in the concept of reform, which opened longer and wider vistas than the notion of restructuring of which he (and others) had spoken until then. Finally, he developed a full theory of reform, to cover political as well as economic reform and to relate the two. In this, he made political reform dependent on economic reform, which was consistent with the classical Marxist scheme of independent economic base and dependent political and cultural superstructure, but contradicted Mao's scheme during the last twenty years of his life. All through, he was careful to describe the characteristics of socialism – he never ventured a full definition – in terms consistent with basic Marxist propositions. This was essential in a situation where many party members were uneasy about the ideological soundness of Deng's programme and troubled by the frequent claims by foreigners that he was leading China towards capitalism.

In practice, reform had got under way well before Deng developed his theory about it. In the countryside, much had been done even before 1982, when he began to speak of building socialism with Chinese characteristics. In particular, the government had raised its procurement prices for agricultural products and frozen the national procurement quotas for each product; and, even more important, it had returned to the peasants the right to cultivate the land as families. The land remained in collective ownership, but it was parcelled out for family use, under arrangements which gave each family the right to occupy and cultivate its holding for a long period of time, in return for undertakings to pay taxes to the state and fees to the collective (usually the production brigade) and to supply a share of the output quotas imposed on the collective. Families were free to dispose of all above-quota output as they wished – by selling it to the government at a price above the price for quota output, by selling it in local markets or by consuming it themselves. The nationwide introduction of this system, known as the 'household responsibility system', produced a situation which differed both from the situation which had existed after land reform in the early 1950s and from the one created by collectivization. In theory, only the use of the land was decollectivized. In fact, the guarantee of long-term occupancy (up to forty years in the end) encouraged the peasants to regard the land as their own.

A second wave of reform took place from 1983 to 1985. In 1983, the household responsibility system was declared to be the national norm (though there were areas in which some of the peasants preferred to stick to collective labour and equalized reward), and in 1984 it was stipulated that the existing pattern of land allocation would remain unchanged for at least fifteen years. In 1985, the old system of quota procurement for all agricultural crops was replaced by a system under which the government set national targets for the purchase of a much smaller number of crops and then negotiated contracts with families to supply amounts satisfactory to both parties. For the peasants, the greatest advantage of the new system was that it allowed them to shift into the production of crops which brought them higher incomes than grain production. They faced no greater risks than under the old (intermediate) system, because the government still promised to buy all 'surplus' output – output above the amounts sold to it under contract or disposed of in local markets – and to do so at or above fixed floor prices.

The impact of these reforms on agricultural output, and on the income and morale of the peasants, was enormous. From 1978 to 1984, the output of grain per head of the (total) population grew by an average of 3.8 per cent per year (compared with 0.2 per cent between 1957 and 1977), the output of cotton by 17.5 per cent compared with a fall of 0.6 per cent) and the output of meat by 9.0 per cent (compared with 1.7 per cent). Rural consumption per head, having grown by only a third between 1965 and 1978, almost trebled between 1978 and 1986. By the mid-1980s, villages all over China were full of stacks of brick, piles of sand and bags of cement bought by their inhabitants to build new houses, and many peasant families had bought bicycles and radios. In less than ten years, much of rural China had been lifted from a condition of deep, and seemingly endemic, poverty to one of modest prosperity, in which many farmers were producing four or five times as much as they needed to feed their families.

Industrial and commercial reform and reform of planning and pricing followed rather than preceded the twelfth party congress. A code for all three was set out in a long central-committee resolution adopted in October 1984. Because its text had been hammered out between reformers who wanted to move decisively away from the Soviet model and others who, to use Chen Yun's metaphor, wanted to give the bird in the cage more freedom but to keep it firmly inside, it was full of ambiguities. But it set an agenda which held until 1992.

The core of industrial and commercial reform was a set of measures to give wider powers to the managers of factories and trading corporations, in relation to staffing, procurement and marketing. The two principal elements in the reform of planning were to restrict the scope of mandatory planning, substituting either indicative planning or complete freedom from planning, and to devolve many powers within the new framework from the central government to provincial governments. The key element in price reform was to create three price categories: fixed prices, prices which were free to fluctuate within limits, and uncontrolled prices. Quite soon, a single commodity often came to be priced in two (or even three) of these ways. The combined effect of the three types of reform was to create large numbers of new markets, black as well as white, to stimulate enterprise but also corruption, and to reduce the ability of the central government to control the composition and circulation of industrial output and the functioning of the national economy. Some provinces began to use their new planning powers to work towards provincial self-sufficiency in important industrial lines, restricting interprovincial exports and imports and spending money on the development of industries whose products were almost certain to be more expensive than those acquired from well-established sources elsewhere. Some factories began to sell their output to new users, so that traditional users found themselves short of essential supplies. Because the national budget tended to be in deficit and (even more) because the degree of control exercised by the ministry of finance and the central bank over credit creation was weak, inflation began to be a serious problem for the first time since the 1950s. Output rose rapidly, but so did the price level. And the balance of payments on current account, which had been healthy until 1984, went into serious deficit in 1985 and 1986.

Deng did not play a large part in framing measures. He proposed the creation of special economic zones, in which foreign investment would be allowed on concessionary terms, in 1979, and remained attached to the concept thereafter. Otherwise, however, he left almost all the work to others. He explained why in a speech to a symposium on China's economic relations with foreign countries in October 1984: 'I am a layman in the field of economics. I have made a few remarks on the subject, but all from a political point of view. For example, I proposed China's economic policy of opening to the outside world, but as for the details or specifics of how to implement it, I know very little indeed.'[3]

Political reform was a different matter. Here Deng was no layman; and here he alone had the authority to propose far-reaching change.

Deng's interest in political reform went through three phases. During the first phase, from 1978 to 1982, his chief concern was to restore the institutional patterns which had existed during the mid-1950s, but whose functioning had been disrupted during the Great Leap Forward and again during the Cultural Revolution. This entailed redefining the roles of the party, the army and the government, in a manner which limited the roles of the first two and enlarged the role of the last. It also entailed reviving the united front between the Communist Party and the eight lesser parties which had rallied to its support in 1949, restoring the legislative role of the National People's Congress and introducing and propagating the concept of the rule of law. Socially, it entailed the removal of discriminatory class and political labels from several million people. Former landlords and capitalists ceased to be described as such and became citizens. So did large numbers of 'rightists' and 'capitalist-roaders', including some who had worn their 'hats' for over twenty years. It also entailed the withdrawal of the party and the security apparatus of the government, which had worked through a mass of police informers, from many areas of life in which they had been intrusive. Private life had more or less disappeared in the cities during the Cultural Revolution. It now came into being again. Hobbies which had been condemned as 'bourgeois', such as stamp-collecting and flower-arranging, were allowed to flourish again; and the ordinary citizen could be reasonably sure of staying out of mischief if he did nothing which could be seen as a challenge to authority.

During the second phase, from 1982 to 1986, Deng was chiefly interested in rejuvenating all the institutions of the state. The central committee elected in 1982 contained quite a few men and women who were neither veterans nor radicals. But it had gone on to elect a politburo whose twenty-eight members were almost all in their seventies and among whom eighteen had taken part in the Long March, nearly fifty years before. As it was in Deng's scheme that the politburo should function as a policy-setting and ratifying body, he was forced to argue with people who tended to look back rather than forward and were in any case not responsible for implementing whatever policies they approved. He therefore spent a good deal of time and energy in 1984 and 1985 on an effort to cajole the majority of his elderly associates to resign. In the end, he was successful and the politburo became once again what it had been in the early 1950s: a committee of people who were either elders of exceptional distinction, like Chen Yun, or executive chiefs. The retired veterans joined the central advisory commission, a body which had been set up as a home for them in 1982.

In the party at large, Deng encouraged the wholesale retirement of the elderly. In 1984, about two million party members who had become officials before 1949 were still in office. By the end of 1986, however, over three-quarters of these had retired, though on their full final salaries and without the removal of most of the perquisites, such as good accommodation and access to official vehicles, which they had enjoyed while working. In the apparatus of government, sixty-five was set as the normal retirement age for ministers and provincial governors and sixty for all other senior officials; and only a few exceptions were allowed.*

In the third phase, which began in 1986, Deng raised his sights. There were some old themes in what he said. One was that the party needed leaders, at every level, who were 'more revolutionary, younger, better educated and more competent professionally'. Another was that the party was trying to do too much, duplicating the work and cramping the style of the government and preventing experts from contributing as much as they could to development. But there was also a new theme: the need to develop 'socialist democracy' by allowing 'grass-roots units' and individuals to participate more actively in decision-making and management. In practice, however, not a great deal was done. Contested elections made their appearance at low levels in the hierarchy of people's congresses and for places on consultative and advisory bodies, in universities and elsewhere, but not among candidates standing on political platforms. The press became livelier and fuller of variety, but new publications could still not appear without official permission. To judge from what he said to foreigners in the summer of 1986, Deng himself both wanted to go further and expected his senior colleagues to agree. But a central committee meeting in September of that year produced no document on political reform, concentrating instead on culture and ideology – and in a conservative tone. It was only in October 1987, at the party's thirteenth congress, that Deng was able to get agreement that political reform should be 'put on the

* Deng, aged eighty-two at the end of 1986, saw as exempt from retirement at fixed ages anyone who had risen above the rank of minister in the government or as far as the politburo in the party.

agenda for the whole party', and even then without clear guidance as to how far and in what direction the process should go.

In speaking about culture and ideology – in the context of building a socialist civilization (the second of the four tasks he had set at the eleventh congress) and in that of threats to political and social order – Deng stuck to ancient orthodoxies. He defined an advanced ideology as one whose core was 'unshakeable faith in socialism and in leadership by the party'. He asserted that socialism was superior to capitalism for moral as well as material reasons: 'We exert ourselves for socialism not only because socialism provides conditions for the faster development of the productive forces than does capitalism, but also because only socialism can eliminate the greed, corruption and injustice which are inherent in capitalism and other systems of exploitation.' The 'advanced culture' which he saw as crowning the socialist system was one in which the people were 'imbued with communist ideals, have moral integrity and a good general education, and observe discipline'. It was also one in which 'the bad practice of putting money above all else' had been eliminated and in which the 'corrupt and decadent ideas of the bourgeoisie and other exploiting classes' found no place.[4] It was characteristically Chinese that Deng should define culture chiefly in moral terms. The irony is that the morality he advocated should resemble the morality preached by the puritans of central and northern Europe during the sixteenth and seventeenth centuries, associated by many Western historians with the rise of capitalism and the bourgeoisie as a class.

Deng took a close personal interest in action to crack down on crime, the fourth task he had set at the eleventh congress. His approach was of a piece with his stern views about morality. All through 1983, the party and the government conducted a drive to seek out, arrest, try and sentence criminals of all kinds. Several thousand of those convicted were sentenced to death. In at least some places, executions were carried out in public. And yet Deng was not satisfied. Two years later, he spoke in these uncompromising terms to the politburo standing committee:

The death penalty cannot be abolished, and some criminals must be sentenced to death. Recently I have read some relevant documents, from which I understand there are a great many habitual criminals who, on being released after a few years' remoulding through forced labour, resume their criminal activities, each time becoming more skilful and more experienced in coping with the public security and judicial organs. Why don't we have some of them executed according to law? Why don't we punish severely, according to law, some of those people who traffic in women and children, who make a living by playing on people's superstitions or who organize reactionary secret societies, and some of those habitual criminals who refuse to reform despite repeated attempts to educate them? Some of them must be executed, but of course we have to be very careful in such matters. Those who have merely made mistakes in the political or ideological sphere but have not violated state law should not be given any criminal sanctions, let alone the death penalty. But some of the perpetrators of serious economic or other crimes must be executed as required by law. Generally speaking, the problem now is that we are too soft on criminals. As a matter of fact, execution is one of the indispensable means of education.[5]

Deng was very much the presiding genius in foreign affairs. Here he broke decisively with Mao's precept and practice. By degrees, he substituted an optimistic for a pessimistic view about the possibility of the world's remaining at peace. He began to talk of conciliation instead of the encouragement of revolution in speaking about China's approach to regional conflicts and civil wars, and about 'opening to the outside world' instead of self-reliance in discussing China's international economic relations. He dropped Leninism altogether, arguing that, far from making conflict between them inevitable, the economic relationships between the rich countries of the North and the poor countries of the South created an interdependence which made it both possible and desirable for them to collaborate. Although he continued for a few years after 1978 to pay lip-service to Mao's theory of the three worlds, his judgements and actions increasingly belied belief in the theory, and he ceased in due course even to refer to it. He began to speak like someone schooled in the central tradition of Western diplomacy: that the chief objects of action by one country in relation to others are to reinforce its security and to maximize its prosperity.

During the 1980s, the chief threat to China was still seen by Deng to come from the Soviet Union. But it was a threat of a new kind – of strategic encirclement instead of invasion or nuclear attack. Over Christmas 1979, the Soviet Union invaded Afghanistan and soon had over 100,000 troops in that country. In the early 1980s, Vietnam moved even closer to the Soviet Union, giving the Soviet Pacific fleet base facilities at two ports on its coast. This, in Deng's eyes, was 'hegemonism' in action – a forward policy to make the Soviet Union the dominant power in Asia and in the process to eliminate all positions of Chinese (and American) strength.

All the same, the restoration of law and order in China, the promising start of economic reform and a sense that the Soviet Union was becoming overstretched combined to make Deng believe that China was relatively stronger than it had been and therefore had less need to rely on the United States. The development of this sentiment coincided with renewed sympathy in Washington towards requests for military aid from Taiwan. In consequence, Sino-American relations went through a bumpy phase, lasting from the inauguration of President Reagan in January 1981 to the conclusion of an agreement between the two countries on American arms sales to the nationalists in August 1982. The six-month long negotiation which led up to the agreement was tough and often acrimonious and took place against the background of frequent Chinese attacks on American foreign policy in general and the American attitude to Taiwan in particular. Once achieved, however, the agreement created a new framework for Sino-American relations – one within which the state of relations no longer depended chiefly on the state of relations between the United States and the Soviet Union, or between the Soviet Union and China, or both, but more on the substance of bilateral relations. This gave both, and China in particular, greater freedom of action. But it also left China with two balances to strike: the balance between political independence at the cost of slow economic progress and rapid economic progress at the cost of at least some degree of political dependence on the United States; and the balance between an open door to Western ideas at the risk of generating political discontent and a door shut to such ideas at the risk of excluding industrial know-how. Much in China since 1982 has turned on the management of these balances.

China now adopted a posture of requirement – which cost little and appealed to national pride – towards both superpowers. It set three conditions for the 'normalization' of relations with the Soviet Union: the reduction of Soviet force levels in eastern Russia and Outer Mongolia (the Mongolian People's Republic), Soviet withdrawal from Afghanistan, and the removal of Soviet political and military support from Vietnam. By degrees, changed international circumstances and changes in the Soviet Union itself brought about the fulfilment of these conditions – without China's needing to do more than help the process along (for instance by giving active military support to the resistance movement in Afghanistan). Its requirement for the United States was that the latter should live up to undertakings in three documents: the Shanghai communiqué negotiated by Zhou Enlai and Kissinger in 1972* and the agreements of 1978 and 1982 about the normalization of relations and arms sales to Taiwan. There was not a great deal it could do to enforce this requirement. But American policy-makers could never ignore a Chinese call to meet it; China possessed the power of veto in the Security Council of the United Nations and was in any case too big to be left out of most international calculations.

In his attitude towards the rest of the world, Deng is no

---

* In this document, issued at the end of President Nixon's epoch-making visit to China, the United States acknowledged that 'all Chinese on either side of the Taiwan strait maintain that there is but one China and that Taiwan is part of China', stated that it did not challenge this position, and affirmed 'the ultimate objective of the withdrawal of all United States forces and military installations from Taiwan'.

cosmopolitan. But he is not a xenophobe either. He takes foreigners as they come, expecting them to be neither more nor less virtuous or intelligent than his own people. He can be very tough, even rough, in talking to them. But he can also display a pawky charm. In October 1986, he greeted the Queen with the words: 'Thank you for coming all this way to meet an old Chinese man.'

Given his passionate nationalism, Mao Zedong took remarkably little interest in the reintegration into China of the British and Portuguese colonies of Hong Kong and Macao. He occasionally referred – disparagingly – to reports in the Hong Kong press about Chinese politics. But he did not make any known plans to recover the two territories, and he is not known to have reacted to a Soviet taunt in the early 1960s that Chinese attitudes towards Russian expansion in Asia in the nineteenth century hardly squared with China's toleration of the 'stinking privy' of Hong Kong at the bottom of its garden.

In the summer of 1967, during the second year of the Cultural Revolution, radical leaders in Peking and in Guangdong issued orders to union leaders in Hong Kong to confront the colonial authorities, with the object of turning a local labour dispute into a situation which would make the colony ungovernable. But there is no evidence that Mao had a hand in guiding the radicals or even in giving them encouragement. Nor, it seems, did he play any part in promoting the destruction of the British mission in Peking by a mob after the British government had rejected an ultimatum about the treatment of demonstrators in Hong Kong.*

Deng Xiaoping, on the other hand, put national reunification high on his agenda. To begin with, it was Taiwan, much the largest of the unredeemed territories, which was chiefly on his mind. In 1981, he told a group of American senators that, under reunification, Taiwan would be able to retain its existing social and economic systems and even its own armed forces. In

---

* The chancery was burned down, the house of the chargé d'affaires was gutted and many members of the staff were physically abused.

September of that year, Ye Jianying proposed a nine-point plan which put flesh on these bones. Two of the key provisions were that Taiwan would be able to enjoy 'a high degree of autonomy as a special administrative region [of the People's Republic]' and that Taiwan's 'socio-economic system' would remain unchanged, as would its 'way of life and its economic and cultural relations with foreign countries'. There would be 'no encroachment' on proprietary rights and political leaders from Taiwan would be able to 'participate in running the [Chinese] state'.[6]

At some stage in the next twelve months, the Chinese distilled from Ye's nine points the concept of 'one country, two systems'. Its authorship has never been claimed by Deng, and no one else has formally attributed it to him. Yet it bears his stamp; he has spoken about it frequently; and Chinese officials have never demurred when foreigners have described the formula as his.

Ye's proposals did not lead to talks. The authorities in Taiwan reacted by declaring that their policies remained unchanged: to have no negotiations with the People's Republic and to interdict any contact with it. In spite of this official reaction, many forms of unofficial contact developed between the island and the mainland as the 1980s wore on. Trade expanded rapidly; and so, after the middle of the decade, did Taiwanese investment on the mainland, especially in Fujian, the province opposite Taiwan. By 1987 it had become a common sight to see conducted groups of Taiwanese tourists in Peking and other cities. Letters in large numbers began to flow in both directions, to begin with through intermediaries in Hong Kong and elsewhere, but later by direct mail. Forms of language were found to allow representatives from the two parts of China to sit together at meetings of international bodies.

In Taiwan, meanwhile, important political changes took place. Not long before his death in January 1988, Chiang Chingkuo, the son of Chiang Kaishek, ended a seven-year spell of martial law and lifted a long-standing ban on the formation of new political parties. This led to the creation of the Democratic Progressive Party, which soon began to function as a largely unfettered opposition to the nationalists. Economically the island, which had enjoyed rapid growth since the mid-1950s, continued to prosper. By the end of the 1980s, its national income per head, at US$6,000, was twenty times as high as income per head on the mainland and it had accumulated foreign-exchange reserves that were the third largest in the world. These developments, and the impact they had on popular attitudes in Taiwan, were watched with mixed feelings on the mainland. They were welcomed to the extent that they symbolized the weakening of the grip of the nationalist old guard on the political life of the island. But they caused anxiety to the extent that they opened the way to the expression of views about the island's destiny which did not assume reunification. Some politicians there began to hint at the possibility of independence, and non-politicians started to talk quite openly about this option. From 1949 on, the one great link between the communists on the mainland and the nationalists on the island had been that they were both wholly opposed to the concepts of 'two Chinas' and 'one China, one Taiwan'. Now there was some danger that the link would snap and, with it, the possibility of a negotiated solution under the rubric of one country, two systems.

Over Hong Kong and Macao, however, diplomatic activity produced formal agreements. In the case of Hong Kong, the first move was made by the British. In March 1979, Sir Murray Maclehose, the governor, broached a specific issue with the Chinese: the uncertainty created by the fact that all government land leases in the New Territories, 92 per cent of the colony's total area, were due to expire three days before 30 June 1997, the terminal date of the ninety-nine year lease under which Britain held the territories, and could not be renewed in the absence of knowledge about the colony's future. It turned out, not surprisingly given the wider issues at stake, that a formula which would allow the Hong Kong government to grant leases beyond 1997 could not be agreed. But the broaching of the specific issue put the whole question of Hong Kong's future on the agenda for discussion within governments and thereafter between them.

Humphrey Atkins, the second-ranking minister in the Foreign

and Commonwealth Office, visited Peking in January 1982. In the language of the White Paper in which the text of the ultimate agreement was published, he was 'given significant indications of Chinese policy towards Hong Kong by Chinese leaders'. These, the paper adds, 'confirmed the view of Her Majesty's Government that negotiations should be opened with the Chinese Government'.[7] The negotiation itself was launched when Mrs Thatcher visited China in the following September. She could not agree with her Chinese interlocutors, Deng included, about the status of Hong Kong – because they took the view that the nineteenth-century treaties under which Hong Kong island and Kowloon had been ceded, and the New Territories leased, to Britain were unequal and therefore invalid – but did agree with them that 'talks through diplomatic channels' should be entered into 'with the common aim of maintaining the stability and prosperity of Hong Kong'. Nothing was said in a brief joint statement about how the two sides wanted the talks to turn out or even about the basis for their conduct. To begin with, all that they had in common was their commitment to negotiate with an agreed social purpose.

The negotiation itself was protracted, complicated and both sensitive to and a source of influence on confidence in Hong Kong. The first British position was that Britain would be ready to restore sovereignty over Hong Kong to China in return for the right to continue to administer the territory. But it soon became clear that the Chinese side was not prepared to accept continued British administration, in any form, after 1997. The constitutional reason was that China had never relinquished sovereignty over any part of Hong Kong, only its exercise, and would therefore gain nothing from the continuation of British administration. The political reason was put bluntly by Deng Xiaoping to visitors from Hong Kong in June 1984: 'We are convinced that the people of Hong Kong are capable of running the affairs of Hong Kong well, and we want an end to foreign rule.'[8]

The British reacted by proposing that the two sides should 'discuss on a conditional basis what effective measures other than continued British administration might be devised to maintain the

stability and prosperity of Hong Kong and explore further . . .
Chinese ideas about the future . . . in order to see whether on this
basis arrangements which would ensure lasting stability and
prosperity could be constructed'.[9] The inducement to the Chinese
side was contained in an undertaking: that the British government
would consider recommending to Parliament a bilateral agreement
which enshrined whatever arrangements could be agreed.
Unorthodox though it is for an international negotiation to take
place on a conditional footing, these proposals proved enough to
open the way to the discussion of matters of substance. Once the
Chinese had accepted the proposals, it was their tactic to ignore
their conditionality. Conversely, it was British policy to underline
it. The negotiating reality was that each piece of progress towards
agreement on a full set of arrangements weakened the element of
conditionality, although never quite to the point where it would
have been impossible to invoke.

A way forward discovered, the British concentrated on giving
the Chinese a very detailed account of the character of the institutions and systems of Hong Kong. The Chinese responded by
elaborating in a good deal of detail on twelve points about the
future of Hong Kong – closely modelled on Ye Jianying's points
about Taiwan except over the existence of independent armed
forces – which they had tabled almost at the outset. By April 1984,
it had become clear that agreement on arrangements acceptable to
both sides was a real prospect. In this situation, the British
Foreign Secretary, Sir Geoffrey Howe, visited China. He had a
long meeting with Deng Xiaoping, during which the latter made
it clear that he looked forward to a successful outcome. On his
return journey, Sir Geoffrey announced in Hong Kong that it
would 'not be realistic' to think in terms of an agreement which
provided for British administration after 1997, and that the British
side had therefore been examining with the Chinese side how it
might be possible 'to arrive at arrangements that would secure for
Hong Kong a high degree of autonomy under Chinese sovereignty
and that would preserve the way of life in Hong Kong, together
with the essentials of [its] present systems'.[10]

There followed the end-game. This was at times very tense. One reason was that the Chinese had at the outset stated that the negotiation must be over by the end of September 1984, so that both negotiating parties – especially the Chinese – found themselves under severe time pressure. Another was that there was a natural tendency for each side to leave the most difficult issues, such as nationality, to the end, in the hope that momentum gained over the solution of less difficult issues would help resolve them. Two big concerns for the British side were that a joint liaison group to be set up 'to ensure a smooth transfer of government in 1997' should not in the meantime be regarded as being 'an organ of power', and that the agreement concluded should have treaty status in international law. A large concern for the Chinese side was that the agreement should state Chinese positions and prescriptions in passages which contained no reference to British attitudes, or to British agreement or concurrence. There was a serious tremor in mid-September, when, for reasons which are still unclear, the Chinese suddenly demanded scores of changes to texts which had been agreed in two drafting groups. If they had not very quickly backed down, their own deadline for agreement could not have been met. On one point the Chinese remained inflexible: that the People's Republic would station 'military forces' in Hong Kong after 1997 (though it was stipulated in the agreement that these would not interfere in the internal affairs of the special administrative region). The subject came up, among many others, during a conversation between Deng and Sir Geoffrey Howe at the end of July, during a second visit to China by the latter, but without leading to agreement, even on the basis that China would possess but not exercise the right to send troops to the territory.

The agreement – in the form of a joint declaration with three annexes – was initialled in Peking on 26 September by the leaders of the two negotiating teams and was signed there by Mrs Thatcher and Zhao Ziyang, her formal counterpart, on 19 December. Deng Xiaoping looked on. Instruments of ratification were exchanged on 27 May 1985, and it entered into force on that day.

The evidence is that Deng followed the course of the negotiation very closely. The fact that seven of the passages in his *Selected Works* for 1984 deal either directly with the negotiation or with the concept of one country, two systems shows that it was much on his mind. He himself declared in October, in a speech to the party's central advisory commission, that he only worked on two 'projects' during the year, one of them being to 'resolve the Hong Kong question through the one-country, two-systems approach'. The Chinese negotiators told their British opposite numbers that they were sometimes required to report to him personally on how the negotiation was going.

Deng spoke a good deal to foreign visitors about the negotiation. He made three main points. The first was that the concept of one country, two systems was one he hoped could help solve problems not of direct concern to China. In July, he told Sir Geoffrey Howe that the 'solution' of the Hong Kong question within its framework would 'set an example for other nations in settling the disputes history has bequeathed them'. His second point was that the concept could be applied to Taiwan and Hong Kong because these territories had (relatively) small populations, so that the persistence of capitalism in them would not affect the survival of socialism in the rest of China. He emphasized this to Mrs Thatcher in December:

I should also like to ask the Prime Minister to make it clear to the people of Hong Kong and of the rest of the world that the concept of 'one country, two systems' includes not only capitalism but also socialism, which will be firmly maintained on the mainland of China, where one billion people live. There are one billion people on the mainland, approximately 20 million on Taiwan and 5.5 million in Hong Kong. A problem arises of how to handle relations between such widely divergent numbers. Since one billion people, the overwhelming majority, live under socialism in a vast area, we can afford to allow capitalism in these small, limited areas at our side. If this were not the case, capitalism might swallow up socialism.[11]

Deng's third point was about patriotism. In a conversation with visitors from Hong Kong in June, he defined patriots in the territory in a way which has continued to echo:

Some requirements or qualifications should be established with regard to the administration of Hong Kong affairs by the people of Hong Kong. It must be required that patriots form the main body of administrators, that is, of the future government of Hong Kong. Of course it should include other people, too, as well as foreigners invited to serve as advisers. Who are patriots? The qualifications for a patriot are respect for the Chinese nation, sincere support for the motherland's resumption of sovereignty over Hong Kong and a desire not to impair Hong Kong's prosperity and stability. Those who meet these requirements are patriots, whether they believe in capitalism or feudalism or even slavery. We don't demand that they be in favour of China's socialist system; we only ask them to love the motherland and Hong Kong.[12]

There is, however, one puzzle about Deng's statements. During the negotiation, the Chinese side was adamant that Hong Kong was not, and could not become, a party to it. The Chinese attitude was often expressed as hostility to the concept of a 'three-legged stool', which a junior British minister had used to describe the character of the (then impending) negotiation. The formal reason for this hostility was that Hong Kong was a part of China and that the settlement of its destiny was a matter of China's sovereign right. Another was to discourage statements by Chinese organizations and individuals in Hong Kong which cast doubt on the proposition, expressed in the first article of the eventual agreement, that it was 'the common aspiration of the entire Chinese people' to recover 'the Hong Kong area'. Yet Deng was quite ready to speak of three interested parties. He did so in a speech to the central advisory commission in October 1984, and again in speaking to Mrs Thatcher in December. On the latter occasion he said:

To settle the Hong Kong question peacefully, we had to take into consideration the actual conditions in Hong Kong, China and Great Britain. In other words, the way in which we settled the question had to be acceptable to all three parties – to the people of China, of Britain and of Hong Kong. If we had wanted to achieve reunification by imposing socialism on Hong Kong, the Hong Kong people would have rejected it and so would the British people. Reluctant acquiescence on their part would only have led to turmoil. Even if there had been no armed conflict, Hong Kong would have become a bleak city with a host of problems, and that is not something we would have wanted. So the only solution to the Hong Kong question that would be acceptable to all three parties was the 'one-country, two-systems' arrangement, under which Hong Kong would be allowed to retain its capitalist system and to maintain its status as a free port and a financial centre. There was no other alternative.[13]

What accounts for the discrepancy between Deng's statements and the official Chinese position? It is improbable that the Chinese negotiators would have ignored any instruction from him to acknowledge the existence of three interested parties. If, therefore, it can be assumed that he gave no such instruction, the conclusion can only be that Deng claimed, and was not challenged in, the right to interpret important events in his own way, but did not insist that others – his subordinates – should follow suit. In other words, toleration of some degree of inconsistency between what the leader said and what was done by the bureaucracies of the party and government had become a feature of the Chinese political culture. And yet it was only some degree. When two senior political figures suggested publicly in the summer of 1984 that there might be some flexibility in the official Chinese position on the dispatch of troops to Hong Kong, Deng was quick to rebuke them in public, declaring that they had no right to speak on the subject.

CHAPTER 14

Tiananmen, 1984–9

On 1 October 1984, the thirty-fifth anniversary of the founding of the People's Republic was celebrated in Peking with immense fanfare. Following the pattern set during the 1950s, when it was the custom of Mao Zedong and his colleagues to watch enormous parades pass from east to west through Tiananmen Square from the platform of the Tiananmen itself on 1 May and 1 October every year, Deng Xiaoping and his closest associates watched a parade which lasted for over three hours. It was led by marching squares of men and women from all branches of the armed forces and brought up by lorries carrying ballistic missiles. In between, farmers, workers, students and representatives of most of the professions marched by in contingents of varying size, many of them around huge tableaux mounted on trucks. A military band of more than two hundred played first the national anthem and then marches from the country's revolutionary musical canon. In the square, a phalanx of many thousand youths turned and re-turned placards to display the slogans of the hour. As the parade ended, thousands of balloons were released. The discipline of all those taking part was exemplary – much better than that of the marchers of the 1950s – the weather was perfect and the combination of order, colour and stirring sound left even hard-bitten foreign spectators with the sense that things were going well in Deng's China.

Deng imitated Mao by making a short speech before the parade began. He broke with precedent by driving out from the Tiananmen in an open car to review the troops who were waiting to march past. Dressed in military uniform, he saluted each contingent as he passed it. The troops responded by shouting a greeting to him. Six weeks beyond his eightieth birthday, he stood without support in a moving vehicle for about fifteen minutes, a show of vigour and style which impressed the foreigners present as much as anything which followed.

Deng's speech was confident, almost triumphal, in tone. On the state of China, he declared:

Thirty-five years ago Chairman Mao Zedong, the great leader of the people of all our nationalities, solemnly proclaimed here the founding of the People's Republic of China. He declared that the Chinese people had finally stood up. In the past thirty-five years not only have we ended a dark period of our history for all time and created a socialist society in China, but we have changed the course of human history. Particularly since the third plenary session of the eleventh central committee of the Chinese Communist Party, when the reactionary acts of the counter-revolutionary Gang of Four were definitely brought to an end, the approach of seeking truth from facts – a way of thinking advocated by comrade Mao Zedong – was restored and developed and a number of important policies suited to the new situation were adopted, the whole country has taken on a new look. On a foundation of national stability, unity, democracy and the rule of law, we have given socialist moderniza-tion the highest priority in our work. Our economy has grown more vigorously than ever before, and achievements in all other fields are widely acknowledged. Today, all our people are full of joy and pride.

On the future, he was no less positive:

The party's twelfth national congress set a goal of quadrupling the gross annual industrial and agricultural product between 1980 and the year 2000. The experience of the past few years indicates that this magnificent goal can be reached. Our primary job at present is to reform systematic-ally everything in the existing economic structure that is impeding our progress. At the same time, we shall carry out the planned technical transformation of existing enterprises throughout the country. We shall redouble our efforts in scientific and technological research, in education at all levels and in the training of workers, administrative staff and cadres. The entire party membership and the community at large must truly value knowledge and let intellectuals make their contribution. All this will ensure that we shall gradually realize our modernization programme.[1]

Deng referred with pride to the achievement of agreement with Britain over Hong Kong and declared that 'peaceful reunification with Taiwan' would sooner or later 'become a reality'. He warned, however, that China existed in a 'seriously deteriorating international situation' and called on 'all commanders and fighters' of the Chinese People's Liberation Army 'to be alert' and to 'upgrade their political and military quality and strive to master the skills of modern warfare'. In a sentence which revealed his pride of race and nation more strikingly than anything he had said in public before, he declared: 'The desire for peaceful reunification of the motherland is taking hold in the hearts of all descendants of the Yellow Emperor.'*[2]

Deng had grounds for confidence. The grain harvest of 1984, at over 400 million tonnes, was the largest, by a wide margin, in China's history. The output of the country's factories and mines was growing faster than at any time since 1978. Retail prices were edging upwards, but more slowly than in the late 1970s. There was no obvious political trouble. Nor was there any obvious social discontent. In spite of Deng's words about a deteriorating international situation, no one believed that China was about to be attacked, by the Soviet Union or by any other country. Hundreds of speeches and articles by foreigners over the previous two years showed that most of the world's perception of China had become favourable. The achievement of agreement over the future of Hong Kong had been widely applauded abroad, as showing that China meant what it said about the settlement of international disputes through negotiation, as well as for removing uncertainty about their future for the territory's five million inhabitants.

---

* A legendary monarch of the fourth millennium BC. He is supposed to have led the Han Chinese to victory against the Miao, a nomadic northern people, and to have taught them a great deal about the technologies of building, agriculture and the control of water resources.

It seemed, too, that Deng was personally popular. During the parade, a group of students unfurled a home-made banner of greeting as they passed the Tiananmen. Its legend, '*Ni hao Xiaoping*' – 'Hello Xiaoping' – conveyed in its impertinence a degree of affection and approval which nothing more formal could have matched. Such a thing could never have happened in Mao's day, and many must have reflected that, if the students were content, then not much could be amiss in society at large.

As it turned out, the thirty-fifth anniversary was a high point, in the fortunes both of China and of its leader. Before even a year had gone by, there were clear signs of trouble. Some of the veteran revolutionaries had begun to speak darkly about the consequences of economic reform and the loosening of controls over writers, artists and the press. Student demonstrations had broken out again, a series of scandals had revealed that many in high places were corrupt, and a new phase of economic reform had led to a new phase of overheating in the national economy.

The two leading critics of the fruits of reform were Chen Yun and Peng Zhen. At a national party conference in September 1985, convened by Deng to force the retirement from the politburo of some more of its older members, Chen criticized the way in which the abolition of the old system of state procurement in the countryside had led many peasant families to switch from grain production to the cultivation of cash crops and declared that he was wholly opposed to any further reduction in the scope of economic planning. He stated boldly that socialism 'required' the primacy of the planned economy. Peng expressed great disquiet about the degree of criticism of socialist methods and values which had emerged in a freer intellectual climate. Deng did not answer their criticisms directly. But he argued vehemently in a winding-up speech that reform should not be halted, let alone reversed, saying he was confident about the party's ability to deal with the problems it would inevitably produce: 'Naturally, some negative phenomena are bound to appear in the process of reform; as long as we face them squarely, it will not be difficult to solve these problems.'[3]

The student demonstrations took place in Peking in the same month as the conference. They were on a small scale and did not spread beyond university precincts. But their occurrence showed that the students, who had on the whole been quiet since the end of the Cultural Revolution, were restless again. They also showed that the students were as much interested in political causes as ever. They complained, certainly, about their own circumstances and prospects, saying that they were forced to live and work in cramped and uncomfortable conditions and that, on past form, many among them could expect to be assigned on graduation to jobs which were ill-paid and in which they would not be able to make use of their talents. But they also complained about foreign, particularly Japanese, economic penetration, and about the privileges enjoyed by high-ranking officials and members of their families and outright corruption in high places.

Corruption was indeed a spreading blight. During the first half of 1985, the press, perhaps prompted by leaders, like Hu Yaobang, who were particularly worried about it, published details of several flagrant cases. The most flagrant of all had occurred in Hainan, the tropical island off the coast of Guangdong, where scores of party and government officials had formed a ring to import foreign goods and then to sell them at greatly inflated prices to other officials on the mainland. To do this, they had used official allocations of foreign exchange, retained foreign-exchange earnings and foreign currency purchased on the black market. The sums of money and the quantities of goods involved were enormous. Between January 1984 and March 1985, 90,000 motor vehicles, 120,000 motor cycles, nearly three million television sets and 250,000 video recorders, costing about US$600 million, were imported into the island. By the end of this period, large parts of these stocks had been trans-shipped to the mainland. At the top of the party, discovery of the scandal produced a backlash against the concept of special economic zones, compelling Deng, who had been an enthusiast from the start, to declare that the largest zone on the mainland – at Shenzhen, on the border with Hong Kong – was only an experiment. For the man in the street, however, the most striking feature was that the leaders of the ring suffered no punishment more severe than demotion to less important posts.

By the end of 1985, inflation was on the minds and lips of urban-dwellers even more than corruption. Largely because of the changes to the system of procurement for farm products made in 1984, retail prices in the cities had risen rapidly in 1985. The final official figure for retail price inflation in the cities was 9 per cent. But the prices of many goods, including meat and vegetables, had all gone up much faster. How to control inflation in an era when all foreign, and much domestic, advice was that a system of fixed prices both distorted and stunted the functioning of the national economy was becoming a central political issue.

The politics of 1986, an even more troubled year, turned on a drive for accelerated and – even more important – open-ended reform by Hu Yaobang and a group of his supporters at party headquarters, and on the reactions to it of society and the rest of the party leadership. Because the drive ended in Hu's disgrace, and so to the exclusion from compilations of official documents of his speeches for the year, it is not easy to know what inspired him to launch the drive or what debates about it took place in party bodies. It is, however, clear that Hu claimed, and for a time got away with, a degree of freedom to set the political agenda which no one promoted by Deng had enjoyed before.

Hu's principal lieutenants were Hu Qili, a member of the politburo and the secretariat who had been one of his deputies in the Communist Youth League before the Cultural Revolution, and Zhu Houze, the director of the party's propaganda department. Within the party, this group of three fought hard to give a liberal tone to a draft central-committee resolution on culture and ideology which had been under discussion since the beginning of the year, though with only qualified success. The document eventually adopted in September was a patchwork of permissive and restrictive passages, which left its readers unclear about the extent to which non-Marxist ideas could be propagated or brought into debates about China's development. Outside the party, the activities of the three had a greater impact. This was particularly true of a speech made by Hu Qili on May Day 1986, in which he declared that China's intellectuals should have the courage to 'break through' Marxist concepts which 'experience had already proved to be outmoded or not entirely correct' and called for more democracy and reinforcement of the rule of law. Economists, sociologists, writers and scientists all responded. At seminars and conferences, and in the press, they argued that the concepts of Western economics could fruitfully be used in analysing China's economic problems, that it was vain to suppose that Western technology could be imported in an ideologically sanitized state and that it was time to draw a clear line between art and propaganda and to allow art to go its own way. Two writers who had been persecuted as rightists in 1957 and who had since explored the psychological damage suffered by victims of the Cultural Revolution, Liu Binyan and Wang Ruowang, insisted that the depiction of real life in literature and art had nothing to do with the canons of 'socialist realism', imported from the Soviet Union in the 1950s.

Politically, the most daring response was made by Fang Lizhi, an astrophysicist who was a vice-president of the Chinese University of Science and Technology at Hefei, in the central province of Anhui. He began to speak to the university's students about human rights. In talks to them, of which recordings were made and circulated throughout the university world, he argued that all human beings were born with a set of inalienable rights including the right to enjoy democracy, and that political rights were bestowed by citizens on their governments and not vice versa. This was dynamite.

Deng Xiaoping's reaction to this outpouring was double-barrelled. He repeated, with greater emphasis, the line he had begun to take in 1985, that the greater threat to China's political unity and social stability now came from the right – bourgeois liberalization – than from the left – dogmatism and sectarianism. He made a particularly sharp attack on bourgeois liberalization during the debate about culture and ideology at the central committee meeting in September:

With regard to the question of opposing bourgeois liberalization, I am the one who has talked about it most often and most insistently. Why? First, because there is now a trend of thought – that is, liberalization – among the masses, especially among the young people. Second, because this trend has found support from the sidelines. For example, there have been some comments from people in Hong Kong and Taiwan who are all opposed to our four cardinal principles and who think we should introduce the capitalist system lock, stock and barrel, as if that were the only genuine modernization. What in fact is this liberalization? It is an attempt to turn China's present policies in the direction of capitalism. The exponents of this trend are trying to lead us towards capitalism. That is why I have explained time and again that our modernization programme is a socialist one. Our decision to apply the open policy and assimilate useful things from capitalist societies was made only to supplement the development of our socialist productive forces.[4]

Deng's other barrel was to answer Hu Qili on political reform. He said very little about democracy and the rule of law, concentrating instead on 'political restructuring'. In June 1986, in a formal statement to the politburo standing committee, he focused on the old issue of the relationship between the party and the government, arguing it was 'not appropriate for the party to concern itself with matters that fall within the scope of the law' and that the leadership of the party would be weakened rather than strengthened if it tried to take responsibility 'for too many areas'. By November, he had worked out a fuller prospectus. At the beginning of the month, he told the Japanese prime minister that reform ought to have three objectives: to ensure the 'continuing vitality of the party and the state' by giving senior posts to men and women in the prime of life; to 'eliminate bureaucratism and increase efficiency', and to 'stimulate the initiative of grass roots units and of workers, peasants and intellectuals' by letting these categories of people participate in management. All through his musing during the summer and autumn, he emphasized that the general purpose of reform was to make it easier for the party to exercise effective leadership, and not to dilute this leadership. In a statement to a group of senior party officials in September, he explicitly ruled out movement towards Western forms: 'We must not imitate the West, and no liberalization should be allowed.'

Curiously, Deng's views about liberalization and reform were not given a great deal of publicity. At least partly in consequence, the impression grew that, the central committee resolution on culture and ideology notwithstanding, policy in action was to loosen party control over political and cultural life. Many came to believe, and not a few to hope, that the four cardinal principles were now chiefly honoured in the breach and that the fizzling out of a short-lived campaign against 'spiritual pollution' in the winter of 1983/4 had shown that the revolutionary old guard was a spent political force.

In this atmosphere, the university students started to agitate again. The first demonstrations took place at Hefei, in Fang Lizhi's university. Others quickly followed in Shanghai, Peking and twenty other cities. Many of the students' demands were related to their working conditions. But others were political, fired by dissatisfaction about the way in which student candidates for election to local people's congresses had been discriminated against by supervisory committees, to the point of being declared ineligible to stand. Soon, many students began to argue in big-character posters (now illegal) and leaflets that this treatment revealed official hostility to choice in the electoral life of the country, and so to genuine democracy. The demonstrations began in early December. By the end of 1986, there were almost daily parades in the central districts of Shanghai and Peking and small contingents of industrial workers had begun to take part in them.

Deng is not known to have pronounced on the demonstrations until they had been going on for three weeks. Then, on 30 December, he spoke out very clearly against them. At a meeting of 'some leading comrades of the central committee', he demanded that (new) regulations to deal with them should be strictly enforced, proposed that Fang Lizhi, Liu Binyan and Wang Ruowang ('so arrogant that they want to remould the Communist Party') should be expelled from the party, and renewed his attack on bourgeois liberalization:

The struggle against bourgeois liberalization will last for at least twenty years. Democracy can develop only gradually, and we cannot copy Western systems. If we did, that would only make a mess of everything. Our socialist construction can only be carried out under leadership, in an orderly way and in an environment of stability and unity. That's why I lay such emphasis on the need for high ideals and strict discipline. Bourgeois liberalization would plunge the country into turmoil once more. Bourgeois liberalization means rejection of the party's leadership; there would be nothing to unite our one billion people, and the party itself would lose all power to fight. A party like that would be no better than a mass organization; how could it be expected to lead the people in construction?[5]

Forbidden to demonstrate in public places, hemmed in wherever they went by large numbers of armed police and often sent back to their campuses in buses when their ranks became ragged, the students abandoned their agitation in early January 1987. None of their demands had been met and they seemed to have achieved nothing. In due course, some of their leaders were arrested, interrogated and punished, creating a mood of bitterness among many more than the one or two per cent Deng judged to have taken to the streets. Fang, Liu and Wang were all formally expelled from the party; Fang was moved from Hefei, to a humble technical post in the Peking observatory.

Politically, the chief effect of the demonstrations was to bring down Hu Yaobang. Blamed by Deng and the other veterans for their outbreak and for lack of resolution in dealing with them, he was forced to make a 'self-examination' and to offer his resignation as general secretary at an enlarged meeting of the politburo in mid-January. The text of what he said has not leaked out. But references in other documents suggest that he confessed to a series of acts which bespoke weak but over-independent leadership. He was allowed to keep his place – for the time being – on the politburo standing committee. He disappeared, however, from public view and ceased to have any contact with foreigners. According to a rumour current in 1989, he moved from his official residence in the Zhongnanhai* to a courtyard house outside, where he spent most of his time studying the annals of China's late imperial history. Perhaps on Deng's motion, and certainly with his strong support, Zhao Ziyang was elected acting general secretary in his place.

Hu's fall destroyed Deng's arrangements for party and government leadership after his own death. Ever since the twelfth party congress in September 1982, it had been assumed, by Chinese and foreigners, that Hu would stay on as general secretary and accumulate real power as Deng and his contemporaries ceased by degrees to be active politically. Now a new heir had to be found, late in the day and from a field in which no candidate had perfect qualifications. The old men were too old. Among the younger men, Zhao Ziyang lacked experience as a central party official and had worked closely with Hu, which was likely to make him suspect in the eyes of the veterans. Li Peng, the senior vice-premier under seventy, had a good administrative record. But he too lacked party experience, and he was as much associated with the veteran revolutionaries – especially Chen Yun – as Zhao was with Hu. Zhao and Li each represented a strand in Deng's way of thought, but neither represented his unique blend of political conservatism and economic radicalism.

It is not known whether Li wanted to be general secretary. Zhao did not. He was chiefly interested in making a success of the programme of urban economic reform which had been launched, very much at his instance, two years earlier and in the management of the national economy, which was causing difficulties. A rather solitary man, he was much happier with the impersonal ways of government than with the uncertainties of life at party headquarters, where the day's work could always be interrupted by a telephone call from Deng or a message from one of the old men without formal responsibility. Chen Yizi, an economist who was close to him at the time, has said that he told Deng three

---

* An ugly modern building, serving also as the general secretary's office, which is an eyesore among the ancient pavilions around it.

times during the course of 1987, when acting general secretary, that he would prefer to go back to being premier, but that Deng would have none of it.

Zhao faced a strong and immediate challenge from the veterans, who saw Hu Yaobang's fall as an opportunity to relaunch the campaign against spiritual pollution which Hu, with Deng's support, had cut short in the spring of 1984. In a spate of articles and speeches, given great publicity by a propaganda department over which they had achieved control (Zhu Houze had been sacked a few days after Hu), they condemned behaviour which reflected foreign influence or a hankering by ordinary people, especially the young, to make life less monotonous. They began to hint, too, that the reform programme itself was responsible for what they saw as China's social ills.

Zhao grasped very quickly that more was at stake than the way in which people dressed and amused themselves, and moved to launch a counter-attack. His method was to make a keynote speech to a public meeting, something which party leaders had got out of the habit of doing since the Cultural Revolution (perhaps because they flinched from the memory of Lin Biao's and Jiang Qing's demagogic use of public platforms). A good opportunity was at hand in the spring festival (lunar new year) holiday, when it had become customary for national and local leaders to mix with the population in parks and other public places. He invited the other politburo members who were in Peking to support him and then announced that the party leadership was united in its commitment to reform and that persistence in reform was the way to deal with unhealthy political and moral tendencies. His words had the effect of staying the hand of thousands of officials who were getting ready to harass, or even arrest, young men and women who had taken to wearing jeans, listening to pop music on tape recorders and dancing in bars and discothèques. It also put an end to the appearance in the press of speeches by senior conservatives.

For the rest of 1987, Zhao seemed to be very much in command and to enjoy Deng's complete confidence. Deng, for his part, spoke frequently to foreign visitors about economic reform and political reform, the objects of each and the relationship between the two. His tone was confident, as if he had shrugged off the shocks of the preceding winter, and he gave no sign of fading intellectual power. On the contrary, he broke more new theoretical ground than he had for years. Now eighty-two, he gave his visitors the impression that he was enjoying himself.

Deng's grand theme was that there must be no trimming or backsliding over reform. Political reform was necessary in order to clear the way for economic reform; economic reform was necessary in order to accelerate the development of China's productive capacity (the 'productive forces'); and the development of the nation's productive capacity was necessary in order to eliminate poverty, the purpose of socialism. In developing his theme, he made out his case against capitalism. Speaking in April 1987 to Alfonso Guerra, a senior Spanish socialist, he said:

If China were totally Westernized and went capitalist, it would be impossible for us to modernize. The problem we have to solve is how to enable our one billion people to cast off poverty and become prosperous. If we adopted the capitalist system in China, probably fewer than 10 per cent of the population would be enriched, while over 90 per cent would remain in a permanent state of poverty. If that happened, the overwhelming majority of the people would rise up in revolution. China's modernization can be achieved only through socialism and not capitalism.[6]

Deng also developed his case against Western democracy, relying more on the argument that its adoption in China would stultify rapid political action than on the orthodox Marxist argument that it would mean a 'bourgeois dictatorship'. He made this point most forcefully to Stefan Korosec, a senior Yugoslav communist:

The democracy in capitalist societies is bourgeois democracy – in fact, it is the democracy of monopoly capitalists. It is no more than a system of multi-party elections and a balance of the three powers. Can we adopt this system? Ours is the system of the people's congresses and people's democracy under the leadership of the communist party. The greatest advantage of the socialist system is that when the central leadership makes a decision it is promptly implemented without interference from any other quarters . . .[7]

The big party occasion of 1987 was the thirteenth national congress, held in late October. Deng had intimated beforehand that he did not want to be re-elected to the central committee and his name was missing from the list of candidates put to the delegates. So were the names of many other veterans, including Chen Yun and Peng Zhen. No longer a member of the central committee, Deng became ineligible for election by that body to the politburo or its standing committee. He was, however, re-appointed chairman of the military commission.* It was strongly rumoured that he had wanted to step down from this post too, but had been persuaded to stay on at the last minute (the party constitution, which stipulated that the chairman of the commission must be at least a vice-chairman of the central committee, had to be amended to make his reappointment possible). The politics behind these moves were that the old soldiers on the commission would not have tolerated anyone without a military record as their chairman, while Deng would not have accepted a chairman who belonged to the military establishment.

Three other veterans, all of whom were to play important parts in the drama of 1989, kept or obtained senior posts: Chen Yun became chairman of the central advisory commission; Bo Yibo became one of his deputies; and Yang Shangkun became permanent vice-chairman of the military commission. Yang's post was a new one, created to make possible the appointment of Zhao Ziyang as senior vice-chairman of the commission, on which Deng had insisted.

At its first meeting, the new central committee decided, on a proposal of the politburo standing committee, that, although Deng had withdrawn from the committee, his status as a party and state leader had not altered. In 1989, one of the charges brought

---

* Under the party constitution, the central committee elected the politburo and its standing committee, but appointed the officers of the military commission.

against Zhao Ziyang was that he had disclosed a state secret by mentioning this decision to Gorbachev. This was wholly unfair. Chinese officials insisted to foreigners in autumn 1987 that Deng was still China's 'paramount leader' and the terms of the decision are clearly reflected in Deng's official biography, published after the congress. The charge reflects only the malice of Zhao's enemies.

There was very little talk in 1988 about bourgeois liberalization or spiritual pollution (or about 'national nihilism' and 'total westernization', two other targets of the old guard). The chief topic of discussion, behind closed doors at party and government meetings and in society at large, was inflation. The prices of both capital and consumer goods were still rising rapidly. In his report to the National People's Congress in March, Li Peng – now acting premier and premier-designate – admitted that the problem was serious: 'The outstanding problem in our economic and social life today is the excessive rise in commodity prices, which has to some extent retarded the improvement of the living standard of the people and has even lowered the living standard of some urban residents.[8] He said that price reform would continue 'step by step according to plan', but also spoke of measures to increase supply and restrict demand, and announced that ceilings would be set for the prices of 'major items' of capital goods. He gave no figures for prevailing rates of inflation, but everyone knew that these were well above 20 per cent for many consumer goods.

Sometime in the spring, Deng intervened in the debate about economic management. He argued that the right way to cure prevailing economic ills, including inflation, was to press ahead with price reform, freeing many of the prices which were still fixed or only allowed to fluctuate – at any rate legally – within limits. Li Peng was opposed, believing that price liberalization would lead very quickly to even higher inflation. So was Zhao Ziyang, for the same reason. But Deng insisted; and Zhao was constrained to announce that there would be rapid movement towards the market determination of most prices. In this way he became associated in the public mind with the new policy, and extremely vulnerable in the party to becoming the scapegoat for its failure.

The consequences were as serious as Li and Zhao had feared. Prices soared. Buyers rushed to buy before they rose even higher and suppliers started to hoard against the day when they did. These reactions drove them further up. By the end of the summer, panic-buying had become a feature of life in Shanghai and many other cities, and there had begun to be runs on the banks. Older citizens were reminded of the hyper-inflation of the last two years of nationalist rule – and of the extent to which the communists had laid claim to the right to rule from their success in breaking this inflation. The whole country now had a monetary economy, which had not been the case forty years before, so that the mood in the countryside became as nervous as in the cities.

The party dealt with the crisis in two steps. In August, the politburo decided that, although price liberalization should be allowed to go ahead, fiscal and monetary policy should be tightened. In September, the central committee put price reform on ice and adopted 'improvement of the economic environment and rectification of the economic order' as the guideline for 1989 and 1990. Deng's part in these proceedings is unclear, but was certainly not heroic. According to one account, he began to indicate in July that he was not totally committed to price reform or to complete support for Zhao in his efforts to put it through. According to another, he stood behind both at the politburo meeting in August, but was one of the minority in a vote on a motion to deprive Zhao of all responsibility for economic policy. Whatever Deng's precise role, he preferred to acquiesce in the humiliation of a man he had pushed into a false position than to protect Zhao by declaring that any criticism should be directed at – and absorbed by – himself.

The great movement which swept the cities of China – not only Peking – during the spring of 1989, shaking the state to its foundations, was neither planned nor provoked. Certainly, all sections of society had grievances. Everyone was disturbed about inflation. In the cities, the intellectuals, having tasted a greater degree of freedom, wanted to extend its limits. Some had begun to petition the authorities in political causes. In January, Fang Lizhi had written to Deng Xiaoping (as chairman of the central military commission, the only party post he still held), asking for an amnesty for all political prisoners, including Wei Jingsheng, the Democracy Wall activist who had been arrested in 1979. He had subsequently been supported in an open letter to the central committee by thirty-three writers and artists and forty-two scientists. The students were discontented about their treatment two years before. Managers and workers in the state sector of the economy were resentful about the higher earnings of many people in the private and collective sectors, and uncertain about their job security. In the countryside, the peasants who had stuck to grain production resented the greater prosperity of those who were now cultivating cash crops and of many who had moved out of farming altogether. There had begun to be a good deal of contact between dissident intellectuals, including Fang Lizhi and his wife Li Shuxian, and students who were interested in forms of democracy far less restrictive than those favoured by Deng. Political clubs and 'salons' had sprung up in many universities; at Peking University, an area of campus known as the Triangle had become a forum for frequent debates and meetings. But there was no plotting, and no organized exchange of views and information between the intellectual world and the worlds of office and manual work.

On their side, the party and government had achieved agreement about how to deal with an overheated economy, at a political cost which must have rankled with Zhao but does not seem to have disturbed Deng, and were turning their attention to subjects, like education, which only come to the top of the political agenda in times of no apparent crisis. There was worry about the trend of events in Hungary and Poland, and about the attitude to these events of the Soviet Union under Gorbachev. But the way had at last been cleared for the normalization of relations between China and the Soviet Union. Gorbachev had accepted an invitation to visit China and it had been settled that he should come in the spring. Deng must have been looking forward to 1989 as the year which would mark his apotheosis as an international statesman, through the settlement of the longest and most bitter of China's conflicts with other states – in China's capital and very much on China's terms. Though pressure from China had only contributed to the result, the Soviet Union had come near to meeting all three of China's conditions: withdrawal of military and political support for Vietnam, military withdrawal from Afghanistan, and reduction of force levels in Mongolia and eastern Russia.

The movement itself was precipitated by an event which was not, and could not have been, foreseen: the death on 15 April, a week after a heart attack during a politburo meeting, of Hu Yaobang. Hu had been a Marxist to the day of his death. But he was widely regarded as a man who had wanted to create a freer political system. He was also seen as a victim of injustice, because he had been forced to offer his resignation to the politburo, a body which was not entitled under the party constitution to demand or accept it. For these reasons, and because the death of a leader the party is bound to honour provides opportunities for self-expression which do not otherwise exist, signs of popular emotion were quick to appear.

By the evening of 15 April, students at Peking University had fixed wreaths – in white, the Chinese colour for mourning – and posters to the trees and walls of their campus. By the end of the following day, they had been imitated by students in many other institutions of higher education. On 17 April, a Monday, a few hundred students made their way from the university quarter of the city, in its north-western suburbs, to Tiananmen Square and deposited a memorial banner at the base of the monument there to the heroes of the people. As they crossed the square, they chanted the slogans which were to become the movement's watchwords: 'Long live Hu Yaobang', 'Long live democracy', 'Long live freedom', 'Down with corruption' and 'Down with bureaucracy'. On the following day, a larger body of students fixed a longer banner to the monument and then stayed on in the square to hold a political debate and draw up a petition to the authorities. In seven demands, it set out a full political programme:

- To clear the name of Hu Yaobang;
- To repudiate the campaigns which had been waged against bourgeois liberalization and spiritual pollution;
- To publish details about the assets and incomes of party leaders and their relatives;
- To allow freedom of speech and a free press;
- To increase funding for education;
- To raise the salaries of teachers and other intellectuals; and
- To lift all restrictions on street demonstrations.

In the evening, to the delight of the students, three members of the National People's Congress emerged from the cavernous Great Hall of the People, on the western side of the square, and took delivery of the petition, promising that it would be passed to higher authority.

If the students had now gone home, there might have been no confrontation and no consequent national movement. But a large contingent decided to stay on in the square. During the night, several hundred students moved from the square to the southern gateway of the Zhongnanhai and there began to jostle a line of security guards. They also began to shout, 'Li Peng come out!' When Li did not emerge, they tried to force their way through the gate, on to the lakeside road which led directly to party headquarters. They were kept out, and their action soon provoked a strong official response. Early the following morning, police loudspeakers broadcast a decree by the Peking municipal government which condemned their behaviour and stated that a 'small number of people' had engaged in 'spreading rumours, poisoning minds and putting up big-character posters which attacked and insulted party and government leaders'.[9]

Hu Yaobang's funeral ceremony was held in the Great Hall of the People on 22 April, just one week after his death. Most of the party's leaders, including Deng Xiaoping, were present, though

Chen Yun and Bo Yibo were conspicuously absent. Zhao Ziyang delivered the eulogy. He was unstinting in Hu's praise, making no mention of errors or weaknesses or of the circumstances which had led to his downfall. Outside the hall, nearly 100,000 students stood or sat in Tiananmen Square, chanting slogans whenever official participants arrived or left, but otherwise staying quiet. They had arrived, in well-drilled columns, during the night, and had extracted from the funeral organization office a guarantee that no action would be taken against them if they stayed in the square for the period of the ceremony. They had failed to obtain undertakings that they could pay their respects to Hu's corpse inside the Great Hall or that an official explanation would be given of the way the police had behaved outside the Zhongnanhai three days before. All the same, they had won what they, the party leadership and the world all regarded as a striking victory. Most of them went home when the ceremony was over. But some stayed on; and the rest decided to go on indefinite strike. Posters which criticized Deng personally began to go up on several campuses.

Deng Xiaoping may have taken a few days to make up his mind about the movement. On 25 April, however, he committed himself to views which became the cornerstone of the official position about it. On that day, Li Peng and Yang Shangkun – now head of state as well as permanent vice-chairman of the military commission – visited him at home to report on an overnight meeting of the politburo. The circumstances in which this meeting took place are mysterious. Zhao Ziyang, as general secretary its senior member, had left Peking the day before, on an official visit to North Korea. It was therefore convened and presided over by Li Peng, its second member. It has been alleged that Li acted without consulting Zhao in Korea, as he could easily have done by telegram or telephone. It has also been alleged that Bao Tong, the secretary of the politburo, was told nothing about the plan to convene it and was not invited to the meeting itself. There may therefore have been a plot. Whether or not there was, the meeting concluded that a 'planned and organized anti-party and anti-socialist drive to produce chaos' was developing, and decided to set up a 'small group' to deal with it and to commission an editorial in the *People's Daily* to explain its nature. According to an unofficial account, Li Ximing, the party secretary for Peking, presented a long report, emphasizing that the demonstrators were attacking the 'old comrades', notably Deng Xiaoping, as well as the party and socialism, but stating (extraordinarily) that their number was small. According to the same account, Wang Zhen demanded that the old comrades should be allowed to have their say when Hu Qili suggested that the opinion of 'the masses' should be sought. Having heard Li Peng's report, Deng said that he agreed with the meeting's decisions and went on to deliver his own verdict: the movement was not a matter of ordinary student effervescence; it was a drive to create a situation of chaos in which party leadership and the socialist system would be 'negated'.

When it appeared on 26 April, the editorial in the *People's Daily* used some of Deng's language verbatim, though without attribution, and insisted that China would sink into disorder, with the ruin of the hopes of its people, if a 'handful of people' were allowed to continue to exploit popular grief over the death of Hu Yaobang. According to a good source, the expectation of Li Peng, Li Ximing and the rest was that the article would have an intimidating effect, as had articles of a similar kind during the crises of June 1957 (the hundred flowers) and April 1976 (mourning for Zhou Enlai), so that fewer students would dare to demonstrate and that those who did would be easier to shepherd back to their campuses. If so, its actual effect was precisely the reverse; on 27 April, larger numbers than ever took to the streets and forced their way through one police line after another on their way to the centre of the city. They were cheered on their way by thousands of bystanders.

Deng must have found the circumstances of Hu Yaobang's funeral ceremony humiliating enough. Those of Gorbachev's visit to Peking, from 15 to 18 May, could only have been worse. Large parts of the planned programme, including a formal ceremony of welcome in Tiananmen Square, had to be cancelled. Instead of being able to drive in state through the flag-bedecked streets of a busy but peaceful city, Gorbachev had to drive under heavy military escort through crowds which were friendly but obviously out of official control. In the square, his portrait had replaced Hu's on the monument and an enormous crowd of students brandished banners which welcomed him as the initiator of glasnost and perestroika and asked where his Chinese counterpart was to be found. Deng saw him twice, at a meeting in the Great Hall and at a dinner given in his honour. Their conversations went well enough. But each must have reflected on the indignity of the proceedings and Deng on the reproach of being unable to offer anything better to the heir of Stalin and Khrushchev. A particularly galling feature for Deng must have been the fact that the world's media, represented by hundreds of journalists and scores of camera crews, were more interested in the activities of an army of political malcontents, camped on the doorstep of the Great Hall, than in what was taking place inside. It was their banners, and not his handshake with Gorbachev, symbolic of so much, which absorbed their attention.

During the first half of May, the movement swelled and became more militant. The students established a formal association, began to publish a daily newspaper and (on 13 May) started a hunger strike in Tiananmen Square. All this took place in the open. Behind the scenes, a bitter debate developed between the party leaders who wanted to crush the movement and those who favoured parleying with its spokesmen. In the politburo standing committee, the protagonists were Li Peng and Zhao Ziyang, who had returned from Korea on 30 April. According to an official account, Zhao had cabled his approval of Deng's analysis of events from Korea and so had by implication accepted the line in the *People's Daily* editorial of 26 April. Even if this is true, he and Li were at loggerheads from the moment of his return. Li told him with malice that the students had attacked his (Zhao's) sons as being among the worst of corrupt officials. Zhao responded by writing a letter to the politburo standing committee, saying that he wanted the law to be applied to his sons in its full rigour if they were to be found guilty. On 1 May, he proposed that his letter should be circulated to senior officials in the provinces. Li blocked his proposal. He also stood out against Zhao's demand that the editorial of 26 April should be disavowed, arguing that there could be no going back on judgements made by Deng Xiaoping personally. Two days later, however, Li suffered a set-back; Yang Shangkun supported Zhao when the latter argued that his official speech about the 4 May Movement, the seventieth anniversary of whose outbreak fell the next day, should not contain any criticism of bourgeois liberalization. Yang's support is not easy to explain. But things turned out as Zhao had wished. Both his speech and an accompanying editorial in the *People's Daily* were moderate in tone and were taken by the students – and the world – as signs that the leadership was ready to talk.

The stand-off between Li and Zhao continued until 17 May, Gorbachev's last full day in Peking. At a meeting of the politburo standing committee late on 16 May, deadlock had continued. Twenty-four hours later the committee met again, this time at Deng's house, and therefore under his supervision. Yao Yilin, who was close to Chen Yun (himself probably not in Peking, but certainly in close touch with events), launched into a long diatribe against Zhao, accusing him of having created divisions within the party by supporting the students, as well as of wanting a fully fledged market economy and being largely responsible for the corrupt behaviour of his sons. Yao and Li then demanded that martial law should be imposed on the urban areas of the Peking municipal district. When Zhao questioned the need for this, they (or Deng) demanded a vote. When this was taken, Yao, Li and Qiao Shi (the member of the committee responsible for law, order and security) voted in favour and Zhao and Hu Qili against. Exhausted by the strain and cast down by defeat, Zhao visited the students in Tiananmen Square at 4 am on the morning of 19 May, telling them that he and Li (who had insisted on accompanying him) had come 'too late' and asking their forgiveness, and then disappeared from view. According to an official account, he refused to attend a meeting of local officials and commanders at which Li announced later in the day that resolute action would be taken against 'all manifestations of disorder and indiscipline'. 'Thus', says the account, 'he demonstrated publicly his separation from the party.'

Martial law was imposed in an order of the state council, signed by Li Peng, on the morning of 20 May. Three decrees quickly followed. One banned processions, demonstrations, boycotts and strikes; another authorized the army and other security to adopt 'means to handle matters forcefully' in cases of need; and the third forbade all journalists, Chinese or foreign, to film in or report from the martial-law area without official approval. The message was very clear: the party and government were determined to break the student movement. What was less clear, perhaps even to the authorities themselves at this stage, was whether the army would be sent into the capital if the movement broke down, through dissension within its ranks – which had begun to develop – or through reaction to the pleading of parents or the appeals of the many intellectuals who feared that its continuation would lead to the destruction of the reform wing in the party.

At this stage only two eventualities could have saved the students if they continued to occupy Tiananmen Square: the emergence at the top of the party of a new group of conciliators or the refusal by a significant number of military commanders to take action against them. During the first week of martial law, both seemed to be on the cards. On 21 May, it was announced on television that Nie Rongzhen and Xu Xiangqian, the two surviving old marshals, had made a statement in which they had denied that the student movement was about to be repressed or that Li Peng had described the movement as a rebellion, and declared that the army was quite unwilling to contemplate bloodshed. On 23 May, a message to martial-law headquarters and the military commission from seven very senior retired officers, including Yang Dezhi, the man Deng had chosen to replace himself as chief of staff, was circulated unofficially. Its language was unequivocal. It declared that the 'people's army' belonged to the people, that it could not repress or open fire on the people, and that it must in no circumstances enter the capital.

All sorts of rumours meanwhile swept Peking. One was that Deng Xiaoping had flown to Wuhan to brief commanders from all or most of the country's military regions. This was probably true. It corresponds with Deng's attitude and his status as chairman of the military commission. It also fits two facts: that the minister of defence, Qin Jiwei, had been silent about martial law and that the headquarters of the Peking military region did not pronounce in its favour until 27 May. Some of the military evidently needed stiffening.

The army finally entered Peking, in massive strength, during the night of 3–4 June. Several hundred civilians at the least were killed, and thousands wounded, as columns of tanks, armoured personnel carriers and lorries carrying armed men and much equipment forced their way towards the centre of the city from points all round its periphery. The casualties were so numerous because the citizens of Peking had been busy building barricades on the main thoroughfares and were in a state of the highest apprehension and alert by the evening of 3 June (a Saturday); and this had occurred because the army had organized provocations during the Friday and the Saturday which produced an atmosphere of high tension without giving it any military advantage. These included raids from the Zhongnanhai to recover weapons 'lost' to civilians by groups of soldiers marooned by crowds. All this was done to give colour to the story that the state now faced a rebellion, and not just 'turmoil' or 'disorder'. The terrible irony is that a perceived need to justify the use of force itself helped to create the need to use it.

Most of those who died were not students. They were office and factory workers, shopkeepers and professional people. Some of the victims were women and children. Many people were shot down on barricades – especially on Peking's main east–west thoroughfare between Muxidi, a western suburb, and Tiananmen Square – and many more as they fled down side-streets from advancing troops. Quite a few soldiers were killed too, and even more armed police, who were mixed up with the population from the start. During the following three weeks, many different figures for casualties were given by official spokesmen. It is impossible to make them tally. In any case, they were only used to underpin political points: that the army had treated the students in Tiananmen Square, on whose fate the world's attention was chiefly fixed, with the greatest restraint; and that ordinary soldiers doing their duty had been set on without provocation by mobs of thugs and criminals. Figures for the number of students killed varied, but remained low (never higher than forty); figures for the number of soldiers and policemen killed and injured rose steadily and eventually exceeded 3,000.

There are many accounts, by students, foreign journalists and official spokesmen, of what happened in Tiananmen Square. The fullest – and most moving – is by Chai Ling, a young woman of twenty-three who had become 'chief of the joint command' (a strictly non-military organization) at the square a fortnight before. In a tape-recording smuggled out to Hong Kong, she described the use of violence by the troops who cleared the square against students, ordinary citizens and a contingent of workers from a newly established autonomous trade union. She (and many others) put it on record that, at the end of the night, the main body of students – about 5,000 strong – was allowed to pass through a gap in the ring of troops in the south-west corner of the square, under an arrangement negotiated between a singer from Taiwan who had been on hunger strike and a local commander, but that those who lingered were attacked. All the radio equipment, tents and personal possessions of the students were destroyed. So was a thirty-foot plaster statue, modelled on the Statue of Liberty, which had been built at the central institute of fine arts and transported to the square in three parts during the night of 29 May. As soon as the students had left, a cordon closed behind them, and from then on only the few who were bold enough to climb trees near its perimeter could watch the gruesome business of tidying up which was taking place behind it.

The evacuation of the square did not put an end to the violence. During the morning of 4 June, an infantry unit in the square fired into a large crowd of civilians which had gathered in front of it, killing and wounding scores. Similar incidents took place throughout that day and into the next. The city, and the world, were swept by rumours: that there would be a general strike, that there was bitter antagonism between the commanders of different military formations, which could soon lead to fighting, and that an attempt had been made on Li Peng's life by a security guard whose girlfriend had been killed. None of them turned out to be accurate. On their side, the authorities had curiously little to say. A joint communiqué of the central committee and the state council on 5 June announced that the situation in Peking was still 'critical' and a beginning – but only a beginning – was made by official spokesmen at a press conference on the following day to build up the case that the army had suffered much more than the civilian population. For several days there were no news programmes on television. Nor were the authorities quick to act against their chief political enemies. It was not until 10 June that they circulated a list of seven intellectuals they wanted to arrest, and not until 13 June that they published the names of their twenty-one most wanted student leaders. Of the intellectuals, four succeeded in leaving China, several of them even before they knew they were wanted men; of the student leaders, at least six, including Chai Ling, escaped from China during 1989 and 1990.

On 9 June, Deng Xiaoping appeared on television, for the first time since Gorbachev's visit. A news programme showed him at martial-law headquarters, addressing the commanders of the troops who by now occupied every important building and crossroads in the capital.

In his opening passage, Deng praised the officers and men of the army, the people's armed police and the security police who had died 'as heroes' in the conflict and offered his sympathy to the wounded. He then asked everyone present to stand in silence for a minute in 'homage to those martyred'. Yet he did not say a word about the conduct of operations by their commanders or about the orders these had received from above. Many outside China failed to notice the omission at the time, and so missed its implication: that Deng was angry about the manner in which the whole operation had been conducted. If so, he had good reason. The whole world had watched a slow-moving and blood-stained process, during which no mercy had been shown to anyone who got in the army's way and in which many had been killed by indiscriminate fire.

That this interpretation is not fanciful is borne out by both direct and circumstantial evidence. As direct evidence, there is a story from a party source that Deng called in Li Peng and Yang Shangkun at about the time of his address to the generals and told them that they had bungled the military operation appallingly. Circumstantially, there is the fact that, when the time came to replace Zhao Ziyang as general secretary, it was not Li Peng, who had decreed martial law and been seen on television giving orders to the population on the evening of 3 June, but Jiang Zemin, the party secretary and mayor of Shanghai, who was chosen to succeed him.

Deng went on to declare that the turmoil would have been bound to occur sooner or later. Its outbreak was the product of the climate in the world at large and in China in particular: 'It was inevitable and independent of all human will.' Only its precise timing and its scale had been open. This was Deng speaking in a new tone of voice. Although his daughter Deng Rong (Maomao) had once written that he was something of a fatalist, one of his chief themes over the years had been that good leadership would always be able to foresee and forestall political difficulties.

Deng laboured the point that the young soldiers of the army had done their duty and that they had not forgotten 'the people, the teaching of the party or the national interest'. They had remained firm in the face of death and had shown that the army was a 'wall of steel for the party and the state'. And then, in a phrase which revealed his hatred for those, just as young, who had defied the party, he uttered the harshest official words of his career: 'We must never forget the cruelties of our enemy for whom we must show no mercy or even an iota of forgiveness.'

Deng devoted the rest of his speech to political and economic strategy. As if speaking to a group of civilians at a work conference, and not embattled military men, he went over China's political history since 1978. He asked and answered a whole set of questions, leading up to the question whether the strategy of the thirteenth congress – known as 'one centre' (concentration on economic development) and 'two fundamental points' (maintenance of the four cardinal principles on the one hand and the policies of reform and opening to the outside world on the other) – was correct or not. His predictable answer was that it was and ought to stand.

The second part of Deng's speech attracted little attention abroad. Yet it showed that an acute political mind was still at work, alive to two dangers: that many among his colleagues would attribute the student movement to his reform strategy, and that the disgrace of Zhao Ziyang would make the strategy dangerously vulnerable to attack by new and old enemies. It showed too that Deng's political method had not altered: it was still to take the offensive before he could be put under attack. He looked old and tired on television that night. But there was more art in his speech than the world understood at the time.

CHAPTER 15

Patriarch, 1989–93

The three men Mao Zedong earmarked to succeed him – Liu Shaoqi, Lin Biao and Hua Guofeng – all came to grief. So did Hu Yaobang, Deng Xiaoping's first choice of successor. Now it was the turn of Zhao Ziyang. At the end of June, Li Peng gave a report to the central committee on 'the mistakes made by comrade Zhao Ziyang during the anti-party and anti-socialist turmoil', speaking harshly about Zhao's failure to uphold the four cardinal principles and oppose bourgeois liberalization and saying that he had 'inescapable responsibility' for the emergence and development of the turmoil.[1] Organizationally, Zhao's fate was precisely the one Deng Xiaoping had suffered in 1968 and again in 1976: he lost his membership of the central committee and all his appointments under it, but – as prefigured by the use of the term 'comrade' – was allowed to keep his party membership. Zhao's punishment need not have been so severe. On 13 June, Deng had sent Yang Shangkun to tell him that he could stay in the politburo if he made a formal confession of error. To his great credit, and unlike Hu Yaobang, who had kept his place on the standing committee in return for making a 'self-examination' in January 1987, Zhao refused. He has since disappeared completely from public view. Once or twice he has been spotted playing golf, which has shown that he is not a prisoner, and there were rumours in 1992 that he might be rehabilitated. But these came to an end in the autumn, when it was announced that the central committee stood by its sentence.

A few others, including Hu Qili, also lost their posts in the politburo and the secretariat. Three men were added to the standing committee: Jiang Zemin, Song Ping and Li Ruihuan; and Jiang became the new general secretary.

Jiang Zemin was an unexpected choice. Like Li Peng, whom he now overtook in the party hierarchy, he was an engineer by profession, and like Li he had held a series of technocratic posts in the 1960s and 1970s. Unlike Li, he was an affable man. Li seldom smiled, and when he did his smile was wintry. Jiang liked to laugh. Brought up in Shanghai, he had learned, and could be induced to sing, English music-hall songs and was fond of British films of the 1940s, like *Waterloo Bridge* (on an official visit to London in 1988, he stole away from the Chinese Embassy one night to look at the eponymous bridge). As a young man, he had escaped from the campus of his university, where nationalist soldiers and police were looking for communists, in the boot of his principal's car; and he had a similar adventure in May 1989, when he thought it wise to disguise himself before passing through a student picket line in Peking. Both party secretary and mayor of Shanghai, he had acquired merit in Deng's eyes by closing a liberal weekly there a day after the publication of the *People's Daily* editorial of 26 April. But he had also impressed Deng by drawing up and launching a programme to modernize Shanghai, a city which had slipped from being one of the most modern in the world to one of the most backward. He was both an enemy of bourgeois liberalization and an enthusiast for development.

Song Ping's promotion was a reward for his behaviour during the democracy movement, when he had played an important part as director of the party's organization department in stiffening the resolve of military men who were hesitant about ordering their troops to enter Peking. Old and dull, he was dropped from the standing committee in October 1992. Li Ruihuan was younger and livelier. He had made his name as a clerk of the works during the construction of the Great Hall of the People in just eight months in 1958 and he had gone on to be an imaginative and efficient mayor of Tientsin. A jack-in-a-box of a man, never still in conversation, he had prevented the democracy movement from bringing Tientsin to a standstill – malicious tongues said by encouraging its many students to take their demands to Peking – but was well known for his desire to encourage foreign investment in his city. Like Jiang's, his promotion was a symbol of continued commitment to reform.

Two months after the central committee meeting, Deng took the step he had been dissuaded from taking in 1987: in a letter to the politburo, he asked to resign as chairman of the party's military commission. There was much foreign speculation over his motives. In one view, he wanted to make sure that the army, to which a divided party had owed its survival, did not come to command the party after his disappearance from political life. In another, he wanted to give Jiang Zemin a source of authority but also of advice which Hu Yaobang and Zhao Ziyang had both lacked. In a third, he wanted to prevent Yang Shangkun, the permanent vice-chairman of the commission, from being his own successor as chairman, which would probably happen if he died in office. Perhaps all these motives were present. One which was not was the wish to quit politics altogether. Deng's way of making this clear was to state that he would continue to serve 'the cause of the party and the nation'.[2] Even if he had wanted to retire completely – which would have been most improbable in a man for whom politics had been the stuff of life for nearly seventy years – he knew perfectly well that there are only two possible fates for leaders who have left office in one-party states: elder statesmanship and disgrace. Unless he has been disgraced, the counsel of the retired leader will continue to be sought.

In his letter of resignation, Deng said that he was still in good health. There is no reason to doubt that he was. Suddenly, however, he began to look a great deal older. It seems that, in physical terms, he had chosen the right moment to do only what he felt inclined to do. How did he spend his time? He certainly continued to see a good deal of his children, now all middle-aged, and of their children. Among the children, he seems to have drawn closest to Deng Rong, his youngest daughter. It was she who walked at his elbow, watching for any false step, when he walked very slowly through the assembled delegates at the fourteenth party congress in October 1992. He continued to play bridge, seemingly with his old partners, including Wan Li and Yang Shangkun. Very occasionally, he received a foreign visitor – Kissinger in the autumn of 1989 and Kim Il Sung of North Korea in 1992.

Deng continued to take a close interest in international affairs. The collapse of communist rule in East Germany, Czechoslovakia and Romania in the winter of 1989–90 reinforced his view that China was up against an organized campaign by the West to overturn socialism everywhere. The implications he saw for China are set out in some 'comments' circulated by party headquarters in April 1990:

Everyone should be very clear that, in the present international situation, all the attention of the enemy will be concentrated on China. It will use every pretext to cause trouble, to create difficulties and pressures for us. [China therefore needs] stability, stability and still more stability. The next three to five years will be extremely difficult for our party and our country, and extremely important. If we stand fast and survive them, our cause will develop quickly. If we collapse, China's history will regress for several tens of years, even for a hundred years.[3]

It was in this light that he (and the party's new official leaders) had already interpreted the imposition of sanctions on China by Western countries after 4 June, and that they now interpreted Western protests about human rights violations and the use of force to suppress demonstrations in Tibet and Sinkiang.

It is natural for a Marxist, who sees the whole of history in terms of conflict, to be a conspiracy theorist, and there can be no doubt that Deng believed that the capitalist countries of the West had worked out a strategy to produce 'peaceful evolution' from socialism to capitalism in the whole communist world. In the Soviet politics of 1990 and 1991, Deng undoubtedly preferred the conservative communists – the conspirators of August 1991 – to Gorbachev, but Gorbachev to Yeltsin. But, east and west, he favoured caution in public Chinese attitudes. 'We should observe developments soberly, maintain our positions, meet any challenge calmly, hide our capacities, bide our time, remain free of ambitions, and never claim leadership (of the socialist world).'[4]

Deng had his way; and policies consistent with his view by degrees brought China advantage. Western economic sanctions faded away; Western ministers began to visit China again; and at the end of 1992 Yang Shangkun received a smiling Yeltsin in Peking. Patience and discretion had paid off, and China had succeeded – with some help from events, notably the Iraqi invasion of Kuwait, which made it necessary for the West to seek its support at the United Nations – in resuming its place at the top international table.

Deng was also able to get his way over economic reform. Thanks to his speech at martial-law headquarters, and to the promotion of Jiang Zemin and Li Ruihuan, there had been no serious backlash against the policies of the 1980s after 4 June. Family farming remained the norm in agriculture; the scope of mandatory planning was not enlarged; and existing incentives for foreign investors stayed in place. Yet Deng wanted to go further, and by degrees there developed a dispute between him and the more conservative members of the new leadership, with Chen Yun behind them, over the role of planning in socialism and development. For Chen – and for Li Peng and Yao Yilin, his disciples in the politburo standing committee – a substantial measure of mandatory planning was essential, both as a badge of socialism and as a means of promoting growth. Deng, on the other hand, began to see planning as non-essential to either.

Because Deng had ceased to make set-piece statements at party meetings or to receive foreign visitors, it is not easy to follow the steps in the development of his views. It is, however, clear that he spoke a good deal about reform to leaders with executive posts between the beginning of 1990 and the end of 1991. He has himself said that he spoke out on the subject eight times. It is also clear that he encountered a good deal of indifference, and even outright opposition. The national press did not even refer to an article reflecting his views which appeared in a Shanghai newspaper in the spring of 1991.

Frustrated, Deng decided to make sure of an impact by using methods rather like those Mao Zedong had used in the winter of 1965–6, when he wanted to turn the tables on Liu Shaoqi, Peng Zhen and Deng himself. At the beginning of 1992, he set out on a long tour of central, southern and eastern China, including places where anything he said was likely to be picked up very quickly in Hong Kong. Travelling with Deng Nan and, for some of the time, several senior military men, he visited Wuhan, the special economic zones of Shenzhen (next door to Hong Kong) and Zhuhai (near Macao) and Shanghai. He made speeches in each of these places, and it was not long before summaries or quotations began to appear in the Hong Kong press and in Hong Kong radio and television programmes. These were picked up by millions in south China who watched Hong Kong television and were soon very widely known about.

In this situation, Deng's associates were bound to react. There is a story that Chen Yun told Deng to his face that his views were non- or anti-socialist. But the timing of reactions in Peking shows that there could have been very little debate there about what to do. Deng spoke for the last time on 21 February; on the 28th the substance of what he had said was issued to the party at large in a central-committee circular. As a great deal of editorial work had been needed to turn (at least) four speeches into a single text, the decision to issue the document must have been taken very soon after his final speech.*

Deng spoke on two general topics, economic development and politics. On development, he argued that the line of 'one centre, two basic points' was correct and must not be changed, that it was vital to be bold and imaginative in implementing this line, and that conditions were particularly favourable for a renewed drive for economic growth. He broke new ideological ground in a passage which would have startled even the most ardent reformers of Hu Yaobang's day:

* A member of the central committee told the author in April 1992 that it had been difficult to produce a single text from several overlapping statements.

The fundamental difference between socialism and capitalism does not lie in the question whether the planning mechanism or the market mechanism plays a larger role. [The] planned economy does not equal socialism, because planning also exists in capitalism; neither does [the] market economy equal capitalism, because the market also exists in socialism. Both planning and market are just economic means. The nature of socialism is to emancipate and develop the productive forces, to eliminate exploitation and polarization, and finally to achieve the goal of common affluence. This should be explained to everybody.[5]

Deng also criticized the critics of economic reform:

At present, some rightist things are affecting us, and so are some 'leftist' things. However, the 'leftist' things are deep-rooted. Some theorists and politicians like to use serious charges to intimidate people. This is not rightist but 'leftist' . . . 'Leftist' things have done terrible harm to our party in the past . . . Socialism may be ruined by rightism, and may also be ruined by 'leftism'. China must guard against rightism, but should mainly guard against 'leftism'. Rightist things do exist. The turmoil was a rightist thing. 'Leftist' things also exist. The opinion which equates reform and opening to ushering in and developing capitalism, and which holds that the danger of peaceful evolution mainly comes from the economic field, precisely represents 'leftism'.[6]

There was no mistaking his message: the reaction against liberalization had gone too far, to the point where development and popular morale were both threatened, and a counter-reaction was needed.

On politics, Deng spoke, as he had many times in the past, of the need to uphold social order ('in cracking down on various criminal activities and sweeping away various evil and ugly phenomena, we must not be soft-hearted'), to stick to the four cardinal principles, to promote younger people to the 'leading group' in the party and to apply Marxism creatively ('seeking truth from facts is the quintessence of Marxism'). He ended by proclaiming his belief that 'more people in the world' would come to favour Marxism, because it was 'a branch of science'. What he did not do, any more than he had done before, was to answer the question which his interpretation of the nature of Marxism must have suggested to millions: what if the quest of truth from facts suggests that the assumptions of Marxism itself are open to question?

The circulation of Deng's remarks, followed by their publication in the *People's Daily* in the early summer, produced a turn in the political tide, and it has since continued to flow in his desired direction. There has been no more talk to reflect the line on planning which Chen Yun took at a meeting of his central advisory commission in early March:

At present there is a dangerous tendency [in talk about] enlivening the economy to shake off state planning. This is a grave tendency. It will certainly create chaos, affect the entire national economy and lead to social turmoil . . . some people are asking if we are going fast or wide or deep enough in reform and want us to lean towards it more boldly . . . Have Yugoslavia, Eastern Europe and the Soviet Union not gone far enough? . . . Our national situation differs from theirs, but our economic foundation is even weaker . . . We simply cannot afford their painful lessons.[7]

The defeat of Chen Yun and the rest was signalled in public when the *People's Daily* reported in June 1992 that all regions of the country had supported Deng's call for bolder reform and within the party when a set of measures to give effect to this call was outlined in a new central committee circular. Quite soon, four of the most zealous campaigners against bourgeois liberalization, spiritual pollution and total westernization, including the editor of the *People's Daily* and the director of the party's propaganda department, were moved to less important jobs.

Deng's triumph was sealed at the fourteenth party congress in October 1992. In his political report, Jiang Zemin described Deng as 'the general architect of reform and opening up and of the modernization drive in relation to socialism in China', defined the task of the congress as being 'to use comrade Deng Xiaoping's theory of building socialism with Chinese characteristics as a guide

... [to] quicken the pace of reform, opening up and moderniza-tion', and stated that the target of structural reform was 'to build a socialist market economic system' (not the 'socialist planned com-modity economy' of which Zhao Ziyang had spoken five years before).[8]

Deng was able to savour his triumph when, carefully watched by Deng Rong, he walked slowly down an aisle of the congress hall on the final day of the meeting. He made no speech and did not stay for long. But the applause showed that the delegates liked him better as an architect than they had ever liked Mao as a helmsman. It showed, too, that they were going to miss him. They knew that many others had helped Deng to plan China's moderniza-tion drive and to work out its underpinning theory. But they also knew that he had been the prime mover over both and that he had no obvious successor as a political strategist or theorist. What would China do without him, during a period when, as he himself had warned, new problems and challenges were bound to emerge? There was no one in the new leadership, or anywhere else in the country, who remotely approached him in stature.

Epilogue

What has Deng Xiaoping achieved in his extraordinary career? And what sort of future does China face when it ends?

Deng's first achievement, the condition for everything else, was to become China's leader. He started his revolutionary career with the advantage of extreme youth; at the time of his conversion to Marxism he was five or more years younger than the other converts of the first generation and he was therefore always likely to outlive them. But he stayed a long way behind many of them in party rank during the 1920s and 1930s, and fell behind some of his contemporaries, like Chen Yun (and the Returned Students for as long as they lasted). He did not reach the central committee, let alone the politburo, until 1945, when he was already over forty, and it was by no means clear when he was transferred from Sichuan to Peking in 1952 that he would rise above the large second echelon of the new national leadership. Even after he had become the party's general secretary in 1956, after very rapid promotion, few Chinese saw him as Mao's successor. And once he had fallen in the Cultural Revolution, the odds were against his ever rising again, let alone rising higher than Zhou Enlai, Lin Biao or any of Mao Zedong's new revolutionary friends. That he did owed much to Mao himself – especially in 1968, when he saved Deng from expulsion from the party, and 1972, when he decided to respond positively to Deng's pleas for rehabilitation – and much to the folly of his political enemies. But it owed a lot too to his own qualities: resilience, tenacity and perhaps above all an ability to win loyal friends. One of the most remarkable features of the period between his disgrace in April 1976 and Mao's death in September is that the Gang of Four were unable to lay hands on him – as they would certainly have been able to do if he had not been protected by friends in Peking (twice) and Guangdong.

As national leader, Deng's two great achievements were to set China on a path of rapid economic development and to bring it into the mainstream of international life. On development, his key contribution, which unlocked the door to everything else, was to put it at the top of the party's agenda. He was helped by others, and he was swimming with a tide which was flowing strongly in the country after twenty years of revolutionary excess. But it was his speech at the work conference of December 1978 which made it possible for the central committee to fix Zhou Enlai's four modernizations as the 'focus of all party work'. It was also his speech which led the committee to reject Hua Guofeng's 'two whatevers' – in front of Hua himself – and to decide to abandon all further talk of class struggle as the 'key link'. Development was thereby shorn of the trammels which had held it back before.

On means, Deng contributed less. He has claimed that he first proposed the policy of 'opening to the outside world', and he certainly took a great deal of interest in the fortunes of the special economic zones which were the most visible symbols of this policy. But even here he left the detail to others. This was perhaps as well. His chief intervention over policy, in favour of accelerated price reform in 1988, led to a rapid worsening of inflation, the disease he had hoped it would cure.

The results of the shift promoted by Deng have been remarkable – even staggering. During the thirteen years from 1980 to 1992, China's gross national product grew at an average annual rate of 8.9 per cent, comparable with the rates achieved by the four 'little dragons' of South Korea, Taiwan, Hong Kong and Singapore and far ahead of the rates registered in the developed Western countries. (In 1992, the chief economist of the World Bank wrote that, if the difference between the recent growth rates of China and the United States, 6.4 per cent, continued to hold, China's output would surpass that of the United States within eleven years.) The value of China's foreign trade rose from US$38 billion in 1980 to US$115 billion in 1990, turning China from a country for which trade was a marginal activity into one which was using trade as an engine of growth. During the same period, China attracted far more foreign investment than any other developing country. By 1990, foreign capital had been used to set up or revitalize more than 30,000 enterprises and the total value of foreign investment was well over US$20 billion (with a good deal more pledged). There were many areas, especially in provinces remote from the coast, where the people still lived in great poverty; but even in them, living standards had begun to rise.

The policies of development produced their own problems. One was inflation. Between 1988 and 1990, the official retail price index rose by a total of nearly 40 per cent, which had a good deal to do with the great political explosion of 1989. And it is clear that renewed growth at an annual rate above 10 per cent, achieved in 1992, is producing renewed inflation. A second concerned the finances of the central government. The government delegated so much tax-gathering authority to the provinces that the share of national income which it took as revenue fell from 47 per cent in 1979 to 16 per cent in 1990, a proportion lower than in the United States and far lower than in any country in Western Europe. A third concerned state-owned enterprises. Saddled with enormous welfare costs, for retired workers as well as workers on their books, and often forced to sell their output at low fixed prices, more and more enterprises became loss-making. In 1990, the total of their losses amounted to US$20 billion, getting on for 5 per cent of national income.

These problems are serious. But they pale beside the general success of China's drive for development – and beside the disasters which have followed the collapse of communism in the Soviet Union and most other eastern countries. What have been the secrets of success? Three stand out. The first was the point of departure in reform: in agriculture rather than industry and commerce. Once the yeast of the incentives in systems of 'responsibility' had begun to work, food and raw materials for light industry became plentiful in a manner never known before; and this relief of shortages created physical and social conditions for change in the cities. The second was the avoidance of a 'big bang' over the removal of price controls. This meant that the innumerable vested interests in the old economy were coaxed rather than driven into a more competitive economic world and that the consumer was not turned into an enemy of reform by being faced by spiralling inflation and a rapid decline in his standard of living. China's highest rate of inflation was 18.5 per cent (in 1988); in the Soviet Union, the official rate of inflation was 91 per cent in 1991, and it has since gone far higher. The third was to make political reform follow economic reform. This of course disappointed many hopes and expectations (whereby hangs much of the dreadful tale of 1989). But it also meant that the opposition of groups which were bound to suffer from reform, such as the planners and industrial workers who had enjoyed lifelong security of employment, could be contained. Without newspapers of their own or independent unions or political clubs, they could exercise pressure only within the state structure, where their pressure would be met by countervailing pressure. This in turn meant that the reform programme as a whole could not be brought to a halt, or shorn of features which were offensive to particular social groups, by external political action and that its least palatable features could be allowed to do their work.

None of this is to say that the proletarian dictatorship of Deng and his associates has been benign. It has not. Nor is it to say that Deng and the others have looked forward to the day when this dictatorship and party leadership can be replaced by a plural political system and competitive elections for executive and legislative power. They have not. But it is to say that its exercise allowed advances which made it more likely that a more open political order would stick when it did come than if it had been brought in earlier. Democracy does best when it grows slowly in a developing country and reaches maturity when that country has achieved quite high levels of prosperity and education.

From 1950 to 1972, when Nixon visited Peking, China was a world apart. It was a distant and mysterious place even for other communist countries (except North Korea, Mongolia and

Vietnam). Its separation from the rest of the world had a great deal to do with its treatment by the United States from the time of the Korean War onwards. But it was also a function of Mao Zedong's extreme sinocentrism. He was not very interested in the world at large and disliked a good deal of what he knew about the Soviet Union, the only foreign country he ever visited. In consequence, the stock of knowledge about China in the rest of the world ran down, and the stock of knowledge in China about the world also dwindled.

Deng has changed all that. He has done this so that China can import the foreign capital, technology and industrial and commercial skills which it needs for rapid modernization. But he has also done it so that China can exercise influence proportionate to its size in the international handling of global and (especially) regional problems. He has also changed China's approach to such problems, moving it far away from the encouragement of revolution and war. For the past ten years, China has worked to take the heat out of 'hot spots', its own description of situations which could lead to war, and not to raise the temperature. China has become a member of a host of international organizations, from the International Monetary Fund (where it took over the China seat occupied by Taiwan) to Interpol. It has sent scholars and students to almost all the developed Western countries – over 30,000 to the United States alone – and has received advisers, scholars and students from all over the world. Set alongside the international airports of Europe and the United States, the international airport at Peking is not a busy place; but there are now dozens of inward and outward flights every day, compared with only three or four fifteen years ago.

And what now? China is so large and is changing so rapidly that prediction is bound to be hazardous. But if the past can be used as a lantern for the future, its light falls on the outlines of four features.

The first is political: that one man (not a woman before the end of this century) will come to the top in the party, and therefore the state, though perhaps only after a period of manoeuvre and dispute, after Deng has gone. Chinese tradition and the dynamic of democratic centralism both require a supreme or paramount leader. This does not mean that the principle of collective leadership will be emptied of content altogether. But it does mean that the new leader's closest associates will be more his lieutenants than his peers.

The second is social: that the appetite of the highly educated class, growing all the time in size and degree of knowledge, for greater social and cultural freedom will increase, but that doubt about the wisdom of China's abandoning one-party rule will remain prevalent, in this class and outside. It is therefore possible that, following the route earlier taken by Hong Kong, China will become a country where many freedoms are permitted – and even entrenched – but where plural democracy follows only slowly.

The third is economic and social: that the size of the population, now well over 1.1 billion, will continue to increase rapidly, exceeding 1.2 billion before the end of the century. This will begin to put new pressure on the food supply, ultimately to the point where the amount of food available for each Chinese household starts to diminish. Sometime in the first twenty years of the next century, China will have to face the choice between reintroducing rationing and importing food on an increasing scale.

The fourth is political and cultural: the Tibetans, the Islamic peoples of Sinkiang and (perhaps) the Mongolians of Inner Mongolia will demand a much greater degree of cultural freedom and political autonomy than they now enjoy. So far, the world's attention has been fixed on Tibet. But it is the peoples of Sinkiang, influenced by Islamic revivalism and the emergence of independent states for their ethnic brothers and sisters across the former Soviet border, who may become the most assertive.

Meanwhile, the people of China will have to pass judgement on the man who has led them for all but two of the years since Mao Zedong's death. Most of them will see blemishes on his record – not least the crushing of the democracy movement in 1989. Some of them will see more black than white. But the great majority will see much more white than black, if only for having lifted them to a standard of life unknown, and undreamed of, by their parents.

Notes

The full titles of the books and articles referred to in these notes are given in the bibliography. 'Party historians' refers to Madame Wang Zuoling and her colleagues in the Research Department on Party Literature of the Central Committee of the Chinese Communist Party. 'Official biography' refers to the thirteen pages of text in the English edition of the photographic biography of Deng Xiaoping published by the Central Party Literature Publishing House in 1988. 'Deng's biography' refers to the photographic biography as a whole.

Chapter 1: Farmer's Son, 1904–20

1. Party historians to author, 27 April 1992.
2. Official biography, p. 42.
3. The author.
4. Party historians to author, 21 April 1992.
5. Official biography, p. 42.
6. Bailey, 'The Chinese work-study movement in France', p. 449.
7. ibid., p. 452.
8. ibid., p. 453n.
9. Franz, *Deng Xiaoping*, p. 28.

Chapter 2: Doctor of Mimeography, 1920–26

1. Official biography, p. 43.
2. ibid.
3. *Washington Post*, 31 August 1980.
4. Official biography, p. 43n.
5. Barman and Dulioust, 'Les années françaises', p. 31.
6. Wang, 'Deng Xiaoping: the years in France', p. 702.

7. ibid., p. 704.
8. Official biography, p. 43.
9. Deng's biography, p. 57.
10. Franz, *Deng Xiaoping*, p. 56.

Chapter 3: Warlords and Bolsheviks, 1926–7

1. Spence, *The Search for Modern China*, p. 323.
2. Official biography, p. 43.
3. Helen Foster Snow, *The Chinese Communists*, p. 229.
4. Party historians to author, 21 April 1992.
5. BBC Summary of World Broadcasts, FE/1346, 3 April 1992, p. B2/6.
6. Mao Tse-tung, *Selected Works*, Vol. 1, p. 25.
7. Cambridge History, Vol. 12, p. 607.
8. Official biography, p. 43.
9. ibid.
10. Party historians to author, 21 April 1992.

Chapter 4: In Peril, 1927–31

1. Cambridge History, Vol. 12, p. 656.
2. Official biography, p. 44.
3. ibid.
4. ibid., p. 45.
5. ibid.
6. Yuan Renyuan, 'A Red storm'.
7. Official biography, p. 45.
8. Franz, *Deng Xiaoping*, p. 88.

Chapter 5: Long Marcher, 1931–5

1. Official biography, p. 45.
2. Party historians to author, 21 April 1992.
3. Nie Rongzhen, *Inside the Red Star*, p. 110.
4. Edgar Snow, *Red Star over China*, p. 177.
5. Official biography, p. 45.
6. ibid.
7. Hsiao Tso-liang, *Power Relations*, p. 242.
8. Official biography, p. 45.
9. Salisbury, *The Long March*, p. 142.
10. Mao Tse-tung, *Selected Works*, Vol. 3, p. 193.
11. Party historians to author, 21 April 1992.

12. Yang, *From Revolution to Politics*, p. 159.
13. ibid, p. 165.

Chapter 6: Soldier in the Hills, *1935–45*

 1. Yang, *From Revolution to Politics*, p. 183.
 2. ibid., p. 224.
 3. Party historians to author, 22 April 1992.
 4. Official biography, p. 46.
 5. ibid.
 6. ibid.
 7. Deng Xiaoping, *Selected Works 1938–1965*, p. 86.
 8. Cambridge History, Vol. 13, p. 608.
 9. Kampen, 'The Zunyi Conference and further steps in Mao's rise to power', p. 132n.
10. ibid., p. 131n.
11. Deng's biography, caption on p. 65.
12. Mao Tse-tung, *Selected Works*, Vol. 3, p. 119.

Chapter 7: Soldier on the Plain, *1945–52*

 1. Cambridge History, Vol. 13, p. 752.
 2. Mao Tse-tung, *Selected Works*, Vol. 4, p. 142.
 3. Official biography, p. 47.
 4. Party historians to author, 22 April 1992.
 5. Nie Rongzhen, *Inside the Red Star*, pp. 585–6.
 6. Schram, *Mao Tse-tung Unrehearsed*, p. 191.
 7. Party historians to author, 22 April 1992.
 8. Riskin, *China's Political Economy*, p. 48.

Chapter 8: The Hundred Flowers, *1952–7*

 1. Official guides to author, spring 1986.
 2. Mao Tse-tung, *Selected Works*, Vol. 5, p. 92.
 3. MacFarquhar, *Origins of the Cultural Revolution*, Vol. 1, p. 5.
 4. Mao Tse-tung, *Selected Works*, Vol. 5, p. 71n.
 5. MacFarquhar, *Origins of the Cultural Revolution*, Vol. 1, p. 7.
 6. Party historians to author, 22 April 1992.
 7. Mao Tse-tung, *Selected Works*, Vol. 5, p. 184.
 8. ibid., p. 304.
 9. ibid., p. 341.
10. Deng Xiaoping, *Speeches and Writings*, p. 2.

11. ibid., pp. 29–30.
12. ibid., p. 21.
13. Official biography, p. 49.
14. Franz, *Deng Xiaoping*, p. 165.
15. *Beijing Review*, 25 September 1989, p. 24.

Chapter 9: Looking after Leaping, 1957–65

1. Mao Tse-tung, *Selected Works*, Vol. 5, pp. 469–70.
2. Cambridge History, Vol. 15, pp. 38–9.
3. MacFarquhar, *Origins of the Cultural Revolution*, Vol. 2, p. 121.
4. Party historians to author, 23 April 1993.
5. *Resolution on CPC History*, p. 29.
6. Zagoria, *Sino-Soviet Conflict*, p. 365.
7. Bowie and Fairbank, *Communist China 1955–59*, p. 599.
8. Deng Xiaoping, *Selected Works, 1938–1965*, pp. 305–6.

Chapter 10: Capitalist Roader, 1965–73

1. Cambridge History, Vol. 14, p. 462.
2. Party historians to author, 27 April 1992.
3. Schram, *Mao Tse-tung Unrehearsed*, p. 260.
4. Cambridge History, Vol. 15, p. 140.
5. Rice, *Mao's Way*, p. 252.
6. ibid., p. 264.
7. Chi Hsin, *Teng Hsiao-ping*, pp. 54–64.
8. Schram, *Mao Tse-tung Unrehearsed*, pp. 266–7.
9. *A Great Trial in Chinese History*, p. 35.
10. *Washington Post*, 31 August 1980.
11. Kok, *Teng Hsiao-ping*, p. 23.
12. Nie Rongzhen, *Inside the Red Star*, p. 747, and party historians to author, 23 April 1992.
13. Party historians to author, 23 April 1992.
14. Official biography, p. 50.
15. ibid.

Chapter 11: Against the Gang, 1973–6

1. Cambridge History, Vol. 15, p. 345.
2. ibid., p. 350.
3. Deng Xiaoping, *Selected Works 1975–1982*, p. 16.
4. ibid., p. 14.

5. *Issues and Studies*, February 1979, p. 96.
6. Spence, *The Search for Modern China*, p. 646.
7. Deng's biography, p. 97.
8. Bonavia, *Deng*, p. 142.
9. *Issues and Studies*, December 1978, p. 93.

Chapter 12: Mending China, 1976–81

1. *Issues and Studies*, March 1984, p. 443.
2. Cambridge History, Vol. 15, p. 372.
3. Deng Xiaoping, *Selected Works 1975–1982*, p. 51.
4. Party historians to author, 27 April 1992.
5. Deng Xiaoping, *Selected Works 1975–1982*, pp. 87–100.
6. ibid., p. 107.
7. Cambridge History, Vol. 15, p. 430.
8. Deng Xiaoping, *Selected Works 1975–1982*, pp. 151–65.
9. ibid. pp. 166–91.
10. Harding, *China's Second Revolution*, p. 66.
11. ibid., p. 58.
12. *Resolution on CPC History*, pp. 56, 57, 32 and 40.

Chapter 13: National Leader, 1981–4

1. Harding, *China's Second Revolution*, pp. 29–30.
2. Li Xiannian to Princess Margaret, May 1987.
3. Deng Xiaoping, *Fundamental Issues*, p. 65.
4. ibid., p. 130.
5. ibid., pp. 137–8.
6. ibid., pp. 197–8n.
7. White Paper of 26 September 1984 (Cmnd 9352), introduction.
8. Deng Xiaoping, *Fundamental Issues*, p. 51.
9. White Paper of 26 September 1984 (Cmnd 9352), introduction.
10. ibid.
11. Deng Xiaoping, *Fundamental Issues*, p. 96.
12. ibid., p. 52.
13. ibid., pp. 94–5.

Chapter 14: Tiananmen, 1984–9

1. Deng Xiaoping, *Fundamental Issues*, pp. 61–2.
2. ibid., p. 63.
3. ibid., p. 128.

4. ibid., p. 154.
5. ibid., pp. 164–5.
6. ibid., p. 184.
7. ibid., p. 192.
8. *The First Session of the Seventh National People's Congress of the People's Republic of China*, p. 16.
9. The documents quoted or referred to in the rest of this chapter are all to be found in Béja *et al.*, *Tremblement de terre*.

Chapter 15: Patriarch, 1989–93

1. *Seventy Years of the Chinese Communist Party*, p. 612.
2. *Since the Thirteenth Congress*, Vol. 2, p. 602.
3. *Zheng Ming, Hong Kong*, 1 May 1990.
4. BBC Summary of World Broadcasts, FE/1346 3 April 1992, p. B2/2.
5. ibid., pp. B2/2–3.
6. ibid., p. B2/3.
7. 'Quarterly chronicle and documentation', *China Quarterly* No. 131, September 1992.
8. BBC Summary of World Broadcasts, FE/1511, 14 October 1992, pp. C1/1–19.

Bibliography

This bibliography lists the books, collections of documents and articles which the author has found particularly useful in preparing this study. It gives details of all the documents referred to in the source notes. Books published in Chinese in China or Hong Kong which, to the best of the author's knowledge, have not so far been translated into English or French are marked with an asterisk.

Histories

The Cambridge History of China, Volume 12, *Republican China 1912–1949, Part 1* (Cambridge University Press, 1983).

The Cambridge History of China, Volume 13, *Republican China 1912–1949, Part 2* (Cambridge University Press, 1986).

The Cambridge History of China, Volume 14, *The People's Republic, Part 1: The Emergence of Revolutionary China 1949–1965* (Cambridge University Press, 1987).

The Cambridge History of China, Volume 15, *The People's Republic, Part 2: Revolutions within the Chinese Revolution 1966–1982* (Cambridge University Press, 1991).

Fairbank, John King, *The Great Chinese Revolution 1800–1985* (Chatto and Windus, 1987).

Spence, Jonathan D., *The Search for Modern China* (Hutchinson, 1990).

Zhongguo Gongchandang de Chishinian (Seventy Years of the Chinese Communist Party) (Central Party Literature Publishing House, Chinese Communist Party Historical Press, Beijing, 1991).

Biographies, Autobiographies and Biographical Dictionaries

Bonavia, David, *Deng* (Longman Group, Hong Kong, 1989).

Boorman, Howard L., and Howard, Richard C. (eds.), *Biographical Dictionary of Republican China*, 4 vols. (Columbia University Press, 1967–1971).

Braun, Otto, *A Comintern Agent in China 1932–1939* (Stanford University Press, 1982).

Chi Hsin, *The Case of the Gang of Four* (Cosmos Books, Hong Kong, 1977).

Chi Hsin, *Teng Hsiao-ping: A Political Biography* (Cosmos Books, Hong Kong, 1978).

Deng Xiaoping: A Photo-biography (Central Party Literature Publishing House, Beijing, no date).

Franz, Uli, *Deng Xiaoping* (Harcourt Brace Jovanovich, 1988).

Goodman, David, *Deng Xiaoping* (Sphere Books, 1990).

Klein, Donald W. and Clark, Anne B., *Biographic Dictionary of Chinese Communism*, 2 vols. (Harvard University Press, 1971).

Nie Rongzhen, *Inside the Red Star: The Memoirs of Marshal Nie Rongzhen* (New World Press, Beijing, 1988).

Peng Dehuai, *Memoirs of a Chinese Marshal* (Foreign Languages Press, Beijing, 1984).

Salisbury, Harrison E., *The New Emperors: China in the Era of Mao and Deng* (Little, Brown, 1992).

Schram, Stuart, *Mao Tse-tung* (Penguin Books, 1966).

Sheridan, James E., *Chinese Warlord: The Career of Feng Yu-hsiang* (Stanford University Press, 1966).

Snow, Helen Foster (Nym Wales), *The Chinese Communists: Sketches and Autobiographies of the Old Guard* (Greenwood Publishing Company, 1972).

Terrill, Ross, *Mao: A Biography* (Harper Colophon Books, 1981).

Terrill, Ross, *The White-Boned Demon: A Biography of Madame Mao Zedong* (William Morrow, 1984).

*Zhou Enlai Juan 1898–1949 (Biography of Zhou Enlai 1898–1949) (Central Party Literature Publishing House, Beijing, no date).

*Zhu De, Nianpu (Annual Chronicle) (People's Publishing House, Beijing, no date).

Studies and Monographs

Barnett, A. Doak, *Uncertain Passage, China's Transition to the Post-Mao Era* (The Brookings Institution, 1974).

Dittmer, Lowell, *Liu Shao-ch'i and the Chinese Cultural Revolution: The Politics of Mass Criticism* (University of California Press, 1974).

Dittmer, Lowell, *China's Continuous Revolution, The Post-Liberation Epoch 1949–1981* (University of California Press, 1987).

Harding, Harry, *Organizing China: The Problem of Bureaucracy 1949–1976* (Stanford University Press, 1981).

Harding, Harry, *China's Second Revolution: Reform after Mao* (The Brookings Institution, 1987).

Jenner, W. J. F., *The Tyranny of History: The Roots of China's Crisis* (Allen Lane, 1992).

MacFarquhar, Roderick, *The Origins of the Cultural Revolution 1: Contradictions among the People 1956–1957* (Oxford University Press, 1974).

MacFarquhar, Roderick, *The Origins of the Cultural Revolution 2: The Great Leap Forward 1958–1960* (Oxford University Press, 1983).

Rice, Edward E., *Mao's Way* (University of California Press, 1972).

Riskin, Carl, *China's Political Economy: The Quest for Development since 1949* (Oxford University Press, 1987).

Rodzinski, Witold, *The People's Republic of China: Reflections on Chinese Political History since 1949* (Fontana Press, 1989).

Salisbury, Harrison E., *The Long March: The Untold Story* (Macmillan, 1986).

Schram, Stuart, *The Thought of Mao Tse-tung* (Cambridge University Press, 1989).

Schurmann, Franz H., *Ideology and Organization in Communist China* (University of California Press, 1966).

Sheng Yueh, *Sun Yat-sen University in Moscow and the Chinese Revolution: A Personal Account* (University of Kansas, 1971).

Snow, Edgar, *Random Notes on Red China 1936–1945* (Harvard University Press, 1957).

Snow, Edgar, *Red Star over China* (revised and enlarged edn, Grove Press, 1973).

Whitson, William W., with Hung Chen-hsia, *The Chinese High Command: A History of Communist Military Politics 1927–1971* (Macmillan, 1973).

Yang, Benjamin, *From Revolution to Politics: Chinese Communists on the Long March* (Westview Press, 1990).

Zagoria, Donald S., *The Sino-Soviet Conflict 1956–1961* (Princeton University Press, 1962).

Collections of Speeches and Documents

Béja, Jean-Philippe, Bonnin, Michel and Peyraube, Alain, *Le Tremblement de terre de Pékin* (Gallimard, 1991).

Bowie, Robert R., and Fairbank, John K. (eds.), *Communist China 1955–1959: Policy Documents with Analysis* (Harvard University Press, 1962).

Brandt, Conrad, Schwartz, Benjamin and Fairbank, John K. (eds.), *A Documentary History of Chinese Communism* (Harvard University Press, 1952).

Deng Xiaoping, *Selected Works of Deng Xiaoping 1975–1982* (Foreign Languages Press, Beijing, 1984).

Deng Xiaoping, *Fundamental Issues in Present-Day China* (Foreign Languages Press, Beijing, 1987).

Deng Xiaoping, *Speeches and Writings* (Pergamon Press, 1987).

*Deng Xiaoping, *Deng Xiaoping Wenxuan 1938–1965 (Selected Works of Deng Xiaoping 1938–1965)* (People's Publishing House, Beijing, 1989).

The First Session of the Seventh National People's Congress of the People's Republic of China (Foreign Languages Press, Beijing, 1988).

A Great Trial in Chinese History (New World Press, Beijing, 1981).

Hsiao Tso-liang, *Power Relations within the Chinese Communist Movement, 1930–1934* (University of Washington Press, 1969).

*Kok, Dr C. B., *Teng Hsiao-ping* (Chinese Cultural Centre, Hong Kong, no date).

Mao Tse-tung, *Selected Works of Mao Tse-tung*, 5 vols. (Foreign Languages Press, Beijing, 1961–1977).

Resolution on CPC History (1949–1981) (Foreign Languages Press, Beijing, 1981).

Schram, Stuart, *Mao Tse-tung Unrehearsed: Talks and Letters 1956–1971* (Penguin Books, 1974).

Shisanda Yilai (Since the Thirteenth Party Congress), 2 vols. (People's Party Publishing House, Beijing, 1991).

Other important sources are *Issues and Studies*, the monthly magazine of the Institute of International Relations in Tapei, Taiwan, which frequently publishes translations of Central Committee and other internal Communist Party documents; and the daily and weekly summaries of broadcast speeches and documents published by the Monitoring Service of the British Broadcasting Corporation at Caversham Park, Reading.

Articles and Interviews

Bailey, Paul, 'The Chinese work-study movement in France' (*China Quarterly* No. 115 (September 1988), pp. 441–61).

Barman, Geneviève and Dulioust, Nicole, 'Les années' françaises de Deng Xiaoping', (*Vingtième Siècle*, Vol. 20 (October 1988), pp. 17–34).

Barman, Geneviève and Dulioust, Nicole, 'La France au miroir chinois' (*Les Temps modernes* No. 498 (January 1988), pp. 32–67).

Deng Rong (Deng Maomao), 'My Father's days in Jiangxi' (*People's Daily*, Beijing, 22 August 1984).

Fallaci, Oriana, Interview with Deng Xiaoping. 'Deng: cleaning up Mao's "Feudal Mistakes"' and 'Deng: a Third World War is inevitable' (*Washington Post*, 31 August and 1 September 1980).

Kampen, Thomas 'The Zunyi Conference and further steps in Mao's rise to power' (*China Quarterly* No. 117 (March 1989), pp. 118–34).

Wang, Nora, 'Deng Xiaoping: the years in France' (*China Quarterly* No. 92 (December 1982), pp. 698–705).

Yang, Benjamin, 'The Zunyi Conference as one step in Mao's rise to power: a survey of historical studies of the Chinese Communist Party' (*China Quarterly* No. 106 (June 1986), pp. 235–71).

Yuan Renyuan, 'A Red storm in Youjiang in Guangxi' (*People's Daily*, Beijing, 9 December 1978, p. 3).

Index